THE

DRAMATIC WORKS

OF

BAYARD TAYLOR

WITH NOTES

BY

MARIE HANSEN-TAYLOR

BOSTON

HOUGHTON, MIFFLIN AND COMPANY

The Riverside Press, Cambridge

1880

Republished 1971

Schoalrly Press, Inc., 22929 Industrial Drive East

St. Clair Shores, Michigan 48080

Library of Congress Catalog Card Number: 79-145324
ISBN 0-403-01235-X

The Riverside Press, Cambridge, Mass.:
Stereotyped and Printed by H. O. Houghton & Co.

CONTENTS.

——◆——

THE PROPHET.

DRAMATIS PERSONÆ.

DAVID STARR . . . . . . The Prophet.
ELKANAH . . . . His Father.
HANNAH . . . . His Mother.
RHODA . . . . . . Afterwards his Wife.
NIMROD KRAFT . . . . Afterwards High-Priest.
LIVIA ROMNEY . . . . A Woman of the World.
SIMEON ⎫
MORDECAI ⎬ . . . Members of the Council of Twelve.
HUGH ⎪
JONAS ⎭
SARAH . . . . Wife of Jonas.
PETER . . . An Orphan, the Prophet's Serving-Man.
COLONEL HYDE . . . . Sheriff.
HIRAM . . . . . A Member of the Church.

A Preacher. People of David's neighborhood. Members of the
church. Women. Colonel Hyde's followers.

Time, 18—.
The scene of Act I. is a New England State ; of the four
following Acts, a Western State.

Between Acts I. and II. there is an interval of two years ;
between Acts II. and III., an interval of one year.

THE PROPHET.

ACT I.

SCENE I.

The porch, front-yard, and garden of a farm-house. Late afternoon.

ELKANAH.

'TIS a good ending of the harvest. Now
   We may be sure that every sheaf is stacked
Ere rain can spoil it. One load more, I think,
Said David. But the farther side is low,
A deeper soil, bears well : he may be wrong,
If on the right side of the estimate.
I always counted less than likely seemed ;
Tried to surprise myself, as it might be,
And so increase my luck. He 's over young
For under-guessing ; takes the most at once,
And discounts profit long before it comes.
The lad is not like me, or times are changed.
I was my father over, he declared,
And liked to say so ; but good stock improves ;
Hey, Hannah ?

HANNAH.

      Nay, I heard you : I must think,
Whether I will or no, about the boy,
As in the anxious time when he was born.
Late fruit is best, they say, — the only kind
Keeps over winter ; but it may get ripe,
Like pippins, when the orchard 's bare of leaves.
Your disappointment and your discontent
You do forget ; but I remember all,
Bearing the blame : and when he came, at last,
I said within my heart, Because of that
The Lord means something. Now I plague myself,
Thinking I see, and straightway seeing not,
The sign thereof revealed in David's life.

ELKANAH.

You could not help such fancies, I suppose,
While he was on the way.

HANNAH.

      I know your thought :
You 've the same right to seek yourself in him,
But will not find it : he is most of me.
Why, forty years have you and I been wed ;
And four and twenty has he been with us.
I cannot say beforehand, thus and so
Will speak my husband, or decide, or act ;
But I must wait : yet, if a woman were
By some strange miracle become a man,
Then I should be our David's very self
In feeling and in purpose. Something moves
His mind beyond our daily round of work :
I know not what it is, and dare not ask,
Lest prying words, before the proper time,
Breed mischief.

ELKANAH.

Wife, the boy is all a man :
He 'll soon spy out what 's wanting.

HANNAH.

Ah, not that !

PETER.

(*Singing at a distance.*)
Sing, blow the wind o' mornings !
Sing, blow the wind, 'igh O !
Sing, brush away the morning dew,
Sing, blow, blow, blow !

ELKANAH.

The last load : otherwise, would Peter sing
Not quite so loudly.   They have built it broad,
Mayhap, and high, to save another.   Well,
Whether it show good luck or management
Makes odds in the end.   There be two ways of work ;
And one is doing it because you must,
And one because you like.   Look when it 's done,
You 'll see small difference, as the case is now ;
And I misdoubt me sorely which it is.

DAVID.

(*Singing, distant at first, but gradually drawing nearer.*)
If one to yonder mountain saith,
Be cast into the sea !
And doubteth not, so filled with faith,
The mount removed shall be.
Though love is first, yet faith is chief :
Lord, I believe ; help Thou mine unbelief !

Behold, He granteth prophecy,
And gift of tongues, to all :

His fullest bounty waits for me,
Though I delay to call.
The measure of our days is brief :
Lord, I believe ; help Thou mine unbelief !

(Rhoda, *approaching the house from the opposite side, pauses at
the gate, and listens. She begins to sing, at first in a low
voice, then louder to the close ; when* David *appears.*)

DAVID.

I thought of you, and straightway find you here.
Was that your prayer, as well ? I 'll not believe
You utter words, as one lets pebbles drop,
To splash in water : you 've a helpful soul,
I think, to make another's faith more firm
By just believing, Rhoda ?

RHODA.

What I am

Can I declare ?

DAVID.

Then I will set you forth.
I 'll say that love in you is one with faith :
The trust you give means an eternal term,
And following through good and ill report,
And with strong heart sustaining where the mind
Would stop and question.   These were woman's gifts,
When she beheld the Master, and obeyed ;
And they are yours ; if I supposed you false,
I should be most unhappy.

RHODA.

No, not false !
Believe me, David, anything but that !

             [*They pass into the garden.*

HANNAH.

They both forget us !   Even his face is strange,
Most strange and beautiful with serious thought ;
While hers is troubled, yet has nought of pain.
I do not understand it.   She 's a child,
Is Rhoda still ; and wise she never seemed.
Can one give counsel, comprehending not
The doubtful matter ?   Surely unto her
He cannot show what he keeps back from me !
Men seek clear notions, whether fair or foul,
When they have pondered anything so long
As he with this.   They take the orchard-path :
The fruit will hardly be their chief concern,
Yet gives fair ground that I may follow them.

[*Exit.*

ELKANAH.

(*Laughing to himself.*)

Ha, ha ! I see no mystery in the thing.
A practised tongue has Hannah, takes her **way**
And justifies it, past my argument ;
Yet now and then, like one in too much haste,
Her notions trip, and throw her flat on mine.
Because the lad was moony, she, forsooth,
Must think him like a Samuel, set apàrt
For this or t' other ; but it 's nothing new.
He goes the way of flesh and blood, that first
Knows hardly what the natural ailment is,
Till each finds out, and then the other heals.
Yes, yes, these women !   Best to give them **line,**
And let them pry a while among the clouds
For what their very noses touch.   She kept
Him close, and preached upon and coddled **him,**
As if a root of wilder oats is killed

When you keep down the top.   The girl, 't is true,
Might have a bigger dowry : let that pass !
High time it is to settle him afresh ;
And Hannah has no call to interfere.

[*Exit.*

(HANNAH, DAVID, *and* RHODA *return.*)

DAVID.

Neither to you nor Rhoda, mother.   Both
Must wait what cometh ; for, if I could say,
Then I should know.

HANNAH.

                    And each of you is sure
You love the other ?   I have seen no signs.
Even neighbor's children do not change so much,
But there is seeking, doubt, and bashfulness,
Which will betray them.

DAVID.

                    None of these are ours :
I did not-seek what was already found ;
And truth in me prohibits doubt of her.
If what concerneth life was once ordained
For others, there must be direction still.
The nearest heart is ever easiest read :
So, reading Rhoda's by the light of mine
And that above, as one may hold pure glass
Before the least of stars, nor make it dim,
I saw that each was chosen.   Rhoda, speak,
And tell me once again your heart is mine !

RHODA.

You know it, even if I answered Nay.

Scene II. — A Camp-Meeting.

A grove of large, scattered oak-trees. Against two, which stand near together, a platform is built, supporting a pulpit of rough timber. In front of the platform are benches of planks, upon which several hundred persons are seated, David, Rhoda, *and* Peter *among them. Tents are pitched under the borders of the grove. Many persons kneeling at the front benches, weeping and shouting.*

HYMN.

There is a fountain filled with blood
    Drawn from Immanuel's veins;
And sinners, plunged beneath that flood,
    Lose all their guilty stains.

THE PREACHER.

(*Resuming his exhortation, which was interrupted by the hymn.*)

Oh, there are more among ye shall be plucked
As brands from out the burning ! By the hair
I 'll seize you, — even by the single hair
That holds you from the pit ! My hands are singed
With loosening the Devil's grip on souls;
And you, who should strike out with fists and feet,
Leave me the fight, the cowards that you are !
You think the Lord can't see you : even so
The ostrich sticketh in the sand her head
To save her gay tail-feathers : pull them out,
And cast them from you ! Though you hide your-
    selves
Under the mountains, it will not be long ;
He 'll send you wriggling forth, as mean as mice ;
And, though you dive down in the deepest sea,

He 'll haul you to the surface like a whale,
Harpooned, and spouting blood.

(*Cries and groans among the people.*)

Yes, gnash and roar
Like lions on the hills of Havilum ;
But, all the same, He 'll ask full price of you.
Come up, ye publicans and sinners !   Kneel,
Pray hard, mourn with the mourners, and be saved !
Strike off the crusted brimstone from your feet,
And swap the Devil's fire for water of life !
Oh ! don't I know you ?   This one's pride of mind,
And that one's wretched fear of what folks say,
And t' other's cold " morality," as if
An ice-house better than an oven baked, —
Oh ! don't I know ?   I had them all myself :
I was a scurvy sheep, distempered, bad
With foot and mouth disease : He picked me up,
And, as it were, greased me with oil of grace,
And washed my spotted fleece until it shone.
You think you 're clean already ; but He sees
Red under broadcloth, silk, and calico, —
Only your livers white !

(*Several more come forward to the front benches, and kneel
down with loud cries.*)

Two, three, four, five !
Each one as nine and ninety righteous men :
Why, these alone outweigh the rest of you !
You give a serpent when he asks for fish ;
And He upsets, as men their wagons tilt,
His four-horse loads of mercies and of gifts,
And buries with them all that say, " I need."

(*His eyes meet those of* DAVID, *who leans forward in his seat
with a fixed, abstracted gaze.*)

I see another sinner !   He 's afraid :

It may be that he magnifies his sin.
But, don't you know, the bigger load you bear,
The greater comfort when you cast it off ?
Oh ! you 'll be pardoned fully, not a doubt :
He likes to pardon.   Trembling brother, come !
You will not ?   Say, then, do you love the Lord ?

DAVID.
(*Rising, as if with a struggle and speaking slowly.*)
Whether I love Him, and how well, He knows.

PETER.
(*Aside to his neighbor.*)
Not quite the answer he expected.

THE PREACHER.
                                        Yes,
He knoweth.   Do you seek a hole in the net,
Caught by the gills already ?   Yes, He knows :
These mourners cry to Him because of that.

DAVID.
Let Him be Judge of me !

THE PREACHER.
                              He is your Judge
Without your letting.   These are Devil's tricks, —
This playing pitch-and-toss with holy words,
To gain a little time.   Come up, choose sides !
The Lord means business.   Where a gnat 's enough
For others, must you have an elephant,
And all His promises rammed down your throat,
Before you know their taste ?

DAVID (*eagerly*).

His promises ? —
The power of miracle and prophecy,
And gift of tongues ?   He promised them to all;
And Paul confirmed it.   Tell me, then, the signs !
The heart within me aches from stress of faith :
I have no need to pray, except for power,
Which is the seal and covenant for them
Whom He has chosen.

(*Movements and exclamations among the people.*)

THE PREACHER.

So take hold on hell
The proud of spirit.   What ! the gift of tongues,
The power of miracle and prophecy,
You ask, without repentance, prayer, and grace ?

DAVID.

For what should I repent ?   Why pray as these
Who cry from secret consciousness of sin ?
I never let a fault against me stand
For day of settlement, then balanced all
By pleading bankrupt, only to begin
A fresh account.   Acceptance, yea, and faith,
Are mine already, tenfold more than yours,
Who neither ask, nor know what ye should ask.

THE PREACHER.

We choose His simple way.   You would mislead :
Be silent !

CRIES AMONG THE PEOPLE.

Out !   A very infidel ! —
No sinner ?   Never prays ?   Why, Antichrist
Could say no more !   To face the preacher so !
Away with him !

PETER.

(*Turning suddenly, with clinched fists.*)

          The preacher drew him on,
And got no worse than he deserved.   I say,
Touch him, it won't be " Glory ! " that you 'll shout,
After a sore repentance.

DAVID.

          If I shake
This dust from off my feet, I do no more
Than was commanded.   Have you privilege
To darken counsel with your cloud of words ?
To teach the lesser part, reject the whole,
And mutilate His glory unto men ?
Woe to the Pharisees and hypocrites,
Even here as there, even in these latter days,
As when upon the paths of Galilee
His feet were beautiful !   My words are said.

   (*He leaves the place amid a great outcry and confusion.*)

Scene III.

A lonely lane, evening.

DAVID (*solus*).

Cast out ?   By them that think they do believe,
Cursed for believing ?   God ! what, then, is truth ?
Why, here Thy minted gold is worn with use,
Sweated in handling, till the head thereon
Is quite rubbed out, the superscription dim.
I did but offer it as freshly coined,
With all its glorious promise legible,
And they cry, " Counterfeit ! "   Ten talents given,
Nine have they buried, and a single one

Divide among the people, who are blind,
And blindly led : shall I not therefore see?

(*He pauses, and looks upwards.*)

How reach the faith so perfect and assured
That every gift must follow ?   I have tried,
Sought evidence in lightest, easiest ways :
Nothing obeyed.   So I have *not* the faith,
Or — O my God ! there is no faith, no power,
Nor miracle ; and never can have been.
But this is madness !   This makes truth a lie,
Makes life an emptiness far worse than death,
Peoples the world with devils, drives men mad,
And substitutes —

(*Another pause.*)

I had not thought of that.

Times changed, conditions changed : hence special
  need
Of worthiness through trial, harder now
Than when all understood what meant belief,
And perfect faith was natural to them.
How can I measure mine by other men's ?
I saw not right : I claimed the highest power,
Unpurchased.   What apostle shall declare,
As then, the fealty of a human soul ?
Not he ; not he !   And are not all alike,
Giving their husks of doctrine for His bread ?
The ground we stand on is too far apart :
Whom seek ?   Why, none !   A hand is on my head,
A finger points the way.

PETER (*coming up*).

I meant to leave
When you did ; but, because I cannot swear
As properly as they, and just let fly

Hard lumps of words like stones to hit and hurt,
They cursed me roundly, — in a holy way;
And one, with hand upon my collar, cried,
" Down, sinner, and repent ! "   I answered him
Between the eyes ; then dashed the rest apart,
And so got headway.   Let us hurry on :
They 're after us.

DAVID.

                    And if they were ?   My right
Is greater.   Did you understand my words ?

PETER.

As much as his.   He did not answer you :
That I could understand.

DAVID.

                        If unto you
So much was manifest, and to the rest,
They only want authority and sign,
Which I must purchase.   Peter, I believe
All men are brethren when they see the truth.

PETER.

You never called me " brother ; " yet you did
Even as a brother.

DAVID.

                    Did I so, indeed ?
I thought not of it.

(*They walk forwards.*)

PETER.

                    Why should you not preach ?
There always must be preachers in the world.

We 're used to them ; and people say that things
Would go to wrack without them ; but I wish
They 'd yell and bang and thunder less.   Somehow
The text is friendly, smooth, and innocent
As seems a flint ; yet soon they knock from it
Thick sparks of hell-fire, and the sulphur-stink
Goes to men's heads, and sets them raving wild.
You 'd preach some comfort, now.

DAVID.

> Would you believe ?

PETER.

Why not ?   Something we must believe, they say.
What I can't understand I take on trust.
It 's getting late : the hogs and cattle know
There 's earlier feeding-time when Sunday comes.

(*He hastens on.*)

DAVID.

The world is peaceful.   There should be no sin :
There need not be, or misery, any more.
Yon blue is loftier than the changing wind,
And spreads serenely back of cloud and storm
To show us what we might be.   Wherefore strive ?
Faith puts contention quietly aside,
Smiles, and is master.

(*Rhoda overtakes him.*)

> I have need of you,
My Rhoda.   Sooner than the signs announced,
The time draws nigh.   Here, walk beside me now
At the beginning, as it were the end.

RHODA.

I was not frightened.   All you said was true.

I thought you answered as one having power;
And so did many others.

DAVID.

                    Rhoda, look!
How yonder little cloud is all afire,
As if a rose unshrivelled so could burn,
That was so gray and dull!   Even such am I.
I cannot help the color, nor escape
The light that shines upon me.   You will be
Yon other cloud, that mingles with the first
While now we gaze; and let the multitude
Spread as the clammy meadow-mists below,
That never saw the sunset!

RHODA.

                    And I feared
That you might be disquieted in soul! —
Your peace and strength leave all the trouble mine.
I can but take whatever light is yours,
That is not wasted from a nobler use.
I will not speak of mine unworthiness;
For that were thankless censure of your heart,
Which finds me worthy.

DAVID.

                    Proven so again!
You are a glass wherein I see myself
Reflected as I change, — now clear, now dim,
And soon (or else, I think, the earth shall cease)
Clothed on with brightness, as a lamp with flame.

RHODA.

I pray that I may read what you intend.
It must be so: how, otherwise, give help?

                    2

DAVID.

Will help be needed?

RHODA.

Will not trouble come?
I have the feeling that foretells a storm
When not a cloud has gathered, — sultry, strange,
And full of restlessness which is not fear.
This is of me alone: untouched are you
By that which you regard not.

DAVID.

Let me be!
Stand off, keep silence, wait and hope! One step
Gives me the pathway; but my lifted foot
Feels in the dark, conjectures an abyss
Where one bold thrust might touch the solid base.
My peace and strength, you said? There's seeming
          peace
When hope, desire, and prayer have done their most,
And wait in agony the answer. Come!
I hardly feel the earth that bears me up.
The sky is blazing; all the air is gold;
And every hill-top is a step to heaven.

[*They pass on.*

Scene IV.

The sitting-room of the farm-house, dusk. HANNAH *seated in
an old arm-chair at the window.*

HANNAH.

If half of Peter's story be the truth,
The thing will make disturbance. Not of that,
As him affecting, should I be afraid,
Were not the place, and manner of his words,

Weapons against him. Brooding men are rash
When forced or cozened to declare themselves ;
And he has made, if more his thought includes,
Unwise beginning. Whither will it lead ?
He angers me, who, in my younger days,
Was often hotly angered with myself
Without such bitter cause ; and, having led
In love so long, I now must lead by blame.
It is a pestilent business, and for nought !
I did not say a word against his choice,
Though higher — he a man so proper, she
As hundreds are — he had the right to look.
And now this useless, flighty piece of work !

ELKANAH (*entering*).

Oh, yes ! you 've heard. Although I hardly see
Your face, I know you know it. Well, this once
I think we shall agree.

HANNAH.

First speak your mind.

ELKANAH.

My mind is yours. I always thought you wise
As women may be : therefore there 's no cause
To make this that, when all is clear as day.
My name and standing in the neighborhood,
And yours, are likely to be touched ; for none
Will side with him.

HANNAH.

How ? None ? Suppose him right
Not rash or flighty, as the thing may seem,
But wise and well-considered, shall he bear
Unjust abuse, and we take no concern ?
Then were our name and standing touched indeed

ELKANAH.

(*Lifting up his hands.*)

Why, wedded forty years (the words are yours),
I cannot say beforehand, thus and so
Will speak my wife, when wisdom, reason, sense,
Have but one language. Did I call you wise ?
I knew not what I said. The moon-struck boy
First cracks the egg-shell of his addled brain ;
And yours, to please him, then begins to split.

HANNAH.

Elkanah, hush ! But, nay ! speak as you list,
And let your anger breathe itself on me.
Though I be sore confounded, I withhold
Untimely chiding, which confirms the fault
Not felt as such by him ; and, if the thing
Be verily justified, avoid a sin.
Be gentle with your first and only born.

DAVID.

(*Entering hastily*).

Father ! Mother !

HANNAH.

Behold us here, my son !

DAVID.

I will not call you any other names,
Though all be granted.

ELKANAH.

As a favor, then ?
Say more, or less, and let your riddles drop.
My wits are dumb.

DAVID.

This *must* be the command.

[*Exit.*

ELKANAH.

If ever! Did you mark his lordly air?
Let us be thankful, that, because he made
A strange disturbance in a godly place,
He still acknowledges he is our son.

HANNAH (*rising*).

Oh, spare me any more! 'T was not in pride
He spake. He scarcely thought of us: his soul
Is moved by madness, or a mighty truth,
Or both in battle. All my blood grew cold:
My limbs are trembling still.

　　　(*She lights a lamp.*)

　　　　　　　I fear the dusk.
There was a bat before the window brushed,
A hoot-owl cried. Well, call me anything —
Mistaken, silly, weak — when this is past;
But now be kind.

(DAVID *comes back. He pauses in the centre of the room, with
a strange, rapt expression of face.*)

　　　　　　　Will you not speak to us,
My son! Declare so much as may be told:
We listen.

DAVID.

(*As if speaking to himself.*)

Quarantania!

HANNAH.

(*After a pause.*)

　　　　　　　Nay, nay, nay,
This is no answer: do not frighten us!

Whatever purpose so disturbs your brain
You cannot speak it, neither shape its form
Clearly unto yourself, give words, but words :
Silence is poison.

DAVID.

(*Louder than before.*)

Quarantania !

[*He passes out the door.*

HANNAH.

Ah,
He 's lost !   My husband, help ! the world is dark.
(*She falls in a swoon.*)

Scene V.

A wild, rocky valley between hills covered with forests ; on the left an overhanging cliff ; a small brook in the foreground.

DAVID (*solus*).

The second day is sinking to its end,
How slowly !   These eternities of thought
Wherein I grope, and strive to lose myself,
Spin to a weary length the glaring hours.
I would the night were come ; for I am faint,
And from my hold the things I pray to reach
Seem weakly slipping.   Night will give them back,
When every star shines comfort, and the air
Is crossed all ways by print of noiseless feet
That on mysterious errands come and go.
Could I recall my vision !   All is clear
Save that—my bed of leaves beneath the rock ;
The doubt if I were still indeed myself,
And any thing was what it seemed ; until

Came languid peace, then awe and shuddering
Without a cause, a frost in every vein,
And the heart hammered, as to burst mine ears.
Something slid past me, cold and serpent-like :
The trees were filled with whispers ; and afar
Called voices not of man : and then my soul
Went forth from me, and spread and grew aloft
Through darting lights — His arrows, here and there
Shot down on earth.   But now my knowledge fades :
What followed, keener, mightier, than a dream,
My hope interprets.   Only his I know, —
The dark, invisible pillars of the sky
Breathed like deep organ-pipes of awful sound :
A myriad myriad tongues the choral sang ;
And drowned in it, stunned with excess of power,
My soul sank down, and sleep my body touched.

(*He pauses, and looks around.*)

The shadows will not lengthen.   All my throat
Seems choked with dust.   I never knew before
How beautiful may be a little brook.
I cannot leave it, cannot turn mine eyes,
So tempting and so innocent it runs.
If I might drink !   The dry blood else may breed
Fever and flightiness.   I must be sound,
Or soon —

(*He stoops suddenly, dips up the water in his hand, and
drinks.*)

                    Oh, sweet as Cana's wedding-wine !
Did He not offer it ?   Such sudden bliss,
Born of the body, penetrates my brain !
I doubt no more : the vision will return.

(*There is a rustling among the leaves. A snake thrusts its head
forth from under a bush, and gazes at him.*)

Temptation, was it ? and the tempter, thou,
In thy first shape ?   I will not be afeared.
If thou hast power, come forth : if I, depart !
I dare the fascination of thine eyes :
Look thou, lest mine subdue thee !   Is it so ?
He veils the glittering, bead-like sparks, and turns,
Startled, and winds in sinuous escape.
Why, this is fresh fulfilment of the Word !
Faint not, my soul : the rest will surely come.

[*He walks slowly away.*

(*After a little space enters*)

NIMROD KRAFT.

Yon must be he they seek : he is the same
I also seek ; but let me not be rash.
If, by the spirit driven that bade him speak,
He hides for meditation, or is verily daft,
As they whose minds take up too sore a load,
He must be humored.   I will watch him close
Until some act or gesture give me hint,
And then approach discreetly.

[*He follows*

(*Enter* RHODA *and* PETER.)

PETER.

Shall I call
(He knows my whoop), or sing the hymn he made ?

(*Sings, but not loudly.*)

" If one to yonder mountain saith,
' Be cast into the sea ! ' "

There !   I forget the rest.

RHODA.

Nay, now ; keep still !

I 've but a guess to guide me ; and it says
He will not see us.   Sure, that word betrayed
His thought.   But can this be the place ? or where ?
Ah, while we wait, perhaps he 's lying dead !
Foolish ! I know he lives.   Some lives are safe,
Because they are not meant for pleasant paths :
Some wits keep sound, to work for other minds.
I must not fear ; he would not have me fear :
If he discover us, I must be shamed,
Showing so little faith.

PETER.

                And so much care !
If this goes on, I 'll shortly preach myself.
I 'll give you sparrows for example, toads,
And stupid owls : no one goes off alone,
And t' other fears to look for 't !   Did the Lord
Put such a powerful pressure on his head,
To leave him, sudden, like a will-o'-the-wisp,
The work unfinished ?   Then 't was not the Lord.

RHODA.

You 've spoken wiselier, Peter, than you think.

PETER.

So wisdom 's cheap !   I never valued much
My random notions : what they call horse-sense
I always had ; and that sometimes will serve
Even folks that prance so high above our heads.
Now, here 's the question : Is he like to starve ?
You think he means to try it.   Well and good ! —
And we must search, but not find openly ;
Feed him, without his knowledge ; watch his ways,
And not be noticed.   So I 've nought to do

But look for tracks, and leave the provender :
The risk is yours.

(*He goes slowly up the brook, with a basket on his arm.*)

RHODA (*solus*).

         I try to force my soul
To follow his, and question not the way.
Within this valley, called the Wilderness,
He must be hidden, if I understand,
To win, in solitude, the faith and power.
'T is pleasant, now : the shadows of the hills
Soothe the hot leaves with dreams of coming dew ;
The crannies of the serpent-haunted rocks
No longer threaten ; and the water here
Runs onward with a soft, contented sound.
I will believe him safe.   And what is night
But as a darksome cloth that covers us ?
Nothing can harm him, for he did no harm ;
And that for which he goes apart from all
Will be vouchsafed, or prayer is fruitless breath.

PETER (*returning*).

I found his track ! — beside yon biggest rock,
On the flat sand, a little water-soaked,
And made so freshly, that I stooped.   You said
He must not see us.

RHODA.

         And you left him food ?

PETER.

Upon a shelf that jutted from the rock,
Smooth as a platter.   There 's no other place,
Up stream or down, but briery thickets grow ;
And, if he pass before the fowls o' the air
Spy out his supper —

RHODA.

Come, it is enough !
So glad am I at having guessed aright,
I crave no more, lest, pressing on too close,
I spoil the certainty of what remains.

[*Exeunt.*

Scene VI.

Another part of the valley ; Nimrod Kraft *near some bushes ;*
David *at a little distance.*

NIMROD.

Behind these bushes I can watch at will.
He thinks himself alone ; nay, not of that
Thinks he at all : his gaze is bent aloft,
Or falls, and roots itself before his feet.
So young ! Yet even here he bears himself
As one commissioned, who but waits the brief,
With seal and clear subscription, ere he act.
Why not ? Has God been sleeping all this while,
Or only men ? They stand afar and strange,
And count their generations Gentile still.
Of Christian parents Christian children come,
Baptized before begotten, then at birth
Set back to ancient heathendom, and spoiled
Of all their hoarded heritage.   Not such
Is he : he claims his birthright, will possess,
And may restore to others, bringing back
The old, forgotten forces of the Church,
Whose right hand is Authority, whose left
Obedience.   But, however he may build,
My coarser strength must hew and set the stones.
If but my purpose can be squared with his !
Since he has entered in this open tract

His spirit wavers : I can see his lips
Move, as do such that know not if they speak.
There is no better moment : I will go.

(*He steps forth, and approaches* DAVID.)

The soul within me hither turns my feet,
And calls upon you.   Guide me, help ; forgive
If that my haste offend !   I come as he,
Lame from his birth, that shouted, leapt, and ran,
When once the gentle touch had made him whole.

DAVID.

(*After a pause.*)

I healed you, then, not knowing.

NIMROD.

Marvel not !
There 's too much virtue in a perfect faith
To take the measure of itself.   You ARE ;
And what you are, not knowing, is the power.

DAVID.

Nay, there !   What I invoke I cannot be.
How know you aught of me ?

NIMROD.

Yourself did make
The revelation.   When I saw your face
Rise from the crowd, I said within my heart,
" There 's one will sign his own free covenant !
He reaches high : my arms are short and strong ;
But they may touch the gifts within his hand."
You spake.   I stood afar ; but in my mouth
Came a sweet savor, though their husks and stones
Still harsh and heavy on my stomach sat.

It needs no thousand words to make acquaint :
There 's something runs in souls more close than blood
Of them that issue from the selfsame womb ;
And so in yours.   I will not guess your prayer,
But its fulfilment surely is at hand.

DAVID (*hastily*).

Make no conjecture !   Speak no further word !
There was a veil within the Temple : grant
I may have lifted up its awful folds,
And stand, not blasted yet, nor consecrate.

NIMROD.

So think of me as one that waits without,
Silent, and hoping much.   But, ere I go,

(*Kneels.*)

I pray you lay your hands upon my head,
And bless me, wishing that to my belief
Be added understanding ; to my will,
The power to serve ; to mine obedience,
Some gracious gift.

DAVID (*aside*).

　　　　　How, then ?   Without the power
Assume the office ?   Yet a blessing dwells
Within the heart of him that calls it down ;
Or else he dare not.

(*To* NIMROD.)

　　　　　As thou askest, so
May it be given !   From laying here my hands
Expect no unction more than I possess.

NIMROD (*rising*).

But more than I am worthy to receive

Is even that, so filled am I with light !
And they, dumb souls, who for a single ray
Shout " Glory ! " and are saved, — how could they bear
The flood that enters me from you ?   Farewell !
A part is granted : you have forced the gate,
And stand with dazzled eyesight.   When you see,
Come back to men.

                                             [*Exit.*

DAVID.

                    A powerful soul ! and yet
Acknowledges authority in me.
Why was I faint or doubtful ?   Have I reached
Too high, perchance, or dreamed commissioned power
Should be by signs and wonders heralded,
Not as the simple consequence of faith ?
Faith is as beauty is : no maiden feels
Through inner sense the glory of her face,
But it shines back on her from who perceives.
" With dazzled eyesight ? "   Darkness comes of that ;
And on the finished shrine He sank in cloud.
If power unconsciously be held, I climb
The while I seem to beat a weary round ;
Possess authority beyond my sense ;
Am blinded, yea, because so near the light ;
And weak, since even now my shoulders bear
The unwonted burden.   Let the vision come !
It cannot fail : the first and largest star
Already glimmers from the expanding vault,
And millions wait behind.   So sure as they
Shall pierce the veil when thickest, even so
The first faint lamp within a seeking soul
Foretells the revelations crowding on.

Scene VII.

A room in the farmhouse ; Elkanah, Hannah, David,
Rhoda.

HANNAH.

I try to understand you : if I fail,
The heart your baby head found comfort on
Is not to blame.

ELKANAH.

It 's all a waste of words !
You look for duty, and it 's asked of you :
Command, or wish, or plead, one answer comes, —
He has "authority !" So much I 've learned :
When once a man says that, you might as soon
Prevail upon a tortoise in the shell :
No words go through it. I have said my say.

DAVID.

If I had given you grief of heart ere this,
Sinned unrepenting, disobeyed your will,
What I have done would bring rejoicing now.
There 's no perversity in whole desire,
Or the receiving of the gifts unused
Because unclaimed. I could not help but reach ;
Then, plucking back my hand, I found it filled.
What said you, mother, all my years of youth,
But " Seek, and ye shall find " ?

HANNAH.

I did, my son.
That you have sought, I know : that you have **found,**
I will believe. But if a healthy tree,
Grafted with apple, bearing apple-flowers,

Should after yield a fruit we never saw,
What man would taste until he knew it safe?
Thus from the hope I nursed springs all at once
A something strange, sheer wonderment to me
That gave your nature most.   How can I say
" Go on ! " not knowing whither, or, " Come back ! '
Haply from good ?

RHODA.

                    Say nothing, then, but wait :
The way is fixed.   I know not how I feel
His purpose ; yet I feel, and follow him.

DAVID.

Caught out of darkness, shall I turn my back
Against the light ? or, spent from wildering ways,
Refuse the path that makes my feet secure ?
I did not seek my struggle : it was there.
Why, men whose souls but burrow in their flesh
To feed, like worms in apples early ripe,
May say to mine : Be fat, and be content !
But me God sent the butterfly instead ;
And it must flutter in the sun, or die.

PETER *(entering)*.

A stranger stands outside.   He 's one of them,
It seems, that you, that they — But come yourself :
Ten steps are easier than my telling it.

DAVID.

What will he ?

PETER.

              Preaching.   There, the word is out !
You 'll guess the rest.

                              [*Exit* DAVID.

ELKANAH.

                The business just goes on
As I expected !   When was notion bred
By mortal brain, that did not set the tongue
In gear, to run full-tilt ?   He'll cackle, too,
So long as folks find something in his egg ;
Then, may be, when the thing's no longer fresh,
There 'll be an end.   He sows religious oats,
A little heavier in the head, that's all ;
But thorns and stony ground will waste the crop,
Or Gospel words mean nothing.

PETER.

(Aside to RHODA.)

                 All the talk
(So this man says) in our and other towns
Is nought but David : there's no end of tales.
The moral of it they don't rightly know,
And bend their ear-flaps, like a restless horse,
To catch some new particular.   If, now,
He has the call to preach, they have to hear.
'T will come to that.   .

                             [*Exit.*

HANNAH.

               I never thought of you
As of a daughter, Rhoda ; yet I see
That in your heart his ways are justified,
As in his own yourself.   Men love the will
That bends to theirs ; and she who fain would guide
Must seem to follow.   I 've directed him
Too long to make a new, obsequious change :
The place is yours.   But, O my daughter (hence
I 'll call you so), remember, never man,
Though gifted, raised, and made a power in the world,
Sufficed unto himself !   Else he were god ;

3

And she, the nearest, first, interpreting
All womankind to him, he, men to her,
Is called, as well, to claim her half of truth,
So testing his.   I may have borrowed care
Where it was not intended : all that's come
Is what my natural sight had long foreseen,
Were it not partial.   I must needs unloose
The precious bond of guidance, let him go,
And pray far-off, where once I held him close,
And breathed my heart in his believing ear.

RHODA.

Grapes cannot come from thorns, but neither thorns
From fruitful vines.   It is his blossom-time,
When storm or sudden chill may stint the fruit :
He should be sheltered.   But my speech is scant ;
And what I say sounds other than I feel.
So new the life is which he brings to mine,
So strange, exalted, I forget myself ;
And, when he needs another's tongue, I fail.
You love him, you will shortly understand.
I will not take an atom that was yours
In all his thought : what he bestows on me
Is only love ungranted otherwise.

SCENE VIII.

*The same as Scene V.   Some of the thickets on both sides of the
brook have been roughly cleared away.   A number of country-
people, chiefly men, are gathered in the space thus made,—
some seated on scattered stones, and stumps of trees ; others
approaching by the footpath from below.   Strong sunshine
and heavy shadow alternately ; an uncertain sky, portending
storm.*

FIRST MAN.

T is a fool's errand that we come, I fear.

SECOND.

He 'll keep his word.

FIRST.

Perhaps ; but was it given ?

THIRD.

Ay, given to me.   I offered him a chance
Open to use or let alone : he took
As eagerly as one that in the road
Sees a stray gold-piece.

SECOND.

Be he cracked or sane,
Four days, they say, he fasted hereabouts,
Then, fresh and fair, went home.   I 'd not believe,
But for accounts of such and stranger things
Before our time.

FIRST.

He 's nowise different
From you or me.   A little fresh conceit,
Like yeast, will puff a brain above its pan.

THIRD.

It 's more than that in him.   He looked straight through
The face I had, and saw what lay below, —
Namely, no faith, but some curiosity,
A little fun, withal ; I hardly know, —
And smiled, but in a queer, forgiving way,
That hurt me afterwards.

SECOND.

Stay, there he comes !
I mark no flighty or conceited airs, —
A plain young man, pale face, and shining eyes :

He mounts the rock.   See how the sun comes out,
And strikes his head !   Be silent, you !   Sit down,
Make no disturbance, let him speak his mind !

DAVID.

(*Standing upon the rock, sings:* RHODA *and* PETER, *below,
join in the hymn.*)

> Oh, praise the Lord, the Giver !
>   Relieve His burdened hands !
> His miracles deliver
>   The congregated lands :
> He poureth as a river,
>   And we but take the sands.
> His fruitful boughs are shaken ;
>   His bounties fall as rain :
> We sit with souls mistaken,
>   In penitence and pain :
> Awaken, world, awaken,
>   And spread His feast again !

SECOND MAN.

A gay beginning !   I could join in that
With all my voice.

FIRST.

                      They sing to lively tunes
In many churches.

THIRD.

                      Yes, but say, the while,
They 're stolen from the Devil.   May be so ;
But then the Devil must be a jolly soul,
And angels doleful as *Begone, dull Care !*

DAVID.

What come ye out to see ?   A reed in the wind ?
But if God's lips unto a reed be set, —

The dryest one that whistles in the marsh, —
There comes a music that can soothe the world.
I make no claim : I tried to understand
The many promises that rust unused ;
And all I asked, was, Are they granted yet ?
Then, rising high as agony of prayer
May lift a mortal, lo ! the answer came.
Show me the term, or limit !   There is none :
Restore conditions, you restore the power ;
And He who waited for a thousand years
Will manifest His wonders.   They who teach,
You say, are silent as to this ?   Why, then
Let them make answer !   Gifts of many tongues,
Of healing, miracle, and prophecy,
Given to His followers, by them to theirs,
Are buried treasures for this drowsy race.
He offering helmet, buckler, sword, and spear, —
Armor of proof, — perchance a shepherd's staff
We take, reluctant, mendicants where He
Awaits the guests that know their welcome sure.
So dust and cobwebs fill the temple ; so
The cedarn beams are rotted in their place ;
The trumps and timbrels crack, and wake no more
The songs of Zion : all is desolate,
As we were Israel that turned away !
'T is time a mighty wind should whirl the chaff
From idle threshing-floors : my breath is weak,
So others not increase it, yet thou, Lord,
Who knowest whether I deserve or no
Thy signs of power, — who, should I point, as now,
My finger at the crest of yonder rock,
And say, " Be thou removed ! " —

(*A part of the rock crashes down with a great noise and re-
    verberation.   Cries of terror, and much confusion among
    the people.*)

VOICES.

It falls ; it falls !

The world is coming to an end ! He spake,
And it obeyed ! A prophet, yea, a prophet !

DAVID.

(Who has remained quietly standing upon the rock, pale and
rapt.)

Be not afraid ! The power that works within,
If it but shiver down one crumbling edge
Of old indifference, is mightier yet.
Therefore, I take it from His open hand,
Who made yon stones to fall. I hurl on you
His arrows, and the shining of his spear :
I bid believe, not me, but what, renewed,
In me is manifest : I call you back
From pools made muddy by the paddling feet
Of darkened generations, to the fount
He cleft, now gushing in a desert land.
He waits, how long ! His summons, day by day —

(*Thunder and lightning.*)

VOICES.

We do believe you. Turn His wrath away !
A Prophet, yea, a Prophet !

DAVID.

There He spake,

Doubt not, as oft of old, — but now attend
The voice within you, which is He indeed.
Oh ! spread Thy banners on the streaming wind,
Come as the Morning, broaden as the Day,
Fill the dark places with Thy healing light ;
And, once Thy reign assured, cast me aside,

So glorified in mine unworthiness,
Because I saw when Thou didst touch mine eyes !
Come, now, in thunder and the clouds of heaven,
And purifying cisterns of the rain,
To wash Thy world, and fit it for the sun !
Thy day is near at hand : the glory shed
With all Thy promises shall doubled be
On all Thy gifts !

> (*A storm arises, — thunder, wind, and rain.*)

VOICES.

A Prophet, yea, a Prophet

ACT II.

SCENE I.

Afternoon. The crest of a rise, or swell, in a broad prairie. To the westward, in the distance, a line of timber, denoting the course of a stream ; a train of emigrant-wagons scattered along the road thither. On the crest a solitary wagon, its canvas cover partly folded back. DAVID and RHODA, with a child in her lap, seated in it ; PETER standing at the horses' heads.

RHODA.

YOU'RE weary, husband : is it far to camp ?

DAVID.

Two hours, — to yonder smoky line of trees.
The signs of heaven are fair: the earth believes
In them, and, glad as any living thing,
Smiles far and wide. The sky is larger here,
And brighter ; other life is in the winds ;
The grass is lost beneath the waste of flowers :
It is our promised land.

RHODA.

At last !

DAVID.

Ah, me !
This weight and perilous sinking of the heart,
That ever looks before, or stubbornly

Tastes the o'ercome distresses of the past!
I gave the guidance of my mind away,
To be uplifted : now, on lower things, —
On trial, parting, woe of ignorant love, —
I dwell, as were they shadows coming on.

PETER (*sings*).

We are swallows seeking the land of spring :
　　We are faint, we have far to roam :
When shall we fold the weary wing,
　　Lord, in Thy promised home?
　　　　　　Home !
　We are bound for the promised home !

DAVID.

How is it that I still upbear their souls ?
The land, the temple, and His coming reign,
Through me and their acceptance of my power,
Fill and content them : I should be content,
If human memories were not obstinate
As human needs.　Do you remember still
The day that tried me most, and mother's words, —
" I cannot follow you, and dare not hold :
Farewell ! we shall not meet on earth again ? "
What I obeyed expunged the seeming wrong,
But not its lingering sense ; for while the wind
Blows softly over these unpeopled plains,
And in the middle watches of the night,
And when the young birds cheep their wish for morn,
I hear her say, and see her tearless eyes, —
" I cannot follow you, and dare not hold :
Farewell ! we shall not meet on earth again."

RHODA.

(Bending over her child.)

Sleep, baby, sleep !   The wind will blow the flowers,
The trees will drop their berries, all for thee !

PETER *(sings)*.

We will build the temple broad and high,
    And crowned with a golden dome ;
For the day of the Lord is surely nigh,
    When we reach the promised home.
                Home !
    We shall dwell in the promised home !

DAVID.

They shame me, who have also left their all,
Save, nurtured with an easier hope, they bear
A lighter sorrow ; yet as day by day
Their hosts increase, so mounts the sum of faith.
There was a woman came, a week agone,
To hear my message : on the outer edge
Of those few gathered in the dusky hall
She sat, and fixed me with her wondrous eyes.
At first I said, 'T is Mary Magdalen,
When sin forgiven still left her virtue sad ;
But, kindled with my words, the while I drew
A picture of the Kingdom, she became
Queen Esther, as in Shushan's royal house
She touched the sceptre, — proud, obedient,
Sure of the end.   A power came forth from her,
As if of wings companioning mine own.
Can she believe, nor follow ?

RHODA.

                Rather think

On these your faithful flock.   If she have power,
Indeed, the greater sin of pride is hers,
Whose gold and gay apparel are her gods.

DAVID (*musingly*).

The light of guidance never was so clear
And then deceived : what instruments I have —
Rough hands of workmen, by whose awkward use
The gifts almost become a mockery —
Still leave me helpless when the finer sense
Would snatch from floating lines a plan supreme.
There must be law, pure discipline of lives,
Foundations set, and pleasant sheepfolds made
In desolate places.   Ah ! were only one
But near me, bathed in equal bliss of faith,
To see, where I am dazzled, and to say,
" Build higher ! here enlarge the pillared front,
There push thy climbing pinnacles aloft ! "
Even light is lonely to a human soul.
Two glories are there ; and but one they know,
Save her who saw, then closed reluctant eyes.

RHODA.

Can you be faint of spirit while by you
We all are led ?   Then is the body weak,
And rest will be your medicine.

DAVID (*to* PETER).
Go on !

PETER.

(*Driving onward, sings.*)
The bolts of the Lord shall fall and burn
On Babylon and on Rome ;

But the chosen seed shall safe return,
To dwell in His promised home.
Home !
We have found His promised home !

Scene II.

Night. A camp on the banks of a small stream. Men, women, and children grouped about fires under the trees. In the centre a tent, before which a pole, stuck in the earth, bears a blazing torch. Outside of the camp a guard is heard to challenge some one approaching. After the password, "Zion," enter Nimrod Kraft. *He dismounts from his horse, and draws near the tent.*

NIMROD.

Hail, Prophet David !   Grace and blessing be
To all the chosen !

DAVID.

Be the words fulfilled !
You come beforehand, like the dove, to say
The waters settle, and the olive-tree
Puts forth new leaves.   We shall possess the land.

NIMROD.

We *do* possess it.   On the highest bluff
That overlooks full twenty miles of stream,
Now stand a hundred cabins : we have staked
The streets, first measured with the holy reed,
And broken cornfields from the stubborn sod,
And set young gardens round about the place,
That much do flourish.   Every work is blessed :
Even the quarry-stones come loose in squares,
As if they hastened to be lifted up,
And made the temple.

DAVID.

Ah ! when once it stands,
A visible sign, a shelter for our ark !

NIMROD.

Even so we feel.   They give their tithing-time
In faith and in rejoicing : I have used
The power you delegated to my hands,
Sifted the wheat, and sent some chaff adrift,
Fixed ordered rule, exacted industry,
And so blocked roughly out what you may shape
To pure proportions : as my work below
Grows up, may yours complete it from above !

DAVID.

Let all the frame-work needful for our flock,
As shelter, or enclosing law, be raised,
And quickly !   I have given you the Twelve ;
Yet they debate, methinks, or seek to know
Who shall sit highest.

NIMROD.

Thus it was of old.
Your headship must remain ; for you alone
Possess direct commission.   Let them see —
They whom your messengers found here and there,
And, not beholding, none the less believe —
What power is yours.   A little thing 's enough.

DAVID.

What mean you ?

NIMROD.

Well, I find it natural.
Your coming will be made a holy day ;
For all shall then be gathered as a brood

Beneath your wings.　And something they expect,
Some sign, or show, as reconfirming faith;
Or revelation, such as ignorant souls
Gape at and glory in.　None promised this:
But they believe, and therefore they expect.

DAVID.

When I was small, I planted once a tree,
Then every second morning plucked it up
To see if it were growing.　Summer came;
And while the others, left alone, were green,
Mine pined and perished.　Give the flock, instead,
This parable.

NIMROD.

　　　　　They would not understand.
Transplanted faith (let me the rather say)
Needs watering, shelter, all the gardener's care,
Till it be rooted.　Ponder this yourself.
Put on your sandals; leave the holier ground,
And walk in dust among the multitude:
So shall you feel their need.

DAVID.

　　　　　　　I never asked
But what is offered freely unto all.
There is no flame, it seems, that of itself
Will burn in earthly air; but, then, is flame,
When fed from coarser aliment, less pure?
Water pollutes itself from what is washed;
But fire takes up its own, and spurns the dross.
If that were possible to me?

NIMROD.

　　　　　　Yourself
Shall winnow, with a finer fan than ours,

Whom we have gathered. All is ready, else.
I will not keep your body from its rest.
With Hugh and Jonas, members of the Twelve,
I must consult, so portioning the homes,
That none shall mark advantage of the rest.
The flock is jealous : softly on the nose
Must we pat every sheep, as well as feed.

[*Exit.*

DAVID.

(*To* RHODA, *who has overheard the dialogue.*)

There goes a sense with which I cannot strive,
So well it builds, and so obediently ;
Yet power is lessened when it touches me.

RHODA.

I did not like the man, when he — I mean
His hardness first repelled ; but now, perhaps,
He is the coarser fuel, you the flame ;
And each may need the other. I, too, feel
That they which follow, never having seen,
Deserve a sign.

DAVID.

If so, the Lord will send.

[*Exit into the tent.*

RHODA.

Not their belief, but who it is believes,
Gives him support. That was a happy time,
When we alone went wandering through the land ;
For few could jeer, though many sore abused ;
And ever here and there a soul was caught
Out from the Gentiles, and was glad with us ;
And Zion with its temple shone afar,
More beautiful, I think, than now at hand.

I must not murmur : we are verily blessed,
Put past the reach of persecuting hands,
And guided so, that this fair wilderness
Already bears the roses as we pass.

SCENE III.

Another part of the camp. NIMROD, HUGH, *and* JONAS, *seated
near a fire.*

HUGH.

He will not, think you ?

NIMROD.

Nay, I said not that.
I only charge that nothing be proclaimed;
Then whatsoever come, if so it come,
Will have more operation. See, the flock
Is over-hungry for continual signs ;
Which, could they be bespoken, would be nought
But independence of the Lord.

JONAS.

Maybe.
But I that chose the gift of healing, I
That have obeyed in all things, I should heal !
If he must husband up his power to spend
On higher miracles, enough is mine
For lesser work : so strengthen, then, my hands,
That they on whom I lay them shall be whole.

NIMROD.

The wish may choose : possession comes by faith.
Know surely that you have it, and you have.

JONAS.

How know without a test?

NIMROD.

                              Ah ! there you lack
The last anointing ; there the prophet stands
Transparent in his own internal light,
While yours is cloudy still.   When you foresee
The healing of your hands, your hands will heal.

HUGH.

So works the gift ?   But, if *his* foresight be
Indeed so perfect, it were well to say,
As cheer to some, and guidance unto all,
This member strays, that rises ; these receive,
Or lose, — that our authority be firm:
For such picked out for higher reach of faith
Will stand, supporting us, above the rest.

NIMROD.

First show them patience !   Gathered here and there,
The dust of other life upon their shoes,
The stagnant blood of other creeds not yet
Purged from their veins, the Gentile taunt still loud
In ear and memory, restless from the change
And long privation of the pilgrimage,
They hear but halfly : we must give them rest,
Fitting their shoulders to an easy yoke,
Filling their cribs, and warmly bedding them,
Till they will rather serve within our fold
Than rule outside of it.

JONAS.

                        Is all prepared

For us who come? The people hear of those
Who, first arriving, may be better placed.

NIMROD.

I did not take my gift of prophecy
In vain : so ye declare it unto all,
Contentment waits for woman, man, and child ;
But to yourselves I promise more belief.
Go, hither bring the tally of your men :
My work is yet unfinished.

[*Exit* HUGH *and* JONAS.
                    All alike !
No one is certain that he has the power,
Unless his neighbor says so. Tell them, then,
They govern, governing myself the while.
So far were easy : yet from him comes forth
The fire that makes their dull cold metal bend;
And when to kindle it is in his will,
Not mine. He has a look of weariness,
And out of languor comes no miracle.
But oft, from very expectation, springs
The thing expected, if a cooler skill
Command the heat of others. What she plans —
If anything, indeed — I cannot guess ;
Not even whether like or dislike looked
From eyes that only seemed to hide her thought.
Turn either way, I 'm poking in the dark.
Well, well ! the morrow is the clearer day.

Scene IV. — The City.

*A street on a high, airy plateau, overlooking the course of a
great river. In the centre stand the unfinished walls of the
temple ; opposite to them a house larger than the others, its
front hung with garlands, and an arch of green boughs span-
ning the entrance. The people, several hundred in number,
are drawn up in lines on both sides of the street, with branches
in their hands. Shouts are heard in the distance, announc-
ing the arrival of the train : then* DAVID *appears on horseback, a little in advance, bare-headed, and wearing a long
white mantle : the people cast their branches before him.*

HYMN.

We have left the land of Egypt
   For the place of our desire:
Fallen is the gated city,
   And the woe thereof is dire :
The boughs of the tree are withered,
   And the women set them on fire !

Lo ! who is he that cometh
   In the name of the Holy One ?
The bearers of gladsome tidings
   Before his pathway run :
He bringeth us out of darkness,
   As the star that brings the sun.

(*The women step forward on each side, and sing,* LIVIA ROM-
NEY, *with a crown in her hand, standing in the midst.*)

Hail, all hail, to the prophet,
   Whose reign begins to-day !
Who hath laid his firm foundations
   In the dust of the world's decay :
He maketh the dry bough blossom ;
   He gathers the sheep that stray.

DAVID (*aside*).

It is herself !   How beautiful she stands,
Forgetful of the stare of wondering eyes,
And filled with promise of mysterious power !
She's Miriam now, and sings deliverance.
I breathe again : the weight falls off my soul,
As poising rocks are started by a sound ;
And I am glad and strong for what may come.

LIVIA.

(*Stepping forward.*)

Thrice hail, O Prophet !   Bow but once before
Thy humble handmaid, not as honoring her,
But that she reach thy consecrated brow.

(DAVID *bends down his head : she places the crown upon it.*)

Forgive me, that, when first I did believe,
I failed to follow : thus it came to pass
I went before to seal mine evidence,
Lest that were vain which I would ask of thee.

HUGH.

(*To* NIMROD.)

Who is the woman ?

NIMROD.

More than is her name
I cannot say.   'T is but four days ago
She landed from the river.   Worldly store
She seems to have, and knowledge of the world,
Notable cunning of the hand and eye,
And influence with her sex — perhaps with ours.
Foremost in planning this array was she ;
Went here and there ; was always first and last ;

And therefore fell to her, by proper right,
The place she wanted.

DAVID.

(*After a pause.*)
                    Thou art one of us.
There is no high or low : each bows to each
In whom the Spirit lives.   I saw thy faith,
And called thee : well it was that thou didst hear.
Not they who yield when buffeted by words,
And shaken by the signs, but they who feel,
Like wandering birds, where lies the summer-land,
And strike their way across the printless air,
Build up the kingdom.   Thine obedience
Is as a soil for planting of the power.
What is it thou wouldst ask ?

LIVIA.

                    The gift of tongues.

DAVID.

(*After looking in her face a moment, beckons.   She comes
                    nearer.*)
Take thou the gift, in measure as thy faith
Shall justify, and even so exercise !

LIVIA.

(*Steps back a pace, keeping her eyes fixed on* DAVID.   *She rises
to her full height, with uplifted head, and points towards the
temple.*)
Aïro pamétha loydór óndis abárka !

            (*Movements and murmurs among the people.*)

A MAN.

What tongue is that ?

A SECOND.

It must be ancient Greek,
Or Hebrew, maybe, as Isaiah spoke.
The sound is glorious.

A THIRD.

Never did I hear
Such mighty words.   Our preacher once came down
With " Armageddon, Pandemonium, Baal; "
But they were nought to hers.

THE FIRST.

'T is prophecy !
He understands : his face is like a flame.

LIVIA.

Oráthmedón ádra, bánnorim ádra slávo !

DAVID.

(*Rapidly and eagerly.*)

It *shall* arise !   The tempests of the world
Shall not prevail against it !   Every stone
Shall testify ! — from its completed towers
A light go forth till darkened Edom sees ;
And here, even here, where our Shechina stands,
When all mankind is gathered to our fold,
Shall angels plant the ladder of the Lord
For his descending !   Be ye not as them
That craved new signs, and were rebuked of Him !
Who feeleth not the presence of the power
Above us, in us, moving in our works,
And only sparing insomuch as saves
From easy heart, slack will, and idle hand,
Let him go forth !

CRIES OF THE PEOPLE.
Nay, nay, we will abide !

DAVID.

Forget that you have ever lived ere now !
As strips the serpent her uneasy skin,
And comes forth new and shining, cast ye out
Old hopes and hates, old passions and desires !
Be as a fallow field that waits new seed :
Take rain and sunshine in their times ; lie bare
To the invisible influence of heaven ;
And be assured from your warm breast shall spring
The holy harvest !   Ye have welcomed me
With faithful hearts and voices : so, henceforth
No more as one that in the wilderness
Cries to the stocks and stones, shall I be heard,
But as a father 'mid his children teach,
And as a brother 'mid his brethren love,
And as one chosen lead ye all to share
An equal power and glory.

THE PEOPLE.
Hail, all hail !

NIMROD.

(*Coming forward.*)

Here is your home : by her on whom the tongue
Descended at your bidding, it was dressed.
The humble house is like a bride that waits
The bridegroom's coming : enter, and be blessed !
I, and my brethren of the Twelve, have charge
That all, ere nightfall, shall be snugly housed,
New brethren mixed with old, but in such peace
And kindly fellowship, as, until now,
Hath not been witnessed, to the world's disgrace !

THE WOMEN.

(*At a sign from* LIVIA, *sing.*)

Make haste, Belovèd of Zion!
  The porch and the chamber shine:
We have gathered the myrrh and manna,
  And filled the flagons with wine :
Now comfort the souls of thy daughters,
  As the Lord shall comfort thine.

(DAVID *waits, standing under the arch, while* PETER *assists*
RHODA *to alight from the wagon.*)

PETER.

Well, here's the end!   Our Zion's rather bare,
But makes a good beginning.

RHODA.

(*Giving him her child.*)
                        Carry him,
But hold him gently : he is tired and scared.
I, too, am wearier than I thought to be,
And hardly happy in beholding home
Till I possess it.   David, come with me !

[*They enter the house.*

SCENE V.

The council-room.   Night.   NIMROD KRAFT, HUGH, JONAS,
SIMEON, *and two other members of the Twelve.*

NIMROD.

All now are housed and sleeping : first their souls
Were satisfied, and then their bodies soothed.
On this rock must we build.   The arch of truth
Requires abutments in the life of flesh :
It cannot hang in air.   See, therefore, ye,

That these the weak foundations of our state
Be firmer settled.   Scourge the drones away;
Over the labor needful unto each
Be labor added for the sake of all;
Let him whose lips are not anoint believe
With hand and sinew !

JONAS.

            If the hand should doubt?
Equality of service and of power
Was promised them ; and many bear the yoke
As they that seem to stoop, and mean to spring.

NIMROD.

Equality ?   Yes, were there equal faith !
Not yet dare I to measure mine by his,
The Prophet's, since the token lies in power.
They sleep ; we watch for them : why, let them watch,
And we will sleep !

SIMEON.

            Then wolves would rend the fold.
The new life must begin : he spake the word.
It will be hard ; but we submit to him,
And they not more so, in obeying us.

JONAS.

How far will he concede ?   The government,
Scarce framed as yet, will he alone direct,
Uncounselled, or be led to side with them
Who, standing nearest, easier prevail ?
Whence comes decision, when opinions clash ?

NIMROD.

By revelation.

SIMEON.

May it come at need!

HUGH.

We, the apostles of the wandering church,
Should be, of right, foundations here.

NIMROD.

                                    He takes,
Lifts up, or sets aside.   You know my work,
If it be good.   I never thought to say,
" Reward me ! " but whatever implement, —
Scythe-blade, or sword, or knife that scullions use, —
His hand has need of, he will find me that !

JONAS.

(Aside to HUGH.)

When one is sword already, sharpened too,
The offer 's glibly made.

NIMROD.

                    I say but this :
It was my providence to know him first,
To see descending on him, like a flame,
The Spirit : near, because alone, I stood,
But am less near than he who more believes.
What use of prying words ?   'T is signs we need,
Accord of all, the temple-walls complete
With roof and pinnacle, the shrine set up,
Symbolic vessels, altar, veil, and ark,
New psalms of praise, and joyfulness of hymns.
All this made visible, their faith is firm,
And their impatient thoughts, now floating loose
In every wind, will settle, and have rest.

                    [*Exit* HUGH, JONAS, *and others.*

SIMEON.

You touched his secret sore, — I name no names, —
Kept tender, as I guess, by discontent
Of womankind.   You 've seen the kind of wife
That never wholly justifies the man,
And, when he follows, straightway shifts her mind
To make new disagreement : such is she.
With brethren one must be considerate,
As you have been ; but those, whom now he makes
Apostles, should not wear a home-made bit.
That I am widowed, nigh a blessing seems,
Though mine respected me.

NIMROD.

                            The words I spake
Were but the Prophet's unpronounced desires.
I am the nearest yet, because I keep
A circle round him clear and unprofaned,
That so his soul be tempered to receive
Continual revelations.   They mistake
Probation, preparation, for the end ;
But that which draws the few is not enough
To sow infection in the blood of all,
And overcome the world.   Much more awaits,
And grander : are you as the fallow earth ?

SIMEON.

Yea, passive as a field the sower treads.

NIMROD.

'T is well : till he shall order otherwise,
Be led by me ! Go, now, and counterwork
The small dissensions : I have other tasks.
It was a wonderous sign that heralded
The Prophet's coming : keep the wonder fresh

In all, yet raise not wild and over-wrought
Expectancy of more.   The woman's power
Renews another ancient virtue lost, —
Zion shall have its prophetess !   I go
To give my homage, and to arm for us
A Deborah, — a chieftainess of the faith.

Scene VI.

A room in the Prophet's *house.* Rhoda *seated near the*
window, sewing; the baby asleep in a cradle at her feet;
David *at a desk, looking over some papers.*

DAVID.

The man must have commission from the Lord,
To plan such perfect system : not the bees
Get wax and honey, build their brittle combs,
And organize their kingdom of the hive,
So faultlessly.   My loss of power through him
Was but a fancy bred of weariness ;
For what he asked of my unwilling soul
Came, half a marvel to myself.

RHODA.

.   I, too,
Have thought him hard : he lacked your sweeter fire.
Yet surely something kindly planned this home,
Not chance, to give the dear familiar rooms
We first were happy in.   Young trees are set,
Like children of the old ones following us,
In the same places, by the southern porch ;
And in the garden — foolishly I cried
To find the cushions of the mountain-pink
And yellow-flags, and fragrant southern-wood.

Can this again be taken ?   Will there come
Aught to disturb us ?

DAVID.

                    Nay, it cannot be.
We build too surely : we are set alone
In a new land.   Why should the Gentiles mock
The boasted precedent whereon they build,
Their right of conscience, by molesting us ?

(*Enter* Peter.)

PETER.

The town is ringing with the miracle.
Whether 't was Hebrew, or the sort of tongue
That Adam spoke, they 're not exactly sure ;
But 't was a prophecy, and will fulfil.
Then, since it seems there 's here and there a man
Talks Dutch, or French, or maybe Cherokee, —
They 're all as one to them that never learned, —
She understood 'em !   'T was a coming down
Of tongues, they say, just like what happened once
Away in Mesopotamia.

DAVID.

                    Given at need !
By this I know the woman's lofty faith,
And eminence of prayer.   Why, save myself,
Not one hath been so visited.   New flames
Circling mine own, kindled in souls like hers,
Will help fend off the slow, devouring chill
That from the fiend is blown.

RHODA.

                    I thought her strange,
Scarce one of us, so grand and beautiful

And unabashed.   I should be grateful, though,
She drew away so many eyes that else
Had stared in wonder I should be your wife.

PETER.

They say, in getting up the welcome-home,
And such pontificals, she steered the raft.
Willing or not, or knowing things or not,
All, somehow, lent a hand : she had a way
To make them satisfied with what they did.
Talk of the — well, it nearly slipped that time —
Of *her*, and she appears.

                                        [*Exit.*

RHODA *(aside.)*

                        I cannot stir,
Lest baby wake ; and sure my place is here ;
Yet would that she were come and gone again !
(LIVIA *enters: she is simply but elegantly dressed in a black
        silk robe, and wears a white veil upon her head.*)

DAVID.

(Taking her hand.)

Be welcome, sister !   If I thank you less
For honor paid than for unstinted faith,
I most am grateful.

LIVIA.

                        What I fain had said
Falls back upon my heart as hollow sound.
Your soul hath read, and, reading, spares me words
That only stammer when my own would sing.
The marvellous light that entered me from you
I cannot fathom, nay, nor merit it,
Except in yielding, in receiving all,

As woman may, in whom the sense is quick
To conquer reason which resists in man.
I was a harp-string, mute until you touched:
If to your ear the sound be melody,
Strike out of me the strong, full-handed chords
To your exaltment!

DAVID.

(*Aside, as* LIVIA *goes forward to* RHODA.)
                    When was ever such?
The clear-eyed spirit, so superbly housed,
The power that bends in soft subservience,
The gift that beams on all except herself, —
Yea, she is chosen!   Yea, from out her eyes,
And from her hands, and breathing forth from her,
Is promise!

LIVIA.

(*To* RHODA.)

            You, whose blessed place it is
To touch and warm the Prophet's weary hands,
And, after shining visions, to restore
The virtue of his dazzled eyes, be kind,
I pray, and friendly!   I would have *your* love,
His confidence.   My life was not as yours,
Ah, me! as simply innocent and pure;
And yet, methinks, for them that meet in truth,
There's but a single gateway to the heart.

RHODA (*slowly*).

I think I never hated such as seemed
Unfriendly: if I fail to love, when love
Invites me first, I were not worthy it.

LIVIA.

(*Turning to* DAVID.)

My lines of life, as they draw near to you,
Lie clearly traced ; yet, as they backward tend,
Lead to confusions which, ere knowing them,
Your pardon touched.   The spoiled child of the world
Was I until I saw you ; born in wealth,
And cradled 'mid the shows and vanities
Religion covers with a modish cloak.
Pride to the right, to left stood Piety :
Each took a hand, and grimly led my life
Along the pavement trod by feet of all.
When I would wander free, as whoso feels
Some independent right of soul, gave Pride
A downright blow that stung ; but Piety
Pinched me in secret, while her leaky eyes
Wept rivers, and her whining voice bewailed.
Then I submitted, lived a ceaseless lie,
Till death and changes had delivered me
From all but wealth.   But, ah ! my fettered limbs
Were dwarfed and shrunken : I was free to move,
When motion was but pain.   I saw the world
As one beholds a casket, and the key
Thereof is lost.   I stood outside of life,
Helpless to reach existence I desired,
Disgusted with existence which I knew,
Until you said, or through your soul I heard,
" Daughter, arise ! " and I arose and came.

DAVID.

Not I, but what in me was manifest.

LIVIA.

It is the same.   By you alone I heard,

Through you am satisfied.   I hardly knew
What gift to claim, till something in your face
Gave me the words.   But now, farewell !   I go
To cheer, perchance to help, the others.

[Exit.

DAVID.

Go !

Delivered, thou, and crowned !   A woman's hand —
I had forgotten — yet it saved of old,
And here may build, as well.

RHODA.

Your lamp is lit
You know whereat ; and theirs are lit from yours.

DAVID.

Fire hath one being : 't is the life that makes
Obscure or luminous ; and hers, suppressed
By darkening hands, breaks out in splendid blaze.
She waited for me : I have bid her shine !

5

ACT III.

Scene I.

A room in the Prophet's *house.* David, Nimrod, *and* Livia *seated at a table upon which lie papers and plans.* Rhoda *at the window looking upon the garden, with some needlework in her hand.*

NIMROD.

IT means not failure.   Still our armor shines,
   Our weapons cleave ; but they whose power we
     shake,
The lazy priesthood of neglected law,
Have clothed themselves with cunning, to evade
Direct assault : so on their flanks exposed
Must we surprise them.

DAVID.

          Yet I would not haste.
Even after goodly battle, here we sit
Not quite secure ; for jealousy of some,
Unreasoning hopes that in denial end,
And selfish fretting o'er each needful curb,
Still task our wisdom : hardly can we spare
The fine, selected strength your purpose claims.

NIMROD.

There is no virtue but fatigues itself.
A sudden truth uplifts with violence
The prostrate human soul ; but once exhaust

The first impulsion, see how weak it stands !
So there 's a crisis this side of success
In highest things : our lot, this hour, is weighed
With that of all neglected, powerless tribes,
That have no life but in the founder's name.
If here we pause, we may become as they ;
But if, accepting every sign of power
As loan, or test, until another come,
We lime new branches, and extend our nets
To snare men's fluttering souls, we shall possess,
In time, the world.

LIVIA.

        Surely no less will you,
Our prophet ; and no atom less will we.
That few are gathered now, and halting minds
Grow restless, casts no shadow on the truth ;
For souls are verily but as frightened birds
That beat themselves against the pane, and shun
The hand that catches them to set them free.

NIMROD.

Well spoken !   Nothing more have I proposed.

DAVID.

I hoped direct, immediate influence —
The power that kindles, burns, and purifies —
Might be all-potent : yet, if men avoid
The touch of healing, must be first constrained,
Till health and gratitude together work
To bring them here, I cannot but receive.

NIMROD.

Then, if they come, why question how they come ?
The life delivered never faulty finds

The manner of deliverance.   I, once,
When caught by drowning arms that would have drowned
Me also, dealt a powerful blow that stunned
And saved the man.

LIVIA.

Deal out your blows to men,
And welcome !   Women claim a gentler touch.
How many are there, discontented hearts
That pine and wither, seeking sympathy
Their sex denies, and yours in half-contempt
Neglects to give !   For virile souls are coarse
And awkward, being selfish : the plain way
To woman's fast dependence (which she thinks
Dependence on her) you would seek in vain,
Unless an Ariadne gave the clew.

NIMROD.

Who, then, was she ?   A Gentile woman, sure,
Whom Paul converted.

LIVIA.

'T is enough that she
Was woman, and enough that also I
Am woman.   Once I dwelt in Rome, it chanced ;
And thither came a spinster whom I knew,
Free of the world, indifferent to love,
secure and calm in high intelligence,
armed at all points ; yet soon the Church espied
neath cold breasts the vulnerable sense.
The haughty priests, whose passionless, thin lips
rarely, but with dangerous sweetness, smile,
dreamy youths, the rosy acolytes,
to her, gave their faith the form of love,
with new passion, as in budding years,

Her woman's heart, sore with long abstinence,
Sent up narcotic heats that drugged the brain,
And she was theirs.   As easily were she ours !
There is no woman lives but in her soul
Demands a bridegroom ; failing one of flesh,
Then one of spirit.   Learn to promise this
In secret visitations, mystic signs,
Make truth seem love, and knowledge ecstasy,
And you will lead our sex.

RHODA.

(*Rising hastily.*)

Who, then, are *you ?*
What mother nursed you on such milk as this ?
I have but scanty words ; but in my heart
The woman, from her simple whiteness torn,
And dipped in scarlet, cries, " Not thus are we !
Not thus the loneliness of maiden life,
The lingering sorrow of frustrated love,
And pure regret, and tender hope outlived,
Seek compensation ! "   Less than moveth man
Gives woman peace.   The aged, innocent lives
Of childless widows and unwedded maids
Softly enclose us, young, and keep from harm :
Denied their own, they guard another's brood,
So gathering bliss.   But of what kind are those
Who find no truth, save men, forbid to wed,
Or wived already, offer it as love ?

LIVIA.

Your innocence takes false alarm : the old,
The gentle, fixed in narrow circumstance,
Good by tradition and temptation's lack,
Resist us most.   Who was it came to call
Not righteous men, but sinners ?   Virtue lifts

A front the braver after knowledge comes,
But is not knowledge first.   I spake of that
Whereof your ignorance is no reproach :
The blessedness of life descends on you,
But not on them you blame.

DAVID.

                    Reject not such !
'T was so commanded : them the Devil traps
It may be lawful that we snare in turn.
We fight the Fiend, my wife : our triumph here
Hath pricked him out of ancient confidence.

NIMROD.

The power is given : the secret of its use
Is left to us.   The first light dazzles men,
And some reach forth, and grasp the guiding hand ;
Then others say, with pupils narrowed in,
" There is no need : we see but as we saw."
Here, husbanding the busy strength of all,
And wasting naught, the comforts we can spare
Invite a double number : let them come !
And if, through weakness captured, they receive
The gift of power ; through greed, unselfishness ;
Through vain delusions, knowledge of the truth, —
What fool will cast away the tested gold
He gets, for promised copper ?

LIVIA.

                  Strange that men
Who most do suffer must be driven to good !
They are as children bribed to take the draught
That saves, even though the prophet's honeyed wine.
Lo ! now the temple's gilded pinnacles
The impatient sun hath kissed : across the land

They sharply shine like arrows drawn to head,
And heavenward aimed ! The signs portend increase :
Shall we alone be lean, while others burst
With useless fatness ?

DAVID.

Call our messengers
To learn a new commandment ! We must stay
Their sinking hands, fill up their flickering lamps,
And sting their souls with courage which o'ercomes,
Since it foresees. One weapon given to all
Were scarcely wisdom : lend the shorter arm
A longer blade, the less-enduring force
Advantage of the ground ! While they exist,
The Gentile churches, must we spread or cease.
I meant not idleness ; but, if so seems
This pause of preparation, let us work
Amid the noises of the ringing steel,
Heat with quick hammer-blows where fire may fail,.
And only rest when faint with victory !

SCENE II.

The council-room. DAVID *seated in an arm-chair at the head of a long table ;* NIMROD *at the foot ; on each side, six members of the* COUNCIL OF TWELVE.

DAVID.

Not every leaf an equal bounty finds
Of sap or sun ; yet rooted is our State
To grow, and not to wither. We must sweep
The troubled waters of the world, henceforth,
In wider circles, luring to our ark
Them, chiefly, for the covenant who yearn,

And would behold, distinct as graven words,
The signs thereof in us. If any here,
In view of such advantage, hath inquired,
And finds a partial answer in his soul,
Let him be heard !

NIMROD.

Some brethren, with myself
(For scattered duties scarce allow, as yet,
Full conference), have found accordant minds.
We, least of all fore-grasping power reserved,
But for projecting lines of present power
To their conclusions in the future, reach
This argument : We dare not mutilate
Our restoration of neglected faith
By preaching only : it must live in us
Until the ancient days and ways He loved
Shall draw Him near, — not simply where the soul
Trims her small chamber, or prophetic lips
Burn from His fiery touch ; but call Him down,
To make His very self endurable
To human sense.   A trance, mistook for death,
Thaws from the blood with struggle and with pang;
And still we feebly move the torpid limbs,
See through a veil, and hear but muffled sounds :
So you, whose hand upon us broke the spell,
Give, pulse by pulse, the life revealed to you,
As we take strength to bear it !

JONAS.

Not to me
Was this imparted, nor to some I know.
There may be times demanding cloudy speech ;
But clearer now were welcomer.   What pulse
Shall first be felt ?   The prophet called on us,
I thought ; and you direct us back to him.

SIMEON.

Without conferring, unprepared as you,
Yet do I comprehend.   The cloud may be
Inside of eyes that blame the sky for it.

NIMROD.

Nay, Simeon !   He who speaks in images
Oft sees the image taken for the thing.
Hear, all !   We mean to purchase power disused,
But never abrogated : on what rock,
If not on this, have we been building here ?
And he who welds again the broken link
Between the Lord and man, who summon us
To twofold lives that speak our waxing faith, —
Ah ! once let morning rise, men soon forget
Their hours of darkness, — he awaits that we
Obey his messages in soul and flesh.

HUGH.

Then what is past is sealed, our work approved
And fresh apportioned ?

DAVID.

                    Is not all one piece, —
Past, present, future, — as a youth in whom
The child expands, the man is possible ?
This restless ferment in the general mind
Must not infect my own : the charge ye bear
I gave, indeed ; but, save by constant guard
And forceful lifting of the soul, I keep
The separate gift, then were ye lost with me.
What I anticipate I dare not speak,
Until commanded.   Voices heard from far,
And shadows thrown, are stammering messengers ;
But when His will, in language and in form,

Arrives, the time of conference is past.
Speak, now, and freely : therefore I withdraw.

[*Exit.*

HUGH.

His words hold promise : he was highly moved.
Yet, if the revelation must forbid
All further question, why confer we now ?

MORDECAI.

In holy discipline. We, too, have felt
The breathing of the Spirit, and our souls
Point, like the smallest flame, the way it **draws** :
So, after him if now our light be cast,
We lead the others.

NIMROD.

Yea : what I declared
Was but direction, not a single path.
Who our accomplished work in truth accepts
Will halt not here ; but, bending yearning eyes
Upon their lives, who owned the heritage
From Dan and Hermon unto Hebron's oaks,
Will scan each custom, pleasant to the Lord,
And choose what fails us most. Let, therefore, **each**
Go back in spirit, serve in Jacob's stead ;
Behold the sons of Aaron with strange fire
Consumed, and stoned the son of Shelomith ;
Tarry with Judah where the way goes up
To Timnath ; find his feet, like Boaz, warm
From her who stole beneath the garment's skirt ;
Or, set in fruitful households, chant the psalms
Of shepherd-kings, and Solomon's high song.
All He allowed — nay, so encouraged, then,
He turned aside, and in the heat of day
Did visit His elected — must be ours,

Ere we, with hands and meats no more unclean,
Dare dress the board for Him.   What first to choose
Of new adornment for the mighty Guest
Is now our task.

JONAS.

You had not said so much,
Save you had chosen.   Let us know your choice.

MORDECAI.

While we aspire, it seems you 'd fain provoke
Dissension : rather to the records turn,
Dead histories so long, but now brought near
For pure example.

SIMEON.

Why, what words are his ?
From our beginning we have trod one track —

NIMROD (*interrupting*).

Which leads straight forward, over cowardice,
And half-belief, and forms of later law
God never gave.   What says the foolish world ?
That place and time and circumstance have changed :
Still those were holy men.   But what they did
Makes us unholy.   Oh ! He loved them well,
Stepped down from heaven upon their herded hills,
Talked face to face — so much priests bid us take,
Then — there they halt ; and all emasculate law
They teach, casts dirt on Israel of old.
Of kings, or prophets, or apostles, none
Forbids our following : every sign bestowed
On our new eyes says, Conquer all by all !

SIMEON.
(*Aside to* HUGH.)

He waxes mighty.

NIMROD.

'T is enough to-day!
The Prophet's words give guidance to our thoughts.
Let each into the closet of his soul
Retire a space, and there, alone, select
Not what the weakening leaven of the past,
And unabolished habit of the heart,
Stir up within us; but the thing he finds
Chiefest in ancient lives, and lacking here.
It may be we shall wander different ways;
But all lead forward, and will surely join.

SCENE III.

A garden in the rear of the PROPHET'S *house.* PETER *digging
a bed.*

PETER.

(*Pausing in his work.*)

I hardly ought to say it; but you can't
Turn one thing into t' other. Leastways, some
Have only changed their devils, not cast out,
And, with the pick and choice of gifts they had,
Are none the wiser. There my old horse-sense
Said, just as plain, " See whether you can use ; "
And, if I 'd opened mouth, and shut my eyes,
The Lord knows whether anything had dropped.
I can't make out : there 's going back and forth,
Like candidates before election-time,
When, with a little sleight-of-hand, a man
May sell two votes. Here, mine will hardly count.
Our David 's always safe, and brother Kraft,
And sister Livia, — each a regiment.
She looked at me in such an asking way,

This morning! what the — Zion — could she want?
Maybe, the temple — more pontificals :
Whichever way you turn, when sundown comes,
It's temple, temple, temple! I was glad
On their account ; but, now it's finished up,
Both him and her go sideling round the house,
As if forever hunting something lost.

(Sings.)

Oh! I've a hundred acres of land,
  And a house to cover your head ;
And in the spring, when the dovey-doveys sing,
  They say it's the time to wed.

Oh! I've an eye that is blue and shy,
  And a mouth that is red, says she,
And a heart at rest in my lily, lily breast ;
  And why should I wed with thee ?

Oh! take your choice when the days are long,
  And be sure you never will rue.
When I'm safe from storm, and it's bonny, bonny warm,
  Say, what will become of you ?

Oh! I'll comb and curl your bright brown hair,
  On a Sunday morning gay ;
For a maid, I guess, when she means yes, yes,
  Begins with a nay, nay, nay !

NIMROD *(entering).*

When birds sing that way, it is time to build.
Good-morrow, Peter !

PETER.

And good-day, high priest !
(Aside.)

I have a vote, it seems.

NIMROD.

Your plants are trim
And forward : that shows liking for the place.
The prophet told me, as an orphan boy
You came to him.

PETER.

Ay, 't was my only home.

NIMROD.

Your silent faith counts more than that of some
Who make a loud profession.   Modestly
You choose no gift; but you may highly serve
The Church, by being fully what you are.

PETER.

Preambles don't get through my head.

NIMROD.

Find, then,
A mate, and add a dozen to our flock.

PETER.

Oho !   That 's good advice.   But here 's my fix:
I stand half-way 'twixt Jane and Mary Ann
(We 'll say), both willing.   Now, to choose for good,
When either took, you might find afterwards
The t'other was the better, — there I stick !
I 'd let our Rhoda pick for me ; but then,
She don't know both.

NIMROD.

(*Lowering his voice.*)
If both were given to you,
As in the days of old ?

PETER.

(*Dropping his spade.*)

That's something new:
You mean it?

NIMROD.

What has been may be again.

PETER.

Well, each is pleasant while she holds the chance,
And would outbid the t'other: make it law
For all of us, the double check would last,
And they'd pull square, I guess.

NIMROD.

What thus relieves
Your own dilemma offers general peace.
But guard your tongue: I've no authority
To promise this, or even so much as hint.
You've read your Bible: what the Lord himself
Established for the fathers of the world
Is justified to us.

PETER.   .

And yet it's queer
To live like folks a million years ago.

NIMROD.

Ay, there you hit it! But the Prophet's power
Was lost as long. The hearts of men, you've seen,
Are like their stomachs, used to this or that,
Shy of the best of food, if other kind,
And some half starve before they taste of it.
Here you can aid: I need not tell you more:
There's ways of finding how a man inclines,
Without declaring much.

PETER.

I understand.

NIMROD.

The Prophet's soul is wrestling with his task.
Guard him from useless trouble, keep him free
From small disturbances !   'T is much for you
To be a faithful watchman at his gates.

[*Exit*

PETER.
(*After a prolonged whistle.*)
It 's half a pity such a man as that
Is out of Congress !   When he means a thing,
It 's safe to bet the thing will happen soon.
So *that 's* the secret ; and they 're flustered both,
Misdoubting, doubtless, how the folks will take !
I 'm mighty 'cute, when I lay out to be,
And here 's good reason.   Oh, I 'll bait my hooks,
And jerk men's thoughts out, fast as hungry pike !
I 'll go ahead where David wants to walk,
And cut a swath, then — Jane and Mary Ann !

SCENE IV.

The council-room.   NIMROD KRAFT *and the* TWELVE
assembled.

NIMROD.

Nine out of twelve — thereto my voice the tenth —
Give clearest title : there 's no room for doubt
(Which, as we stand, means nothing else than fear) ;
For each, in silent seeking, urged by none,
By none persuaded, found the truth.   We meet —
Against all secret understanding guard —
Declare in writing : speaks the Lord, or not ?

Who else hath made so many of one mind ?
And if the Prophet's light indeed be ours,
Shed on the law he means to give us next,
'T is as a chosen field should plough itself,
So eager for the seed !

SIMEON.

Who are the three ?

HUGH.

The question tells where you belong, at least.

NIMROD.

They know ; so shall the Prophet ; 't is enough !
The temple's dedication, now at hand,
Demands relaying of a basis built
Of what came nearest.   Thin and crumbling stones
Must be removed, and those of solid grain
Replace them ; 't was intended from the first.

JONAS.

I make no secret of dissent.   Your words
Imply a threat : so speak it honestly !

NIMROD.

Dissent may live, while disobedience dies.
I did not threaten : it may be myself
Shall be rejected first.   If you require
The human logic of the call divine,
To settle new misgivings, none will blame,
So, afterwards, acceptance follows.

MORDECAI.

Lord,
Enlighten them that wander in the dark !

6

SIMEON.

So near accordance, let us cease to strive !
The law we pray for gives new power to man,
Takes old reproach from woman, multiplies
Inheritors of truth, as born therein,
And heals perversions that distress the world.
Oh, may it come !

JONAS.

     Yes ; come to tear down homes,
And leave us tents instead, pitched wide apart !

NIMROD.

Even so they dwelt ; for Zion was their home ;
And thereunto they gave what you deny,
The riches of their loins.   Make end of talk ;
The Prophet waits.   Go, Simeon, bid him here !

(*Exit* SIMEON. *Immediately afterwards* DAVID *enters, and
takes his seat at the head of the table.*)

DAVID.

If I foresaw the form of your desire,
I left you, none the less, uninfluenced prayer,
And ample freedom.   Whither tend your minds ?

NIMROD.

One here impeaches my sincerity :
Let Mordecai declare !

MORDECAI.

     We ten are one.
Three choose another sign, or ours distrust.
We would restore that patriarchal home
The Lord preferred, — its fair, obedient wives,
Its heritage of children ; as He gave,
So giving now, that none be left alone

Or fruitless : thus the chasms of Gentile life
Wherein they fall, or pine on either side,
Shall all be closed in us.

DAVID.

          This makes a chasm
Impassable between us and the world.
Have you considered ?

SIMEON.

          They that follow you
Already crossed, and hurled the bridges down.

NIMROD.

Such test were all too easy.   In our hearts,
By long transmission of the narrower love
Make shrunken, is the field of sacrifice.
Who offers there, in cheerful company
With her who for her sisters' sake submits,
And for the Lord's high pleasure, hath prevailed,
Forgets that he has ever lived ere now
(Thus you commanded), and is surely blessed,
Save bankrupt be the treasury of Heaven.

DAVID.

Oh ! send us, Lord, Thy keenest tongues of fire
To burn out reason, greed, and appetite,
And leave, clear gold, the knowledge of Thy will !
There 's truth in your concurrence ; there is faith
That loves a trial ; yea, so much as this
Lies, as a tree, within our planted seed.
But — in His own good time !   What I declare —
Believe me, brethren ! — comes through sore travail
Of mind and spirit : I am set as one
Beneath deep waves, who, looking for the day,

Sees watery lights, and ever-shifting gleams,
Till, in a calm betwixt the billowy tides,
The sun a moment pierces.   Press not close :
The purest counsel may confuse us here.
Look ye, how many hearts are frozen yet,
Which, until thawed, must be withheld from fire !
But if —   Nay, this is all.   I charge you, wait !
On mine own soul I take the stress of yours,
To climb therewith : a finger stretched to help
May shake the balance : stand aside, and wait !

SCENE V.

A room in the PROPHET'S *house.*

DAVID.

(*Walking up and down.*)

I felt it come : within me and without
The signs agreed.   One influence said, "Postpone !"
But something else — what was, what is it ? — cries,
"No cowardice ! the leaven of the world
Works in thy nature."   Yet the inner sense, —
So pure it seems, even set against His light,
So simply strong, where old, insidious lust
May otherwise find entrance, — yea, it makes
Me coward !   Here might woman offer help,
Had she but reached that statelier modesty
Which takes all mysteries of love and life
As God's enactments.

RHODA (*entering*).

                    You have walked so long !
Your face is vexed with thought.   What is it fills
The very air ?   I have forborne to ask,

Knowing the burden of the fate of all
Weighing upon you ; yet, if those are right
Who counsel most, so soon to be relieved.

DAVID.

It is not that, or only in such wise
As manifest direction of the past
And present blessing may increase the load.
For triumph makes afraid : it stings and stirs
All sleeping evil to a new assault ;
Yet flatters so the self-exalted soul,
That what descended seems to dwell within.
They hope a further message, and with right :
The time is ripe ; but whether purified
As who accepts a truth re-making life,
Or half with us, and half, unconsciously,
Swayed by an ancient conscience —

     (*He pauses.*)

RHODA.

        Dare the truth,
As first you dared.   I know no other law
Than I have learned of you.

DAVID.

       There spoke my wife !
Yea, if all women were so sweetly strung
To trust and follow us, the task were light.

RHODA.

The women ?   How ? you doubt their equal faith ?

DAVID.

(*Slowly, walking up and down, and closely watching* RHODA.)
Not equal faith, but equal — shall I say —

Self-abnegation ?   Nay, the word escapes.
'T is one to either sex, yet opposite ;
For man accepts, without a harm to love,
What unto woman seems its fatal hurt.
Such were not those of old, the strong and proud,
The stately mothers, favorites of the Lord.
What wife was Rachel, when she Bilhah gave ?
Who now would yield, to multiply our tribe,
And take reproach from others, nuptial right ?

RHODA.

I fear to understand.   Who asks the " right " ?
What men demand the license ?   Surely you
Denied them ?

DAVID.

     Wherefore use unseemly words ?
Faith is not license, save in nobler sense ;
And prayerful questioning is no demand.
Say revelation, clear as any given,
Should this confirm : what then ?

RHODA.

      'T will not be given,
To strike the life from all true women's hearts !
Nay, hear me, David !   Do not turn your face.
You are so good !   They have misled your mind,
Those two, themselves misled, who cannot reach
Your purer height ; but this is not of you.
Were we alone, and some strange sacrifice —
'T is foolish, speaking thus !   Put me aside,
But think of innocent wives, whose joy of life,
So satisfied with trust in one man's truth,
Sustains them in long weariness and fear,
That end in pangs, and endless, narrowing cares :
No, no : you will not rob them !

DAVID.

                                    Have I robbed
All these of home, to leave them shelterless ?
Of ignorant faith, to send no power instead ?
If care be less for each, yet love remain
Enough for all, I give, not take away.
To set her delicate heart in common breasts,
And so interpret, is a woman's way :
Were all as you are —   Nay, there 's little good
Conjecturing thus : I have a single path.
Shall He desert me, after glorious signs
Given from the first ?   Why, that undoes my work !
Who was it sent me to the wilderness,
Unsealed mine ears until the distant voice
Drew nearer, and a vision of the night
So seized and shook my helpless human soul,
That breath forsook me ?   Yea, almost I brake
The spider's thread dividing earth and heaven ;
But such was not His will.   When morning came,
And, lapped in faint indifference to life
I lay, the barren rock before mine eyes
Was as a table, spread by angel-hands !
He gave me food : I ate, and I was saved.
As well refuse the food he offers now,
And let faith, starving, die !

RHODA (*eagerly*).

                                    Who saved you then
May save again !   'T is nought to offer food ;
But I obeyed a voice, this moment clear,
And charged, I feel, with all the Lord's high will
In woman manifest.   I pray you, take,
Even from my hands, which then were hid from you,
Now, openly, my evidence from Him !

DAVID.

What double sense is in your words ? I hear,
Not comprehending.

RHODA.

How could I refrain ?
Two days had passed : I dared not interrupt
Your solitude of soul, and prayers that fed
Upon the life of your forgotten frame ;
But, guided near you, oh, thank Him for that !
I left the food —

DAVID.

You ? you !

RHODA.

As was His will.
What ails you, David ?

(*Aside.*)
He is deadly pale ;
There 's something fierce and strange within his eyes :
He frightens me.

DAVID.

You brought me food ?

RHODA.

I did.

DAVID.

What else ? What more have you in secret done ?
Who taught you so to counterfeit the Lord ?
Woman ! to burrow underneath my feet,
And make a hollowness where rock should be !
How dared you cheat me ?

RHODA.

　　　　　　　　Slay me with your hand,
Not with such face and words ! If I but saved
(You say it saved you), how could love refrain ?
I have obeyed, believed all else in you,
As I believe and worship still : forgive !

　　　　(She falls on her knees before him.)

DAVID.

Not unto me, your husband, David, man ;
But, if I be a Prophet of the Lord, —
Yes, *if !* It seems to you a little thing :
Rise up ! I cannot answer now : the house
Rocks to and fro, the temple's pinnacles
Dance in the air like devils' shuttlecocks :
There's nothing stable. Rise, I say again !

　　　　(She rises to her feet.)

Now take your seat, and sew ! I 've heard it said
Women think better when the hand 's employed :
If 't is so, think !

　　　　(He moves towards the door.)

RHODA.

　　　David !

DAVID.

　　　　I go to pray.

　　　　　　　　　　　　[Exit.

RHODA.

Come back ! He 's gone. O God ! what have I done ?

Scene VI.

Midnight. The interior of the temple: a row of columns, on either side of the nave, throws the side aisles into shadow. A huge baptismal font of stone, resting on four rudely-sculptured figures, — a lion, an ox, a griffin, and a ram, — rises from the floor: behind, on a platform of stone, an altar bearing the ark, on each side of which lights are burning in seven-branched candlesticks. A veil, partly lifted on one side, conceals a semicircular chancel, which is the Holy of Holies.)

DAVID.

(Slowly pacing along the nave.)

And this complete, a house to give Him joy!
So near, so great, the triumph, and the dread
Forerunning it! But, while I feared a bolt
From heaven, the earth, without a warning, heaved.
She cannot see the harm, nor I translate:
O doubt of soul, so often trampled down!
O highest faith, as oft renewed in pain!
Why comes your fiercest battle now? *She* fed;
An accident upset the toppling rock;
The vision was a dream: the flock I lead
Is fooled by me, as I have fooled myself!
Howe'er I turn, I stand as girt by fire;
And all in me which seemed divinely good
Is changed to poison, made a scorpion-sting,
To pierce my soul with death. Oh, hearken, Lord!

(He buries his face in his hands. A shadow glides swiftly from pillar to pillar, and pauses opposite to him.)

LIVIA.

(Aside, in a whisper.)

He's nigh despair: I know — there's but one source —
Whence comes it. Fail me not, my woman's heart,
Or he and I are lost.

DAVID.

(Lifting his head.)
                    He will not speak!
Doth He not know how terrible it is
To ask, and not be answered? Why, one soul,
For sin so tortured, would make justice weep;
But this is good, this seek a million souls.
What, then, is He? Hold, hold! There lies a gulf
Whose awful darkness frightens worse than flame.
The thought's a serpent, coiled round heart and throat,
And crushing life, save one dull spark that burns
In suffering only.

(He staggers to one side and leans against a column.)

LIVIA *(aside).*

                    This is deepest woe
Of doubt, that vibrates back to faith again,
Can I but loose the string. He must not see,
Nor hear, as yet; but, stay! one chance remains.

(She steals forward, and vanishes in the darkness.)

DAVID.

Thus all accomplished crumbles, slides away!
Power lost, authority's a puff of smoke;
Respect becomes its angry opposite;
For each an insult in my failure feels,
Spying a cold intention where I gave
In self-forgetting faith.

                    This dare not be:
Am I set back, to seek His face again?
Through heat and haste of youth, too ardent hope
Of large acceptance, was confusion born,
And still I stray? Even for the sake of men,

Should I appear as I believed I was ?
One line of light, — one little entering thread,
As through a worm-hole in a shutter probes
A darkened chamber, — that would save my power.

(*The bass-pipes of the organ begin to sound, scarcely audible at
    first, but gradually increasing in volume ; then, after a few
    simple, alternating chords, a faint, flute-like stop is added.*)

Is this an answer, out of weary sense
Awakened, to delude me as before ?
Not so !   I cannot dream such harmonies :
That shuddering of the air, that far-off sweep
Of myriad voices, hiding what they sing, —
I feel, I hear again !   Come near, and speak !
Fold up your fluttering wings, that shake the sound,
Or soothe my passion, loosened through the eyes,
Till I distinguish !   Oh ! some pity breathes
In your celestial sweetness, melting me
To such self-sorrow, I can bear no more.

(*He covers his face and weeps : the music gradually ceases.*)

My soul is quieted, and yet so sad !
It seems to wait, not all disclothed of hope,
But passive, like the silence of a child
Shut up alone, whom love may soon release.
But I, — will love release me ?

LIVIA.

(*Stepping noiselessly forward : in a low voice.*)

Prophet, yea !

DAVID (*starting*).

Ah !   What is this ?   How came you here ?

LIVIA.

He called.

DAVID.

He called ?   What said He ?

LIVIA.

> First, " Prepare a chant,
> Meet for the dedication of My house."
> I rose, came hither ; and the organ-stops
> Compelled my fingers to the strain you heard.
> As in a dream, the solemn, breathing chords
> Filled all of space beneath the hollow sky,
> Above a valley ; trees and rocky crests
> I seemed to see ; and one awaiting soul
> Was there, and listening.

DAVID.

> Livia !   This you saw ?

LIVIA.

Dimly, and far away; but you were near.
Within the temple something wild and strange,
A sense of agony, a dread appeal,
So pierced my soul, I wept.   I felt whence came
The subtile influence, — felt, and yielded all
Receptive tablets of magnetic sense
Which woman keeps, the substitute for power;
Till what, unconsciously, you wrote thereon
Brought me to you.

DAVID.

> I wrote ? and you know all ?
'T were miracle ! and yet, within your eyes
I read the knowledge.

LIVIA.

> Also that my faith
Finds surer triumph planted in your doubt ?

This is the prophet-nature : such were they
Whose lips became live coals of kindled truth,
Dipped in the hell of an uncertain mind,
To fit them for the bliss of certainty.
What you esteem more keenly, dreading loss,
You will attain : your very fears are hopes ;
For, if the signs of power be accidents,
Then accident is greater miracle !

DAVID.

Ha !

LIVIA.

Thus, each side, your feet are firmly set.

DAVID.

And what I ponder, — is it known to you ?

LIVIA.

Ay, known and pondered, as a woman weighs
Her share in law, her half of destiny ;
Not coldly, but with warm, impressive mind,
That shapes its living features.   Would you see
Their form in mine ?

DAVID.

I feel it, ere you speak ;
And yet I would behold.

LIVIA.

Within my heart
Truth purer is than educated shame.
Unteach this last in woman, she will love
Not selfishly, as now, — possessing less
By claiming more, — but with a proud content
In yielding home and honor to the rest.

(*She speaks in a lower tone.*)

Here might I help : my heart suggests a way
It shrinks from, save extremity of need
Demand all sacrifice.   If I confess
One timid prayer, and justify the law
Through my desire, I do but shut the door
On its fulfilment.

DAVID.

Livia !

LIVIA.

Bid me speak,
And by obedience other bliss may come.

DAVID.

Livia ! fulfilment of your prayer, and mine !
So many hearts, as birds in mating-time,
Draw near each other perched on hedge and spray ;
But ours, like skylarks, met above the cloud !
When first I saw you, there was touch of wings,
Far up in loftier solitudes of air
A warm companionship.   You cannot sink
Below our partnered light, nor I, alone,
Aspire beyond it.   Come, and be yourself
The law, the revelation !

(*He stretches out his arms:* LIVIA *throws herself upon his
breast.*)

LIVIA.

David ! now
My Prophet and my love !
(*Kissing him.*)
Oh ! nevermore
Shall I, thus beckoned, falter on the way ;

But when your weary spirit leans on mine,
And draws such life as once, from hers he gave,
The Roman father, 1 am all fulfilled.
This is the place, the purpose, and the power
For me ordained : be not less bold to take
Than I to give !

DAVID.

(*Returning her kisses.*)

    This sign shall triumph.   Lo !
The Enemy but made his last assault :
My power comes back : the temple stands complete !

SCENE VII.

Midnight.   A bed-chamber in the PROPHET'S *house.*   RHODA
*seated near a small table, upon which is a shaded lamp ; the
New Testament in her lap ; the child asleep in a crib near
her.*

RHODA.

(*Closing the volume.*)

It is not there ; or else my troubled mind
Fails to detect it.   All the precious words,
All, all, I find ; that, like a mother's kiss
And healing breath upon her baby's hurt,
Make the poor heart forget its bruise, — all, all !
The sweetness of the Life that loved the world,
So hallowing human love ; the promises
That keep a nobler justice still alive
Beneath each wrong ; the nearness of the Lord,
As of a wing that covers and defends, —
They shine upon me.   Only this unsaid ?
He *must* have said it : they forgot to write.
It was so small a thing for Him, — ten words

To help all women, — yea, enough were three !
A single breathing from His lips divine,
And we were saved ; for, though He meant so much,
Not thus commanding, men will dare deny !

I saw the text so clearly in my soul, —
Already marked, and laid the open book
On David's desk.   He could not help but see,
And then the power within him would be firm,
I prayed, to conquer other counsel.   Ah !
What course remains ?   My tongue deceives my heart ,
I speak but foolishness, and vex him more.
But hers makes beautiful a darkened thought,
Makes purity a secret selfishness,
And holy love an evil.   Oh, 't is false !
Why, what did he declare me at the first ? —
That faith and love are one !   Give me a line,
Clear, pointed, piercing, from the armory here,
And I will use it as a sword.   I reach,
But they are hung too high, or over-weight
My hand ; and I am helpless to contend,
As if the Lord opposed me.

> (*The child moves restlessly in his sleep.*)
>   You are safe,

My baby, even from the world's reproach, —
Of love begotten, ere its nature strayed.
What waits for you and me ?   Confusion comes
When that which in the universal heart
Alone is holy finds no reverence.

> (*The child wakens, and begins to cry.   She takes him from the crib, folds him warmly in the bed-clothes, and rocks him upon her breast.*)

Hush, darling, hush !   If that thy mother's woe
Hath pierced thine innocent, unconscious rest,

7

And wakened thee in witless trouble, hush !
Thou art too young for anything but joy,
Too dear for shadowed pain ; and some old song
Must cheat my sorrow till thou sleep'st again.

(*Sings.*)

" My baby smiles, at last awake :
　　The curtains let me draw,
And on my happy bosom take
　　The child he never saw.

" He 'll come to-night : the wind 's at rest,
　　The moon is full and fair ;
I wear the dress that pleased him best,
　　A ribbon in my hair.

" So lately wed, so long away !
　　But, oh ! between is joy :
He left a wife ; he 'll find to-day
　　A mother and a boy.

" Be still, my heart ! the sound I hear
　　Is not the step I know ;
But hope so perfect turns to fear,
　　And bliss is nigh to woe.

" What voices now delay his tread,
　　Or plan a sweet surprise ?
Come, babe ! and we shall wake, instead,
　　The rapture of his eyes."

The moonlight, through the open door,
　　Upon her forehead smiled.
Still feet and frozen heart they bore :
　　He never saw his child !

(*She breaks into a passion of weeping.*)

ACT IV.

Scene I. — The Temple.

Grand ceremony of dedication : the main aisle is thronged with people, — men, women, and children. The baptismal font is filled with water, and decorated with garlands. Lights are burning in the seven-branched candlesticks : a flat bra- zier, containing live coals, stands upon the altar. The Holy of Holies is concealed by a dark purple veil. Upon the plat- form, in the centre, on the right hand of the altar, stands David, *in robes of white, embroidered with gold ; on the left hand,* Nimrod Kraft, *as high-priest, in robes of violet, em- broidered with silver, and a tall silver mitre upon his head ; behind them ten members of the* Council of Twelve, *in robes of pale green, bordered with crimson : they bear symbols, representing the gifts and attributes of the Church. Four boys, standing below, in front of the altar, hold censers in their hands.*

DAVID.

THIS having heard, — commanded to receive,
  By Him who speaks through me, — do you possess
As somewhat unto them whose hearts are strong
To plant His service in devoted lives,
Permitted ; not as ordered unto all.
The sword of Truth is only terrible
Against defiant wills : whoso obeys
In spirit, though his human reason fail,
Shall yet perceive in spirit, and be glad.
It is the highest faith that tramples down
Rebellious intellect : while this is blind,

That sees ; and even where the softer heart
May tremble, in its delicate habit jarred
By harmonies of love that first disturb,
'T is Faith that soothes our bosom's frightened bird,
And says, " The nestlings and the nest are safe."
Remember this ; and still exalt your souls
To light that purifies, while fancied warmth
May stream from darkness.   That revealed, I give ;
Not that expected, or of men preferred.
And Thou who gavest, symbol of whose truth
These living coals upon Thine altar glow,
Take, from the hands of the anointed priest,
Our first burnt-offering !   As it melts in flame,
And radiance out of darkened dross is born,
So melt from us, in this Thy holy house,
All understanding, feeling, thought, and love
Not meet for Thee, till every soul, refined,
Burn in an upward glory !

NIMROD.

                        If strange fire,
Hated of Thee, the food of heathen gods,
Come forth from what we offer, quench the flame,
Or turn it back, consuming these my hands !

(*With both hands he casts something upon the coals. A clear,
rose-colored flame arises, steadily increasing in brilliancy,
until all the interior of the temple is tinted by its radiance.
The boys swing the censers ; and the clouds of perfumed
smoke are illuminated as they rise.*)

CHANT.

(*With full organ accompaniment.*)
Hosanna ! harp and song
   Proclaim the consummation :
Homeless on earth so long,
   Thou hast an habitation !

As was of old Thy bid,
Thine holy place is hid :
Descend, and dwell amid
Thy chosen nation !
Hark to the voice of Thy welcome, Jehovah !

Make this Thy city proud,
And this Thy sacred river !
Guard us with fire and cloud,
And arrows from Thy quiver !
Increase us where we stand,
That we possess the land ;
And from our enemy's hand
With might deliver !
Dwell in the house we have builded, Jehovah !

JONAS.

(Among the congregation, to HUGH.)

The most are caught.   I marvel at myself,
Like one, who, entering on a company
Filled with deceitful wine, tongues thawed and hearts,
Feels an unfriendly soberness of blood,
Until their folly rights him.   This alone
Were harmless luxury for stinted souls,
Save for its rootage in their homely lives.
The evil waxes strong.

HUGH.

And weak, thereby,
Our chances.   Note the women's faces, here !
At first I thought them troubled : now the bait,
Self-sacrifice, upon the hook of faith,
But gently frightens : they already feel
Consent approach, and shyly play with it,
To gulp more perfectly at last.

JONAS.

Be still !
The priest, through all his haze of sanctity,
Fails not to watch us : meet me three days hence.

NIMROD.

(*Addressing the people.*)

Even as He charged, sojourning in the coasts
Of Gadara : tell no man this ye saw !
Who come to us must their belief attest,
Ere they be worthy of the signs.   Dull ears
Misread the revelations : clouded eyes
Behold them darkly.   Wherefore, you that know,
Be as encloséd gardens to the world.
The highway is no Tabor, meet for saints ;
The market-place is no Gethsemane.
Keep the exceeding nearness of the Lord,
This day, and when again in voice and flame
He visits us, like secret holiness
We share as brethren, but none else than we.
I gave you once the Prophet's parable,
Here verified : the tender roots of faith,
That feed such glorious summer-leaves of life,
Lie deep below, and wither when laid bare.
A happy bond, indeed, is speech of that
Which moves the heart ; but holier, sweeter far,
The bond of silence, guarding truth revealed !

MORDECAI.

(*To* SIMEON.)

Wise words, and most devout !   But wherefore now
Adds he this law, when, publishing the first,
We gather thousands ?

SIMEON.

      Not to any one
May I declare, even that I know his mind.
I say not that I know it; be assured,
No less, that also wisdom orders here.

DAVID.

(To the people.)

Once more my mouth is opened ere ye go.
In every house the fatness of our land
Prepares your feast; the shawms and sackbuts wait,
With lighter measures, for rejoicing feet;
The day is made a glory, far and wide,
On shore and river.   Issuing forth to these,
Let not your perfect exaltation sink
Even to the gladsome level of the time.
Behold in all, as out of nothing wrought,
What here the soul commanded, and the hand,
A willing slave, fulfilled!   As it hath been,
So, with increasing forces, let it be;
And, from the loins of us that humbly serve,
Shall start the lineage of millennial kings!

(Sound of the organ.   The Prophet, High-Priest, *and members of the* Twelve *come forward to the front of the platform, and lift their hands, while the people gradually disperse.)*

Scene II.

A room in the house of Jonas.   *Night.   A small lamp burning upon the table; the shutters closed.* Jonas, *his wife* Sarah, Hugh, *and* Hiram, *a member of the Church.*

SARAH.

Walls hear, 't is said; but they 've no tongues to blab.
Up street and down, so far as I can see,

'T is lonely as a graveyard : use your chance,
And well, and quickly !

JONAS.

        Many more are ripe
For what we may determine : all they need
Is certainty of equal power opposed ;
And this, within the compass of our flock,
They see not, neither is it found : so strong,
So as with Devil's wisdom skilled to work,
Is Nimrod Kraft.   But one thing hath he taught
Whereby we profit, — to keep counsel close,
Direction in a single pair of hands,
And move, when ready, backed by secret force.
Why, such a man profanes conspiracy,
So using it !   His weapons, in our hands,
Scoured by the better purpose, are made sure.

HUGH.

The hands are yours that shape the counter-plan ;
And mine are idle till you bid them do.
Whence comes the equal power ?

SARAH.

           If men are weak,
Then women easily may foil the law.
It were the rarest show, good faith ! to see
The battle left to us ; our recompense,
To own their weakness whole, which, but for us,
Would be divided.

JONAS.

        Nay, you haste too much.
Already half the leaven of discontent
Is kneaded up in their submissive clay ;

And that which drew us, and we still accept,
Grows one with what we loathe.   Thus open war
Were vainly ventured: leaving them, we lose
Possession and its chances.   What remains ?
The help abiding in the outer law, —
A hand still stretched, to smite where it forbids,
As this, yet spare whatever else we hold.

HUGH.

Then, as I guess, you guide the Gentile law
To his confusion only ?   Can you stay
Its meddling there, nor open other pleas,
Which, in the end, may set us where we stood
At the beginning ?

JONAS.

                There my secret lies.
The world is pressing on us : right and left
New colonies have passed the prairie lands,
To settle on the river-bluffs, and build
Some cabin-city they believe shall be
A centre of the world.   The chief of one,
And potent in their county government,
Is kin of mine ; and messages have passed.
That half the plot, and most of danger, falls
To them who work outside, not seeming leagued,
Demands advantage.   What were ours to give,
After success, and what were fair to give, —
So that the leadership secures to us, —
Needs final parley : time and place are fixed.

HIRAM.

As here and now declared : this day I bore
Your message and its answer.   Colonel Hyde
Sees lighter work in leading on his men
Than holding back : the excitement grows apace.

Give evidence to make pretence of law
A legal movement, should the law inquire :
He asks no more.

HUGH.

The revelation, say ?

JONAS.

Just that ! With all the priest's freemasonry
To keep the usage secret, here and there
Are leaky souls : the raftsmen, as they pass
The landing ; firemen, wooding up their boats ;
Or peddling agents, prowling through the land, —
Catch hints of it, and bear disfigured forth.
Thus interference threatens either way ;
But we avert a ruin possible,
And seat ourselves in power, to change and save,
By pointing the attack.

HUGH.

And yet I 've heard
How one, that, in the guns against him fired,
Had rammed blank cartridges, forgot a ball.
Your plan is perfect, if the guidance holds —

SARAH.

(*Interrupting him.*)

What man are you, to fear the lesser risk ?
The thing is coming.   Standing now to us,
You lose no more, though interference fail,
And gain by any change.

JONAS.

The fact of kin
In him whose hand must grapple with the priest
Is my security.   Full match is he,

As you shall know. We meet, to settle all,
Beyond the river-bend, just where the bluff
Turns inland, and the little brook comes down.
'T is thickly wooded : there the Indians made
Their final stand; and rows of bleaching ribs
Shine, like the fangs of steel-traps, from the grass.
Even border hunters, bold to hug a bear,
Avoid it after nightfall : we are safe
From even suspicion's ear, conferring there.
Will you go with me ?

HUGH.

                    Coward am I not,
Though cautious, as befits a man full-grown.
But woman's virtue caution never was :
Only the rash are brave to her.   I 'll go !

SCENE III.

Night.   A street in the city.

HUGH.

(*Walking slowly homewards.*)

Were he alone, he might conspire alone,
And welcome !   This is shrewdly done, if his ;
The more, if hers.   I thought her not so wise.
If interference menaces indeed,
And one might make conditions, then, why, then
Comes chance to seize o'erthrown authority, —
No matter whose, — and let it stick to me.
So much there is of wisdom in the plan :
We lose by quiet, and we can but gain
By new disturbance.   Had he promised aught —
But 't is the same !   What as an offer fails,
Can I exact : which side goes up or down,

One moment both are balanced evenly,
And then a hand decides.   The man's a fool
Who thinks to cheapen revolution's cost,
And feed enthusiasm upon itself,
Without the hope of benefit: go to !
I may be made a cat's-paw, but sharp-eyed
To grab one chestnut, — let me see it first !

NIMROD.

(Suddenly appearing at his side.)

I 'll show you !   What !   you meditate escape ?
Stand still !   I will not touch you, since you must.
How left you Jonas ?

HUGH.

In his usual mood ;
Dissenting, yet not disobedient.

NIMROD.

And yours the same ?   Should I repeat his words,
While every tone is in your ears alive,
You would deny them : so I waste no breath.
I would have suffered you to take the leap
To that fair quicksand-scum you think is turf,
And said, " Good riddance ! " — save that you can
serve ;
And that you *will*, is truth, when I declare
You shall not serve unpaid.

HUGH.

A Devil's brain
Is yours !

NIMROD.

A brain that once he owned, perhaps ;
Now by the Lord, to his discomfiture,
Tuned otherwise.

HUGH (*aside*).

Why, even here, to me,
With both hands full of treachery and bribes,
He says such things !   That 's genius, on my soul !

(*Aloud.*)

The Lord directs you ? well, then also me,
If I should do your will.

NIMROD.

My instrument
Is surely His, in spite of halting faith.

HUGH.

What would you have me do ?

NIMROD.

Stay what you are,
A traitor ! plot and plan our overthrow,
With him and others ; only, as a spout
Collects, from every shingle on the roof,
What rain it sheds, to fill the thirsty tank,
Convey to me your knowledge, me alone !

HUGH.

The Lord commands at will what He forbids,
It seems, or you interpret loosely : be it so !
I 'll grant His purpose better known to you,
And let you patch the breakage in His law ;
But, if the open virtue earns reward,
This claims a higher payment !

NIMROD.

In your work
Will soon be shown the form of your desire,

Which, being seen, I 'll make reality.
Though partly known to me, I dare not speak
The Prophet's mind, but bid you ponder this :
If you were set aside, not faithless charged,
Nor any virtue lacking, but for use,
As one unjustly to conspiracy
Compelled, by justice to be beckoned back,
And crowned by honor when the plot is crushed,
How then ?

HUGH (*aside*).

                This is a touch beyond me.   Driven,
While will and purpose wholly seemed my own,
To do the thing he wanted, — can it be ?

(*Aloud.*)

" How then ? "   'T is just another miracle.
There have been men whose tongues or hands obeyed
Some dark, mysterious force, and did the things
Their souls resisted : am I one of such ?

NIMROD.

It well may be : the working of the power,
Itself, is mystery.   Weary not your mind,
As if to your account were aught set down,
Even seeming treachery.   So much we know,
Source, pretext, object, chance, and means of aid,
That, had your virtue yielded, we were safe ;
But time is gained since you endure the test,
And labor lessened.   Here your service lies.
First, come with me, and state the very truth,
Mindful that, if you swerve, my knowledge waits
To prop your memory.   This rehearsal made,
And duty fixed in what concerns us next,
We 'll talk of your exaltment and reward.

[*Exeunt.*

Scene IV.

Livia's *house.*   David *seated in a cushioned arm-chair:*
Livia *on a low stool beside him.*

DAVID.

The restlessness that stirs in feet and limbs,
The dull confusions that besiege the brain,
The strange uncertainties of heart, pass off
When you are near me : overhead in blue
The sun comes out ; and life is like a land
Where tempered winds kiss buds, and make them
         flowers.
What is your magic ?   Nay, it is yourself !

LIVIA.

It is that I, who follow and believe,
So spared the high anxieties of soul
In you that cleave your passage to the truth,
Am ever fresh, a little way beneath,
To stay your weariness from further fall.
The light your being brings transfuses mine
With strength and gladness ever to uphold
Myself, upholding you.

DAVID.

                 The gift of tongues
If I bestowed, yet scarce the gift of song.
Whence come your hymns, as eloquent of faith
As Miriam sang, between the sea and Shur, —
Rejoicing strains, that suit our cheerful laws,
And shame the Gentiles' wailing psalmody ?

LIVIA.

'T is consecration of a skill profane

Wherein my soul found foolish peace.   I sang,
In that dark time before I saw your eyes,
Of knightly harps, and willow-wearing maids,
Of jewelled crowns, red swords, and evening stars,
And lonely tombs, and ghosts that wept and went,
One burden beat through all.   Such songs betrayed
The lack of that which sweeter is than song,
Now found ; but raptures of believing bliss
Seek the same passage, and the single voice,
Chanting in them, becomes the speech of all !
Stay, would you hear a ditty which yourself,
As one whose arm may brush accordant strings,
Nor mark in passing, did awake in me ?
A secret, else, and dumb for other ears.

DAVID.

Oh, sing !   Though David's craft you exercise
In being silent, yet my soul demands.

LIVIA.

(*Takes a guitar from a table, tunes the strings, and after a
soft, subduing prelude, sings.*)

Let words be faint, and song refuse
　　To frame the speech divine :
Look on me, love, and all they lose
　　Your eyes shall sing to mine !
I ask no voice to breathe my bliss,
　　Or bid its answer come ;
For lips are silent when they kiss,
　　And meeting hearts are dumb.

A wave that slides to clasp a wave,
　　On mine your being flows ;
The pang you took, the peace you gave,
　　Must wed in such repose.
So, love, your eyes alone shall tell
　　What else were unconfessed ;

And, if too fondly mine compel,
Oh, hide them on your breast !

DAVID.

Livia !   What are you ?   What triumphant force
Flows out from you, and knits my blood with yours ?
How is it that the liquid dark of eyes
I gaze on grows a broadening sphere of light,
Enclosing me forever ? — touching so
Your hand, that suddenly a warmer world
Beckons and wooes as if it might be mine ? —
That in your cheek the blossom-tender flesh,
As it were spirit, sanctifies my lips ?
Oh ! you are beautiful.

LIVIA.

Because I love !
All happiness prints beauty on the face.
I cannot keep it like a bridal-dress,
Laid in a drawer, with fragrant orris-root,
And wear my working-gowns again.   I 'm bold,
And proud of boldness, glad because of pride,
And love the more for gladness !   Thus my heart
Beats in a ring, beginning as it ends, —
A magic circle, and you dwell therein !

DAVID.

My love !

LIVIA.

You say it, and I echo back.
What more is freedom to a beaten slave,
Than this to me ?   Oh ! I could sit, as now,
And study all the beauty of your eyes,
Where nameless color brightens here to blue,
And there turns brown, until the dusk should leave

8

Their sparkle only.   I could part your locks,
And from my fingers shake their wandering gloss,
To seize again, and soothe with creeping thrills,
Till you should dip in slumber ere you knew.
I am as one that scarcely can believe
Past poverty is o'er, but ever spends,
To teach himself his hands are verily gold.
If you have feared, lest shame and danger wait
To blight the second marriage of your heart,
Leave me to meet them, and to tread them down !

DAVID.

I fear no more ; I wait no longer : come !

SCENE V.

The council-room.   DAVID, NIMROD, SIMEON, *and* MOR-
DECAI *in secret conference.*

DAVID.

The danger's real : shut within our camp,
Would perfidy, in time, consume itself ;
But thus, in league with outer ignorance
That easily breeds hate, it threatens harm.
Have you assured yourself how much of truth
In this alliance lies ? — with how much power
It arms itself ?

NIMROD.

　　　　　Last night my messengers
Came back from close espial of the land.
With tongues disguised to speak the Gentile mind,
They won so much as Colonel Hyde sees fit
To let his followers know ; and strangely shows

Our Church's image in their looking-glass !
Hereof they speak : a faction needing help
Among us ; hints of strange, unholy rites
To be suppressed ; and promised evidence
(For he, considerate of future place,
First means to lift the banner of the law) ;
Then, last of all, his godless crew expects
Plunder and ravage ! They would snatch away,
With unclean hands, the Lord's high heritage, —
They careful of the faith ! The Devil laughs,
Methinks, to see such Christian volunteers
Assail our industry with hands of theft,
Our laws with sinful bodies, and our prayers
With tongues that cast defilement when they speak.

MORDECAI.

Oh, sons of Belial ! But the Lord shall raise
His hand to smite, as at the gates of Aï.

NIMROD.

What have we done that should alarm their law ?
Lo ! strife and murder in this border land
It scarcely chides, is patient of free lust,
Yet makes a culprit of the sanctioned love
That broadens home. It waits for evidence.
I would not counsel rashness : let it wait,
And not receive !

DAVID.

       Then is their pretext vain ;
For we, appealing to the selfsame source,
Possess law's shield, to hold against its sword
Wherewith they threaten. That were best of all ;
But how prevent the tales, if true or false,
Which may be carried ?

NIMROD.

(*After a pause.*)

　　　　　　　　He who governs us
Once smote directly : will He do so now?
The liar once fell dead ; the enemy
Was slaughtered, and no child of all his seed
Renewed the race : even mercy was reproach,
And Moses felt the anger of the Lord,
When human plea persuaded him to spare.
How much the more than what was punished thus
Doth Jonas purpose !　Why delays the bolt?
Why rusts the blade in God's closed armory?
Or, waits He for our call? means He to test
What zeal and courage guard His holy place?
Then, cry aloud !　As it was said of old,
They were not, for the Lord had taken them,
So in your soul command, Let him not be !

SIMEON.

Ay ! that were shortest passage to the end :
Let him not be !

MORDECAI.

　　　　　　Who from the Anakim
His hosts delivered, over Arnon led,
And gave the men of Heshbon to their hands,
Will, from exceeding smallness of this prayer,
Be merry in his mind !　No giants here
Oppose our path, but one malicious dwarf,
Whose pointed tongue may verily stab to hurt :
Let him not be !

DAVID.

　　　　　　If some mysterious ail,
Even while we speak, should palsy all his frame,

Yea, stop with sudden check the wheels of life,
The thing were good ; but thus to stretch a hand,
And beckon, consciously, the fate on watch —
Why should it seem so different ?   What sense
Makes us so thoughtless when we plant a life,
Knowing the awful sanctity it holds,
When we would take away ? Yet, if life serve,
Fulfilling as it may His will in man,
Then why not death ?

(*He pauses, looks upwards with an expression of profound
    abstraction, and continues, as if speaking to himself.*)

       I see the poor beast's eyes,
And that tremendous question hid in them,
I tried to answer.   Like a human life
I loved the dog's ; but when the other came,
With certain madness in his slavering jaws,
And sprang upon and bit and tumbled him,
Then staggered forward, seeking where to die,
My hands were armed with pitying cruelty.
And he, so doomed, forefeeling all his doom,
Crouched down, and, whimpering, read some fatal change
Set in my face : the liquid, lustrous eyes,
So sad with yearning after human speech,
With love that never can declare itself
So tender, now so wild with dumb despair,
Implored in vain : it was a tragedy,
O God ! and I the unrelenting fate.
'T was kindness, in the shape of monstrous guilt
Disguised ; and, for his sake and mine, I prayed
That, through continuous being, he might know
And pardon.

    Even so doth God prevent ?
Is moral madness, some implanted seed

Of harm to all, thus hindered in our lives,
Though by the uncomprehended blow should bleed
A thousand loving hearts ?   I thought so then.
It seems not much, when such an aim demands :
" Let him not be ! "   The words themselves seduce
With seeming innocence, — and each a stab :
" Let him not be ! "
(*Nimrod makes a sign to Simeon and Mordecai, who steal
quietly out of the council-room.*)
                                   I shrink from asking that
Which in my secret soul I hope may come :
Why should I shrink ?   The days wherein we live
Allow no Moses-nature ; but for him
The Lord descended, counselled face to face,
And hallowed slaughter with direct command.
Am I so far from ancient holiness,
I dare not pray His hand should touch the man
Who plots my ruin ?   How bring, otherwise,
Conditions which make sure the covenant ?
Here lies a *must :* it calls me to subdue
My frightened fancy, and forget the heart
Which tries to make itself accomplice : yes,
I will implore *His* vengeance, — but no more.

NIMROD.

And should He answer, as my faith expects,
The prayer is justified unto your soul.
Your dread is but the birth-pang of the law
Reborn in you ; and when in living flesh
It smiles, and waxes strong, you will forget
All save the glory.

DAVID.

                       Be your words fulfilled !
The thing you counselled is already done.

What in the soul one fleeting moment stands
Is asked beyond recall : let us go hence !

                                        [*Exeunt.*

SCENE VI.

A narrow, wooded ravine between bluffs crowned with rock.
Late twilight. JONAS *and* HUGH *under a tree.*

HUGH.
(*Aside, looking around him.*)
A pokerish place !   There 's something in the air
Breeds thoughts of murder ; and I 'm cold with creeps
That pinched my flesh, from stepping on a spine,
Wherefrom the skull, so loosened, rolled away.
Were but the business done !
                    (*Aloud.*)
                              He 's in no haste,
Or we too hasty : he outstays the time.
Once more reflect upon the thing you do :
Is it well done ?

JONAS.
                    I settled that at first.
There 's safety in surprise : if Nimrod guessed
The range of popular impatience, then,
I grant you, were some hazard to be met.
But he is idle, seeks additional wives,
And feels as certain of the power he holds
As doth a man of money in his fist,
While at his back the robber's club is raised
To stretch him dumb.

HUGH.
                    A strong comparison !

JONAS.

It suits his case.   You think I underrate
The man's intelligence ; why, not a whit !
Our lucky chance is his security,
Which we must use before a breath disturb.
                    (*A low whistle is heard.*)
The Colonel's signal !
                    (*He whistles in answer.*)
                    Mark you, when he comes,
How perfectly he understands his work,
And sets all parts together till they fit !
That 's where the lawyer tells.

COLONEL HYDE (*approaching*).

                    Good even to both !
Your friend this, Cousin Jonas ?   Here 's my hand ;
And now, to business !   Something must be done,
If done at all, before the week is out, —
That is, as you and I, and this your friend,
Desire to happen : something else is sure.
The excitement grows ; and soon your priest, fore-
          warned,
Will organize resistance ; then comes war
To waste the property we want to save.
Have you the evidence ?   A document
Were best ; but witnesses will answer here.

JONAS.

The written revelation which he read
Was laid within the ark : that you must seize,
And bear away ; resistance then will stop.
Our witness must be forced, unwillingly,
After arrest : I bring you here the names
Of them who can be driven to testify.
You understand ?

COLONEL HYDE.

If they the practice prove !
The revelation shows intent, no more,
And violates no law.

JONAS.

To all of these
The fact is patent: where you need one case,
We give you five.

COLONEL HYDE.

As fingers of a hand
That soon shall clutch them !   'T is enough for law,
Which started, many accidents may chance
Before the process finds a legal stop.
And now, conditions !   You demand the power ;
I, its equivalent, a part secured,
A part reserved for possible future need,
So you gain influence —

JONAS.

And you assure
The chance of power !   Neither can promise all.

HUGH (*aside*).

Where two so bargain, there 's not margin left
To hold a third.

COLONEL HYDE.

The time for huckstering 's gone.

JONAS.

Missing my aim, comes little ; winning, all !

COLONEL HYDE.

Then here 's an end of parley : let us go !
This is no place for pleasure.

JONAS.

So, farewell !
Your stipulations hang on my success.

[*Exit* COLONEL HYDE.

Come, Hugh ! the night is cloudy : I must seek,
More with my feet than eyes, the ticklish path.

[*He moves away.*

HUGH.

Go on, but slowly.   I have dropped my knife,
And look for 't with my hands.   Before you reach
The slippery corner where we climb the bluff,
I 'll overtake you.

[JONAS *disappears in the gloom.*

Shall I overtake
Indeed ?   I 'm not so sure : yes, Colonel Hyde,
An accident, if prayed for, might occur !
They told me nothing ; but the gift of guess
Remains to me ; and, ugh ! 't is horrible.
I 'll neither see nor know !   The skull I kicked,
Used as a pillow, would not breed such dreams.

(*He moves onward, cautiously.*)

Ha ! what was that ?   Along the darkened path
Something, still darker, moves !   I hear no sound,
And yet the silence seems a piercing cry !
I feel the lifting of my hair : I 'll stop
Both ears, shut eyes, and think of anything,
Till I can count ten thousand, then, go on !

Scene VII.

A room in the Prophet's *house.*

DAVID.

No, you are not the same !   The simple trust
Which found content in what I was — and this
Includes whatever more I am become —
Hath left your eyes : your tongue is silenter :
You speak but matters which compel your speech,
And in your ways make hints of things unsaid.
I say not this in blame : you cannot be
More than you are, or other : I had hoped
There were a force in faith, a warmth in love,
To hold your nature side by side with mine,
And take a larger property in me
Through that which only seems to lessen it.
My hope is vain.

RHODA.

        Oh ! wait a little while,
My husband, — as you still and ever are.
I vexed you sore in what I thought was good,
And that seems evil which you ask of me :
It was not so at first.   I lean on you
With all my weight; when you would rest, in turn,
I 've nothing but my simple, loving heart,
To stay your weariness.   I cannot urge
Your spirit forward on its loftier ways ;
Nor did you ask it, save my faith be aid,
When first we loved.   Take what another brings,
You will not find me selfish : take so much,
But keep your heart for me !

DAVID.

                   Why, it is yours,
No less than then !   A very ghost of change
Is what you fancy.   Shut your eyes, and call
My face into your memory : 't is the same.

RHODA.

Ah, David, David ! I would shut their sight
Forever, could you in my ears again
So live.   There 's something in a woman's heart,
I think, so delicate, so soft a force,
That it will cling like steel, nor feel a bruise ;
Yet, loose one fibre, it may bleed to death.

DAVID.

I have not loosed, nor will !   Nay, I have grieved,
Bent down to human sympathy with you,
And hoarded tenderness you have not claimed,
To soothe you till you see.   What can I more ?
Take back the revelation and the law ?
Reverse the advancing work, and, step by step,
Make all things as they were ?   I see your eyes
Lighten at this, as they had nigh forgot
To shine : I do believe you wish so much !

RHODA (*slowly*).

No, no !   Not if your happiness depends, —
Not less of power, — not all the work undone —
Oh, understand me, David !

DAVID.

                  Patience, first !
Suspend your feeling till around us springs
The newer life, then judge if it be false.
But if, indeed, arises primitive peace,

And all that in the patriarchal years
Made manhood pure, and womanhood content,
Then I, by others, not of mine own faith,
Am justified to you.

SARAH (*entering*).

     Where have you put
Jonas, my husband ?   Give him back to me,
Or I will raise a tumult in the land !

DAVID.

Your husband ?

SARAH.

    Ay, and I 'm his only wife.
You have him hidden : set him free, I say !

DAVID.

Wild words are these.   I know no more of him
Than those report who hear his discontent.
He hath not sought me ; nor should I receive,
Unless he came with penitence.

SARAH.

     You *know,* —
I 'll not believe you !   Since he held to me,
Nor with strange women would pollute my house,
You mean his ruin !   Help me, Prophet's wife !
Although, perverted by his tongue, you take
Your rival home —
  (RHODA *starts, and turns away her face.*)
     — yet you are woman still,
And my distress may somewhat touch your heart.
Find out what they have done with him, give back,
And we will go !
    (*She weeps.*)

DAVID (*aside*).

It is no acted fear:
Has he been taken?   Is the answer come
To what I prayed, — come swiftly back to me
With all its helpless woe of consequence,
To make the wish a terror?

RHODA.

In my heart
I feel your grief, and pity, and will help,
Can you but show the way.

DAVID.

But I declare
Mine ignorance !   I speak no further word,
Since you believe not.

SARAH.

Nay, I will believe !
His fear was less of you than Nimrod Kraft,
Whose tongue — but that might anger if I spake :
I know not what to do !

DAVID.

Why, go to him
Whom most you fear !   But, stay ! no evidence
Of evil in your frightened clamor lies.
Come with me, and confess the things you know.
                    [*Exit with her*.
RHODA (*solus*).

Already ?   My prophetic heart declared,
Then called itself a liar !   Not dare tell ?
Such cowardice conceals a little love !
The winter sun, that for a distant land
Makes summer, cannot turn all warmth away,

And slowly comes again : let me not be
A frozen field, but gather every beam
He may allow me !   Oh ! I 'll prove my right
By life or death ; but now, on this alone,
I dare not brood.   That woman, wild with fear,
And charged with reason for it, which alarms
Because unspoken — something lurks behind,
A further outrage to be sanctified,
A guilt thrust under David's innocence !
The thought confuses me : I only feel
The danger closing round us like a mist,
Cold, formless, chilling to the very bone ;
And he is helpless, save I love him still.

ACT V.

SCENE I.

The street in front of the PROPHET'S *house.* PETER *at the gate, talking with two citizens.*

FIRST MAN.

IT 'S floating loose, as one might say : it comes
From everywhere and nowhere.

SECOND MAN.

That 's the way
To make things happen.   Say they 'll surely be,
And all the causes of them set to work.

FIRST MAN.

I 'd check ; you 'd let alone : which starts a cause,
Or hinders it ?   There 's talk because there 's fear.
What says the Prophet ?

PETER.

Nothing !   If I asked,
And he should answer, something would be said ;
But that we neither do.

SECOND MAN.

Until he calls,
Confessing danger, in your pockets sheathe
Your restless hands, and whistle back your faith !
Their name is not yet Legion.

[*Exit.*

FIRST MAN.

No, nor yours
A watchman of the Lord !   There are no signs
Of Jonas yet ; but people think him fled,
And plotting mischief in the enemy's camp.
The Twelve hold council : knowing these reports,
Which make alarm, they have not silenced them ;
And thus suspicion grows.

PETER.

I see it does.

FIRST MAN.

You keep close-mouthed : I do believe you 're primed.
With far more knowledge than you let leak out.

PETER.

I 'm honest only : ignorance need not talk.

FIRST MAN.

As I do, you would say ?

[*Exit.*

PETER.

He 's in a huff,
But can't help counting me the wiser man.
Why, shut your mouth, and shrewdly move your head,
And stare right hard at him who speaks to you ;
And, when he says, " It *is* so ! " answer, " H'm,
Is it, indeed ? " — and there 's your capital
For thriving business in the wholesale trade
Of leading people.   If I 'd half a gift
To save from awkward usage of their minds,
I 'd make them think me great.

9

RHODA.

(*Coming from the house.*)

What have you heard?
This is no time for keeping back the truth.
There's danger somewhere.

PETER.

One was sure of that,
The t'other not; but all I know is this, —
Some say the Gentiles mean to interfere,
Upset the Prophet's law, and him, the head,
Make chargeable for what the others do.
But that they can't: we're drifting on one raft;
And none but fools would ever try to take
The helmsman prisoner, till they smashed the crew.

RHODA.

And all are faithful?

PETER.

Well — they think they are.

RHODA.

This was my fear: you mean that all are not?

PETER.

It comes of management: the priest, and her—
Each is alone a match for any law;
And, if they work together —

RHODA.

Nay, they *must!*
You are worse troubled than you care to show;
But I'll not question more.   One way to help —

The hardest way that ever woman walked —
Is set before me, and I take it now !

                                             [*Exit.*

PETER.

I don't know as I 'm gladder that she went,
Or sorrier that she seemed to think my wits
Of small account.   Here 's one that, as I guess,
She means to pump as deeply as he 'll let.
He comes this way ; he 's got a blunted axe,
And I must turn the grindstone.

NIMROD (*entering*).

                              Have you seen
Sarah, the wife of Jonas, pass this way ?

PETER.

Not I.

NIMROD.

          She still may come.   Wait not for me,
Or any officer, but hold her fast !

PETER.

There must be two of me, to do so much.

NIMROD.

Large-boned, and strong of arm, she is, in fact.
You 'll find a watchman yonder by the wood ;
But scatter, lest she take another path !

PETER.

Why, what 's the row ?

NIMROD.

                    No more than you have heard.
Put what you know, and what you think might be,

Together, and you 'll find disturbance comes
Through her alone, and she can silence it.
The Prophet and the Twelve have that to ask,
Which, having answered, she disarms herself.

[Exit.

PETER.

No use of pumping there!   The water comes
Just even with the spout, and then it stops.

SCENE II.

A room in LIVIA'S *house.*

LIVIA.

(*Slowly pacing the floor, with a letter in her hand.*)

Renounced, and half forgotten, still the world
Has power to hurt!   I know the mirror false
Which makes a grim distortion of my face,
And yet it pains me while I look.   What creed
Is theirs, to whom my love gives more offence,
Man's habit broken, than hath done my faith,
To them a fatal heresy of soul !
Those Pagans, to their monstrous idol bowed, —
Once Moloch named, but now Society, —
Defile, when turned to their forgotten Lord,
His altars with false fire.   Ah ! had I found
One pure male soul among them, not ashamed
To seek, believe, aspire, and overcome, —
With love's white heat to clarify my own,
And dear dependence on my differing force, —
I had remained !   But thus, forbade to seek,
Insulted by insipid tenderness,
That into weakness fain would coddle power,
That shuts men's brains lest ours should be confused,

And hides strong aberrations of the sex,
Which, knowing, we might guide to purity, —
Why, what was left me but a fierce escape ?
Thank Heaven, the line is passed !   I 've not to do
With threatened shame, or vain self-questioning, more ;
I give my being for a large return.

(*Enter* RHODA : *both stand for a moment, looking at each other, in silence.*)

Forgive me, Rhoda, if I show surprise ;
Forgive me, also, that my doubt deterred
The due approach, which now your coming here
So gently chides !

RHODA.

Do not mistake my heart,
Or set it lower, for the thing I do.
Save you perceive me as I verily am,
I cannot speak my message, or may mar.
I come, by sore necessity constrained,
Or I had never come.

LIVIA (*aside*).

Her words awake
A new surprise : is this the fond, weak wife
I thought her, petulant instead of proud,
And simply sulking over fancied loss ?

(*Aloud.*)

Your speech is bitterer, surely, than you mean ;
But, seeming in the wrong, I must endure.

RHODA.

Be not offended !   I must needs suppose
Some curious resemblance in our hearts,
Else — yet it *must* be said ! — you had not loved.

Let there be more, in this, — that, loving him,
You know no better service of your life
Than guarding his.

LIVIA.

　　　　There read me by yourself !
I 'll not explain my passion, since the words
Might sting with needless pangs.　I thought you weak,
And find you strong : thus, silence is enough.
You come because of him ; forget the rest,
For partnership or rivalry in us
Has here one aim.

RHODA.

　　　　I feel before I see,
And that which shakes me with continual dread
Dissolves when I would closelier scan its form.
The missing man, his wife's most real alarm,
The Gentile rumors, threatening David's place,
If not his freedom, and the ruin of all, —
These have a link which must be found and cleft.
Help me, therein : I am not quick of thought,
But I will follow, letting you direct.
You cannot, surely, unobservant be
Of each least danger, when you watch for him !

LIVIA.

Less I may see, because I fear it less
Than you do.　He must triumph as a chief,
Ere love can peacefully possess his life.
Unhelping there, love in its duty fails,
And all too anxiously may guard itself ;
For opportunity wears danger's face
When first it comes ; and now it may be so.
What you declare, I knew : I muse thereon,

To save, if the occasion shrinks to that;
But, if it broaden, to exalt as well!

RHODA.

And you delay? to gain I know not what!
How can you thus so coldly, proudly talk
Of triumph won by risk? Ah! yes, I see
My heart's distress is folly unto yours:
I am a woman, and you know me not.
I show you all I dread; I give you chance
To set yourself above me in desert,
And on the remnant of my bliss to feed,
And you — seek "opportunity"!

(*She turns to leave.*)

LIVIA.

Not yet, —
You do mistake! and I should only wound
By picking words more nicely: all are edged
Which we two use. Twice have you made reproach,
Perhaps not meaning; I will let it pass,
And answer, since I pity your alarm,
With offered help: you may accept or leave.
How much of faith in Nimrod, the high-priest,
Do you preserve?

RHODA.

(*After a pause.*)
If one's right hand could be
Unfaithful to the will? for so it seems.
But service, then, would measure treachery;
And that's too monstrous!

(*Aside.*)
Ah! what have I said?
Her words provoked the doubt I should conceal,
And this may do a mischief.

LIVIA.

'T is enough.
I know the thought, that, frightened, hides its face
Even from itself ; but I will look on mine.
 T is well you came to me : some sheltered plants
First note the distant changes of the air,
And here — the thing is possible : I thought
It might be later —   Ha ! if it be now,
I must to work !

RHODA.

Give me a little part
When you have found it ! so much is my right.

LIVIA.

Ay, ay ! I promise : now, I pray you, go !
For *his* sake, then !

[*Exit* RHODA.

Oh ! she may have her share ;
But I, that dare and save and win and crown,
Shall sit by him as Zion's rightful queen !

SCENE III.

The council-room. NIMROD, SIMEON, *and* MORDECAI
present.

SIMEON.

I find them more disturbed than timorous ;
Still in good heart, the most : but that we keep
Continued silence, while the threats increase,
Bewilders them.

NIMROD.

'T is time, indeed, to act ;
For our intent must be conveyed to all,
Or we shall fail in secret unity.
The Prophet halts : I 've purposely left free
His spirit, praying for a path revealed
Where we, between the waves on either hand,
Dry-shod may walk : the revelation lags.
If unto me, less gifted, were transferred
The leader's office, I should exercise
With human wit, perchance, but also will
To wring success from stubborn circumstance.

SIMEON.

Oh ! were it so transferred ! Can you not claim,
If we sustain you ?

NIMROD.

No, I will not claim !
What my devotion and obedience earn
Should I receive.

(*A knock is heard :* MORDECAI *goes to the door. As he opens
it* LIVIA *is seen.*)

(*Aside.*)

But to invite the trust,
So that the giver thinks he gives unasked,
Is always lawful. What she seeks is plain :
I 've marked her keen ambition, and can use.

(*Aloud.*)

Admit the sister.

(LIVIA *comes forward to the table.*)

Opportunely come !
And hence the rules of council we suspend.
If you have knowledge, or your woman's wit

Works, with result, for our deliverance,
Be welcome, speak, and we shall gladly hear !

LIVIA.

My knowledge is not more, my zeal not less,
Than yours ; my skill to work with minor arts
Which must prevail with individual wills,
Ere, as a body, all are moved one way,
Perchance as great : so much is known to you.
This is no time for testing special power,
When any weapon, be it wielded well,
Becomes a rightful arm.   Our danger lies
In suffering our young order to be jarred
Too suddenly, or slowly undermined
By such defence as leaves the end a doubt.
Between the two we need steer carefully.
You have the rudder ; give an oar to me.

NIMROD.

You apprehend the crisis, and have guessed
Why, measuring it, we have not spoken yet.
'T is purposeless extremity of fear
Begets submission : what were best to do,
Too soon declared, is lightly criticised ;
But, now they cry for guidance, we present
Calm fronts of unperturbed authority.
We crave to act : the Prophet only fails
In revelation, which may be denied,
If human craft suffice : or, unto you
Hath he declared his will ?

LIVIA.

     Not unto me,
Surely, ungifted with commissioned power.

NIMROD.

Yet that pretence of law which threatens us
Concerns you most.   Our body is not yet
The giant it shall be : the covenant,
Now made an accusation, must be kept
By secret truth, the evidence held back, —
So, nothing proven, all their charges fail.
We best oppose by seeming to submit.
Unaided, they examine : not a tongue
Profanes the mysteries of Zion's house ;
And, once so foiled, our skill and industry,
Our peace and order, only, noised abroad,
They will not haste to court a second blame.

SIMEON.

The wisdom of the serpent speaks in that !

LIVIA (*aside*).

And leaves the serpent's slime !

(*Aloud.*)
                              You, then, accept
Their whole procedure, — law, and court, and judge,
And twelve such fools as never heard of us,
Arrest, and trial ?   First, of course, they seize
The Prophet !

NIMROD.

                    Me, instead !   I will so lead
Suspicion from its present course in them.
My craft of brain, that cannot reach his gift
Of prayer and vision, hath its office here :
It will exalt my soul with holy joy
To triumph o'er the Gentiles !

LIVIA.

Prophecy
Is that : the power awakes in you : I thought
Your gift was "craft of brain."   Why, 't is a scheme
Where every wheel must with a hundred *ifs*
Be cogged, or none of them will bite !   The law
Takes any shape it likes : by prejudice
It moves the eleven, and wearies out the one
Within whose brain some dream of justice lives.
Yes, were our danger, law !   But, while you wait
Your own arrest in all decorous form,
Whose hand shall stay the ruffian horde behind
From force and outrage ?

NIMROD.

Woman's brain is quick
To make a part the whole, and for her wits
Work easy triumph.   I but told you part.

LIVIA (*aside*).

Too quick, indeed !   I should have cheated him
By feigned acceptance, till I learned the whole.
He may cajole by truth, as others do
By falsehood.

(*Aloud.*)

Nay, if hastily I spake,
The cause lay deeper than my woman's brain.

NIMROD (*smiling*).

I saw it beating, faster than your words.
I but consider, not decide : the plan
Waits for the sanction of our Church's head,
Which he, in strange uncertainty, withholds.
If to the movement of his mind your own

May give direction, bid him not delay ;
Or, still irresolute, set free my hands,
To work for him.

MORDECAI.

The Twelve are as one man.

SIMEON.

The priest speaks for us.

NIMROD.

And the people wait.
Decide to help, where all is known and weighed ;
Or, knowing little, work your random will,
And bring us ruin !

LIVIA.

You would weigh me down
With much capacity.   If you believed
My power, you would not threaten such result,
But coax and flatter me to shift my part.
Deal fairly, priest, and you shall have my aid !
You 're certain of success : you only need
Unhindered leadership (the Prophet's place
Transferred, in seeming, that he 'scape the risk),
And then, submissive where they look for strife,
You will confound the Gentiles !   Far too bold
For any brain but yours !   Were not your blood
So passionless, your keen intelligence
So coldly watchful, I should doubt the end ;
But now — I go to do the work you set !

MORDECAI.

That 's a beginning !

SIMEON.

　　　　　　How you bent her will!
I never saw the like.

NIMROD.

　　　　　　Ay, ay! The power
Sometimes is with me: may it oftener come!
　　　　　　　(*Aside.*)
The work I set? She 'll do the opposite,
Or else her lying candor lies again.
" So passionless!" — ha! ha! The time may come
When she shall say of me, " Too passionate! "
I think I 've striven to turn away the storm;
But, if they will not see, so let it burst!
They 're all mistaken: 't is no thunder-cloud
That rattles half an hour, and rolls away;
But something that will tear us from our roots,
And sweep us far into the wilderness.
My own device might gain a little grace
To dull the blow: yet our prosperity
Tempts, as upon a counter scattered gold;
And, though the first wave strike us harmlessly,
A second one will follow. Better now
Set matters where they needs must terminate!
I 've learned to rule, even while obeying most;
And I shall surely learn to bind and seal
By revelation, as my gifts increase.

Scene IV.

In front of the temple. A number of people collected; DAVID, NIMROD, *and various members of the* TWELVE, *among them.* LIVIA *moves from one to another of the restless, excited groups.*

A MAN.

They should have armed us first!

A SECOND.

　　　　　　　　The priest is shrewd
To keep his knowledge till it's time to use.
He has something ready: mark his quick gray eye!

A THIRD.

The secrecy they lay upon us means
That we may be examined: more than that
It's hard to guess.

LIVIA (*whispering*).

　　　　　　　Keep you the peace, unless
They would arrest the Prophet, — then resist!

　　　　　　　　　　　　[*She passes on.*

A MESSENGER.

(*To* DAVID.)

There are but four: their head is Sheriff Hyde.
Our watchmen stopped them at the wood below,
And now are leading hither: they would speak
With you, and with the Twelve.

DAVID.

　　　　　　　Go, bid them come!

NIMROD.

Have you considered our united mind ?
Here is it urgent that a single voice
Declare the answer.

DAVID.

First must come demand,
Which, save its words and full intent were known,
We cannot meet beforehand.   I will wait.

NIMROD.

This only, let me speak !   Exact delay
For consultation, when demand is made :
They are but four ; yet each doth represent
A hundred more in ambush !

DAVID.

Are you sure
Of Hugh's fidelity !

NIMROD.

As of his life !
And whether Jonas did escape to them,
Or by the Lord was silenced, — either way
He served us first : so far have we been helped
To their discomfiture !

(*Movement in the crowd.   The people fall back, and* COLO-
NEL HYDE, *with three companions, guarded on each side
by the watchmen of Zion, come forward.*)

COLONEL HYDE.

Which man of you
Calls himself Prophet ?

DAVID.

                 Chosen of the Lord
Am I, and Prophet called by these, my flock.

COLONEL HYDE.

You 're he I seek.   The law, that freedom gives
To manifold belief, now takes alarm
At vicious usages, by you proclaimed
As holy.   You are called to meet the charge
Of wilful crime, with others, whom to this
You have persuaded.

          (*Murmurs among the people.*)

DAVID.

               And should I resist
Such intermeddling with permitted faith ?

COLONEL HYDE.

Though loud report of your licentious lives
Commands my action, we are armed with proof,
And here resistance would be added crime.
Will you submit ? or shall I raise my voice,
And call the County's power ?

        (*Tumultuous movement among the people.*)

VOICES.

               Go back ! go back !
We guard the Prophet !   Touch him if you dare !

NIMROD.

Be quiet, brethren !   Law should not be rash
To hasten conflicts which she might allay.
You, Colonel Hyde, have spoken ; we demand
A space for counsel ere we make reply.
Come three days hence —

       10

COLONEL HYDE.

One day, no more !

(*Struggle and confusion on the outskirts of the crowd ; mingled voices and cries.*)

SARAH.

Let go !

I have done nothing !   Let me free, I say !

DAVID.

Hold, hold !

COLONEL HYDE.

My cousin's wife !

SARAH.

(*Rushing forward wildly, her hair streaming over her shoulders.*)

You have not seen
Jonas ?   No need to answer that : he 's dead !
Oh, save me ! take me with you !

NIMROD (*aside*).

Curséd luck !
I thought she had escaped, but this is worse.

COLONEL HYDE.

What means your terror ?

SARAH.

Jonas never came
From *you !* I thought him held, at first, and made
Vain outcries ; then I feared for mine own life,
And hid till now.   Upon my way to you
Came two, and held me fast with violent hands,
The Prophet's serving-man —

DAVID.

It cannot be !

Peter ?

SARAH.

— and one the high-priest often calls
To do his secret work.

NIMROD.

I ordered them.
The woman's grief, the Prophet's sympathy
Therewith, gave me desire to question her.
If thus our kindness frightens, let her go,
And you may test the value of the tongue
That speaks such folly !

COLONEL HYDE.

Sarah, come with us !

(*To* DAVID.)

To-morrow, at this hour, expect me here !

[*Exit with* SARAH, *his companions, and the watchmen.*

NIMROD (*aside*).

There go the Gentile torches, all ablaze,
Which shall consume the temple !

DAVID.

Peter, here,
If still you owe me service !

[*Exit.*

LIVIA.

So, high-priest,
The court is opened, and the jury called ;
Only the culprits have not reached the bar !

NIMROD.

Some walls are built with clear design to stand
For ages ; but the finger of a child
May pick a stone out ere the mortar dries,
And leave a crevice for the wedge of frost
To slowly split the fabric.   You exult
As such a child might do.

LIVIA (*aside*).

He frightens me.

SCENE V.

Sunset.   An outer street of the city.   A number of men assembled : PETER *in the midst.*

SEVERAL VOICES.

We will not yield !

A MAN.

The Lord should send a sign,
If ever, now, when to His flock dismayed
The wolf comes howling !

PETER.

'T is n't just the howl.
He means to pounce upon our leader-ram,
Then lazily bite our throats from day to day.
The priest says, " Let him ! "   But you run down hill
To law, and up steep rocks climb out again.

VOICES.

Ay, that is truth !

PETER.

                    And he, to boot, mistakes
Through over-sharpness.   Doing what he bade,
I harmed the Prophet in the sheriff's eyes ;
And that wild woman will improve the tale,
Until they see — the Lord knows what — in him.
I 'm bound to make my blunder good.

LIVIA (*approaching*).

                              You are !
I 'll show you how : there 's little time to lose.
How many here have arms ?

VOICES.

                    I have !   And I !

LIVIA.

And, had you not the hearts of fighting men,
You would not answer thus.   They think us weak
Or timorous : let them come in that conceit !
One sharp repulse will so confuse their plan
That time is gained; and what protection lies
In martial garrisons the nation plants,
For need, along the lawless, wild frontier,
May come to aid us, or to stand between.

VOICES.

That 's to the point !   Such talk we understand.

LIVIA.

Shall we submit to scarce the name of law,
Much less its substance ?   Who are they that shake
The sword of justice, which would pierce themselves
If they let go the hilt?   What ! suffer them
To seize at will, until our strength is shorn,

And Zion's riches to their hands lie bare?
Not you!   I know you!

VOICES.

No, we 'll fight them first!

LIVIA.

You will!   And, if no man dares lead you forth,
I 'll be your captain : there are Jaels yet!
Let each his neighbor summon ; scour your guns,
Run even your clock-weights into bullet-moulds,
And tell your wives that milk from manly veins
Looks worse than blood!

(*She beckons to one of the men following her, who comes forward, and unrolls a banner, with a golden lion on a red
ground.*)

Behold our banner spread,
Yours and the Prophet's!   See that first it float
Amid the smoke, which, when it drifts away,
Leaves victory behind!   You want a song,
To set the courage of your hearts in words,
And bid it ring beneath the echoing heaven.
Hear, then!   I 've made it for you, and will sing!

(*She sings.*)

Children of Zion,
Crouch as a lion,
Eager to fly on
  Foes that deride!
Rise for the Prophet!
Arm for the Prophet!
Fight for the Prophet!
  Fling his banner wide!

ALL.

(Enthusiastically repeating the last lines, as chorus.)

Fight for the Prophet !
Fling his banner wide !

(The men gradually disperse.)

LIVIA *(solus)*.

I live at last !   'T was more than love inspired
This counter-plot, though love like mine were more
Than cause and needful spur.   I live and move,
Bid others live and play the parts I set,
Concentrate petty forces to one end
Which grandly must succeed, or grandly fail, —
But, either way, I act !   The top of life,
Methinks, is action, when the field is broad ;
For power of nature cannot truly be,
Till it is proved on others.

                   Ah, he comes !
My dream was that I work for him alone :
Why, since both power and passion wed, I do !

        (DAVID *approaches.*)

Lift up your front, my Prophet !   'T is the eve
Of strength secured : the test, the hostile charge,
Draw near the moment when they sink in dust ;
And, after one dim bar of cloud, your sun
Will hold the sky !

DAVID.

        'T is dusk : the sun is down.
Old habit says the day will dawn again
After a certain darkness : have you thought,
What if it should not dawn ?   'T is possible.

LIVIA.

Yes, when no triumph calls the daylight up;
When human souls, in all God's world, are dumb;
When hope is choked, and, like neglected fire,
The spark of prayer dies out, and even love
Awaits no morrow sweeter than to-day, —
Then, then, 't were possible !

DAVID.

                  Can light be drawn
Even from the spirit, as the warmth from blood?
You seem to shine, as you possessed the glow
I thought was mine : you see where I am dark ;
And, where I walk confounded, you rejoice.
Whence comes your confidence ?   What near success
Fore-glorifies you ?

LIVIA.

               Pardon, if to you
I still keep silent !   Faith, no less than love,
May have its budded secret, soon to bloom.
For some few rapid hours endure your place,
As now, while others work, — I least, perhaps,
Though most in will : the lower necessity
Is ours to meet, yea, ours to overcome.

DAVID.

They wait my word.

LIVIA.

             I know it.   They best learn
Now, when their minds are sore perturbed, to wait.
Can you bestow on clouded eyes and brains
Your perfect gift ? or justify each step,
Greater than Moses, to the murmuring throng ?

The human with the godlike essence strives
In you ; and, when your soul would sanction, straight
The heart stands up in protest : heed it not,
While others can be merely man !

DAVID.

Go, then !
I cannot meet your words, and will not ask
What hope sheds brightness on your face.   Farewell !

LIVIA.

Farewell !

[*Exit* DAVID.

And for the last time, half-apart
And half-acknowledged, do I say, Farewell !

SCENE VI.

Night.   A room in the PROPHET'S *house.*   DAVID, *seated at a
desk, with his back towards* RHODA.   *He opens papers,
looks at them mechanically, lays them aside, and at last rests
his head upon his hand.*   RHODA *sits in another part of the
room, with her hands clasped in her lap.   Once or twice she
lifts her head, looks at* DAVID, *and seems about to speak.*

DAVID.

(*Turning suddenly.*)
You're watching me !

RHODA.

Nay, waiting ; and, besides,
Wishing that you would speak.   To-day's affairs
Leave me in doubt of what the morrow brings.
There's something in a charge that frightens me,

Though vilely made : I never dreamed that crime,
Even as a painted threat, could be so flung
Into our faces.

DAVID.

Into mine, not yours !

RHODA.

It is the same : the threat, the impossible fact,
One like the other, at my honor strikes.
I do not think of that.   Oh, were the day,
And all its horrible aspects, safely o'er !
Were you a nameless servant of the Lord,
Somewhere with me and with our helpless child,
A taper burning calmly, not, as now,
A bonfire whirled and beaten by the winds,
What peace were mine !

VOICES.

(*Outside, singing in passing.*)

Fight for the Prophet !
Fling his banner wide !

RHODA.

But, no ! you dare not fly
Though yet the chance is free.   The frightened flock,
In its devoted faith, appeals to you,
Who, having led to this, must lead beyond.
An hour's enough : the river's middle stops
Pursuit and summons ; but, were you and I
This moment seated on the farther shore,
We needs must cross again.

DAVID.

Do you say that ?

Do you set duty higher than our lives?
Why, she could say no more!

RHODA.

(*In a low voice.*)

Ah, spare me, David!
(*A long silence.*)

DAVID (*musingly*).

Were we together, Rhoda? yes, we were!
One day in June; long, long ago it was:
Wild strawberries along the clearing's edge
Were thick that year; but we grew tired at last;
And I, stretched flat among the fragrant vines,
Looked at the sky: I saw no other thing.
The blue retreated as my vision reached;
And as a pebble slowly deeper, deeper sinks
In still, dark water, up and upward sank
My soul, and sank, and still there was no end.
Somewhere, at last, beyond the invisible stars,
A hoary brightness gathered from the void,
And from the midst there looked a single Eye,
Compact of all ineffable light, — His eye!
And did not blind me.

RHODA.

David! and I cried:
You would not speak: I thought you vexed, unkind!
I could not know, till now.

DAVID.

We came from school
One day, when, from a rising arch of cloud,
The tempest strained the black-oak on the hill.
You feared to pass: I shouted, through the roar,

"You will not hurt us, God !" and then a bolt
Split with red fire the surging firmament.
But you were pale with terror; on my breast
You hid your eyes ; while I, in solemn joy,
Chanted aloud, and waved my arms aloft,
And felt strange fingers pluck my beaten hair,
As one may tease in fondness.   Say, do you
Remember, Rhoda ?

RHODA (*weeping*).
Oh, I do !

DAVID.
How now,
You cry for memory of it ?   Ah ! I see,
Your memory wears another hue than mine.
You tremble : I exult !

RHODA.
Upon us sweeps
A blacker tempest now.

DAVID.
Go you to rest ;
If struggle come, so gather strength for it.
Fret not for me : my body must be as dead
Before my soul is verily alive.

[*Exit* RHODA, *slowly.   A pause.*
They look to me : if I, in turn, look up,
What help is certain ?   Yea, but first to look !
I urge my thought ; but, swerving from its aim,
It backward speeds, and paints anew the past
In colors which confound me.   'T is not doubt;
'T is no renewal of old agonies :
But something cold, that wears the shape of Truth,

Treads down with heavy step, along my path,
The springing harvest, and with fateful hand
Makes sign, " Go on : I follow ! "

                                        Get you gone,
Device of Satan !   Is His law a lie ?
He made the covenant a perfect chain,
Which, link by link, am I restoring, soon
To gird us round about, — a lesser world
Where He may reign : one flaw, and all must go !
One flaw ?   There is no torture known in hell
Enough for such malevolence, if so !
I 'll put Thee to the test : our strait is sore ;
Thine intervention, since the world began,
Never so needed : — do Thy miracle !
Or stand aloof, and let Thy thunders growl
In leash, Thy lightnings flash a distant threat ;
But breathe one word of counsel, — give my soul,
Passive before Thee, one victorious thought !

(*He paces the room for some minutes in great excitement, then
suddenly stops.*)

My prayers rebound, as from a solid wall ;
My brain refuses to anticipate
The coming problem ; and my very hope
Strains, like an eye in darkness, foiled of use !
What palsy thus disorders every sense
Wherein the spirit lives ?   I cannot see
A hand's-breadth forward, nay, nor fancy aught :
The light burns backward over what has been ;
And its last glimmer, fading at my feet,
Leaves all the future darkness !

                                        Oh, my God !
The mortal anguish of a life at bay,

Escape cut off, the certainty of doom,
All that is visited upon the flesh, —
Methinks were easy.   Mine is death in life;
The sinews severed, and the strength as dead;
No power to reach, not even knowledge left
Of how or whither, but the soul a corpse !
I 'll strive no more; I 'll neither think nor pray:
Let accident become my deity !

SCENE VII.

The interior of the temple.   Men, women, and children gath-
ered in groups.   NIMROD, on the platform in front of the
Holy of Holies, trims the lights burning in the seven-
branched candlesticks.   SIMEON and MORDECAI, near the
door, conferring with two messengers.

FIRST MESSENGER.

I counted them as they came o'er the rise,
And nigh two hundred were they.

SIMEON.

                              Did you mark
Some in advance ? — signs of a summons first,
Preceding force ?

FIRST MESSENGER.

          Their march was orderly.

SIMEON.

(*To* MORDECAI.)

Then it would seem he has them well in hand;
And, whether violence be done, depends
Chiefly on him.   But who went forth from us ?

SECOND MESSENGER.

This side the border brook, I saw go out
Three Members of the Twelve : John surely was
The first, Elisha and Zerubbabel
I thought the others.

MORDECAI.

(*To* SIMEON.)
By the Prophet sent ?

SIMEON.

By him allowed ; for neither Yea nor Nay
He answered them or me.   His gifts grow weak
When most we need them ; but the day may cast
The power in stronger hands, and save us all !

(*Sound of drums and trumpets outside.   Voices singing.*)

Fight for the Prophet !
Fling his banner wide !

SIMEON.

Hark, there !   Who leads them ?   Follow, — bring report !

[*Exit Messengers.*

NIMROD.

(*Coming down from the altar.*)

My hands are tied : all ye who hear me, note !
Bear witness, that, if blood be shed this day,
My garments are not stained.   I would have given
Myself as pledge, so using human craft
(Which, for His glory, sanctifies the Lord)
To foil the Gentiles ; now it seems too late ;
But, when all other virtue is outworn,
Then turn to me.

WOMEN.

Go forth, and hold them back !

NIMROD.

Though driven to ruin's edge, I still obey :
Heed ye the lesson !

(*Enter* DAVID, *pale and troubled :* RHODA *follows him, bearing the child in her arms.*)

DAVID.

(*Looking on the frightened groups.*)

     Save all these, high-priest !
I give them to your hands : take boat, and cross
Beyond the reach of this authority
Which smites them with disorderly alarm.
'T will soon be settled whether you return,
Or we must join you.

NIMROD.

    Suffer me to wait,
While aught of peril menaces yourself !

(*Sounds of firing in the distance : cries and confusion among the people.*)

A MAN.

(*Rushing in.*)

They 're firing, by the wood !   Theirs, on the plain ;
Ours, covered by the timber : some were down
Before the smoke got thick !

DAVID.

(*To* MORDECAI.)

     It must not be !
Quick ! — something white ! Within the chancel, there,
My prophet-mantle, as the sign of truce !

(*While* MORDECAI *obeys this command, the sound of firing draws nearer.*)

PETER.

(*Enters, wounded in the arm.*)

First, give me water !

(*It is brought from the baptismal font.   He drinks.*)

Scarce there 's time to tell :
Get over the river ! — that was what she said.

DAVID.

Who brought this on ?

PETER.

They wanted you, — no less
Would answer : we refused to give you up,
And blocked their marching nearer ; then — they fired !
Our volleys tore and scattered them a bit,
But they 're too many.   She went here and there,
Put heart in all, and like a general led,
And not a bullet touched her : then, when I
Was hit in turn, she sent me posting here.
We 're falling back, but slowly, facing them :
Don't lose a minute — ugh ! the thing 's no fun :
My arm feels ugly.

(*He faints.*)

DAVID.

Rhoda, look to him !
My place is at the front : 't is me alone
They seek, and they may have me !

[*Exit.*

RHODA.

(*Giving her child to one of the women.*)

Lift his head,
Undo his collar !   There !   I 've bound his arm,

11

And bathed his brow with water from the font:
He soon will breathe again.   I pray you, give
My child your tenderness, if I should die !

> [*Exit, following* DAVID.

NIMROD.

You heard ?   He gave you to my hands : I charge,
By him commissioned, that your fears be still !
If there be traitors here, let flame from Heaven
Their tongues make cinder, that they cannot speak !
We will submit, in all external forms,
Even to the Gentiles ; then in secret pass
The river, bearing our most precious goods
Beyond their reach : our spies have gone abroad,
And found another Eshcol in the West.
Within our hands lies all we builded here,
And they, upheld by faith, shall build again !
This is no time for lamentation : hope
As ye have never hoped, have confidence
Ye never felt, await triumphant signs
Reserved for you, His people !

VOICES.

> Yea, we will !

(*Scattered musket-shots outside the temple : wild, piercing
cries are heard. Immediately afterwards the chancel-door
is torn open, and a number of armed men, some of them
wounded, enter the temple.   Then* DAVID *appears, shot
through the breast, and held up by* RHODA *and* LIVIA,
*supporting him on either side.   Cries and lamentations
among the people gathered in the temple.*)

DAVID.

Forward ! to the altar, to the altar !

CRIES.

Lord !
Save him, Thy Prophet, for Thyself and us !

(DAVID, *supported by* RHODA *and* LIVIA, *totters forwards,
and is upheld by them, leaning against the altar.*)

DAVID.

Oh for a little life ! it fades so fast !
Hear me, my brethren ! I will only speak
Words needful : not too late, the shadow falls
That veiled mine eyes : confusion has an end.

NIMROD.
(*Aside.*)

What means he ?
(*Aloud, to the people.*)

Silence, all !   The Prophet speaks,
In this extremity, to you !

DAVID.
(*With difficulty.*)

Be still !
Each word you utter steals a word of mine,
And few are left me : let me but begin !
I see so much at once ! all things are clear ;
But speech grows weak.   Ah, hearken, brethren
    mine !
How say it all ?   I pray you, bid your souls
Rise quickly up, and save me half !   O God,
It is for Thee ! — leave me one moment here !
See, I am dying !   On the edge of life,
Truth's lightning flashes backward and beyond :
So hear !   First —   Hold me firm, I slide away !
Lord, Lord, be merciful ! no time is left !

I see no more — but, yes ! one blesséd face :
'T is yours ! — you 're with me, Rhoda ! — *you*, my
   love !

(*He turns towards* RHODA *as he speaks, and falls upon her
   breast, with his arms hanging over her shoulders.*)

LIVIA.

Help ! Lift him up ! he faints.

RHODA.

                       Nay, he is dead !
Leave us ! You have no more a part in him :
He is all mine at last !

(*Clasping* DAVID *to her breast, she sinks slowly down at the
   foot of the altar.*)

NIMROD.

                       So death cuts short
The weakness which had nigh betrayed us all !
His gift and power become our heritage ;
And Zion lives, and shall be strong, through me !

(COLONEL HYDE *and his men force an entrance into the portal of the temple. A wild scene of confusion among the people.* NIMROD KRAFT *snatches the ark from the altar, and
   escapes through the chancel-door.*)

THE CURTAIN FALLS.

THE MASQUE OF THE GODS.

DRAMATIS PERSONÆ.

———◆———

A VOICE FROM SPACE.
CHORUS OF SPIRITS.
ELOHIM.
IMMANUEL.
JOVE.
APOLLO.
BRAHMA.
ORMUZD.
AHRIMAN.
ODIN.
BAAL.

PERUN.
MANITO.
MAN.
THE SEA.
THE MOUNTAINS.
THE RIVERS.
THE TREES.
THE SERPENTS.
THE WOLVES.
THE CAVERNS.
THE ROCKS.

THE MASQUE OF THE GODS.

SCENE I.

The high table-land of Pamere. Midnight. The distant snow-peaks of the Himalayas, the Hindoo-Koosh, and the Küen-Lün shining in the moonlight. At first, silence ; then, slowly and indistinctly,

THE ROCKS.

WE scarcely change, though wind and rain and thunder
 Blow, beat, and fall, for many a thousand years ;
And yet we miss the dread, the ignorant wonder,
 The dark, stern being, born of human fears.
The stains of blood, upon our bases sprinkled,
 Are washed away ; the fires no longer flame :
The stars behold our foreheads still unwrinkled ;
 We were, and are, but Man is not the same.

THE CAVERNS.

With murmurs, vibrations,
With rustlings and whispers,
And voices of darkness,
 We breathe as of old.
Through the roots of the mountains,
Under beds of the rivers,

We wander and deepen
In silence and cold.

But the language of terror,
Foreboding, or promise,
The mystical secrets
That made us sublime,
Have died in our keeping:
Our speech is confusion:
We mark but the empty
Rotations of Time.

THE SERPENTS.

We glided once with crowned and lifted head,
Our supple grace a wonder to the wise,
Power in our starry eyes,
And sacred mystery o'er our being shed,
But grace and power and mystery are fled.

Our smooth, cold undulations gave the sign
Of fate to nations; fanes for us were built,
And blood of victims spilt,
To win a favoring answer at our shrine:
Silent were we, and thence, of right, divine!

Are we aught else?   Yet now we crawl instead,
Crownless, and shorn of power we did not crave,
But they unbidden gave:
Held once as gods, we shrink to shapes of dread,
And writhe abased, with bruised and trampled head!

THE WOLVES.

Prowling on the highlands
In the ghastly dawn,
We scent the steam of slaughter,
Ere the sword is drawn:

Sated with the corpses,
 'Neath the moon, at last,
We sleep, and let the vulture
 Finish his repast.

Where delay the wizards,
 Who were wont to claim
Fur and fang and fleetness,
 And the fearful name ?
Heart of man within us,
 Hate of man to speed,
More than ours the terror,
 Terribler the deed !

ODIN.

Be silent !   Ye are not sons of Fenrir's race,
The huge, the fierce of fang !   What will ye here,
Where even Gods grow dim, and scarce behold
Themselves, or hear the echo of their speech ?
Methinks I slept, but for how long a time
I know not : dreams, or memories of a home,
Surround me still, and something cold, remote,
Some rude resemblance of the world I swayed,
Revives my waning power.   Once more I speak,
And marvel at the accents, sealed so long.
But who art thou, the dark of aspect, here
Confronting me, no less a shade, but more,
Though lost capacity for wrath would fain
Assert itself, and shape thine ancient threat?
I fear thee not.

PERUN.

   Yet was I feared erewhile.
Older than thou, and mightier, I but gave
My footstool, not my throne, when came thy reign.

I held my sceptre still; and on black stones,
The natural altars tumbled from the cliffs,
Frost-carved and thunder-polished, took the blood
Of secret worship, heard the fierce appeals
That half implored my favor, half defied.
I ruled by right of eldest cruelty:
The savage strength of man renewed my life,
And still renews, though all my frame is lean
And racked with hunger, — but I am not dead.

BAAL.

Nor I, whose temples mimicked once the hills.
For those strong lusts of men I kept alive,
They gave me splendor and a mighty name.
None older is than I.   When Man came forth,
The final effort, wrung from monstrous forms,
And Earth's outwearied forces could no more,
I warmed the ignorant bantling on my breast.
We rose together, and my kingdom spread
From these cold hills to hamlets in the palms,
That grew to Memphis and to Babylon;
While I, on towers and hanging terraces,
In shaft and obelisk, beheld my sign
Creative, shape of first imperious law.
Thou, Odin, lord of strength, and thou, Perun,
Of fear and fierceness, never touched the springs
Of life, your faint existence there to feed.
It must be you shall pass: your forms are thin
As incense-smoke: what made you shall unmake.
But I beget, not slay, — grant overplus,
Where you are niggard, — drink from hidden founts,
That flow through channels of the riotous blood,
And keep men at the level of their source.
I may be weakened, but I cannot die.

MANITO.

If I be old, I know not : ye are strange,
Yet kindred, — long conjectured, here beheld.
I have some fitful power, which now is dread,
Now merciful, and, as I think, is good.
The smokes I breathed are shrunk and almost spent ;
The shouted hymns but faintly stir mine ears ;
The blood of dog, and bear, and buffalo,
Gives me but scanty life ; and through the lands
I governed, seated in my hunting-grounds
Above the sky, my messenger the swan,
My slaves the beaver and the crafty fox,
The voices which address me slowly fail.
But ye, of other worlds, declare me this,
Am I myself, or am I made of them ?
If, as I fear, their simple souls had need
Of One supreme, and therefore I became ;
Or if, alone before them, I have drawn
Through ages of unchanged companionship —
Since lonely Gods must stoop to play with men —
Their color to my face, their joys to mine,
And to their prayers the expected answer given,
Declare me this !

ODIN.

   Who shall declare the thing ?
Dost thou, the lowest of us all, provoke
The chill that made me shudder on my throne
In Asgaard, when the gold-haired Freya wept,
And the sweet light of Balder's eyes grew dim ?
Are we, then, born of those who kneel to us ?
Shall we the doubter slay, who doubt ourselves ?
Or cease to be, who grant the sacred gift
Of the immortal banquet ?   I am faint
With more than craving for forgotten rites,

And even might perish, did not something burn
In mine impoverished being from above,
As if Man's shadow met a light in me,
Coming, I know not whence : but it is good.

BAAL.

Dost thou confess it, Odin ?   That we live,
Outliving name and prayer and sacrifice,
Save such as in the heart and limbs of Man
Unconsciously is rendered, tests the truth
Of ancient godship, yet dependent still
On something strange, and mightier than ourselves.
Were we but servants, then, instead of lords ?
Did blood and odor, sound of harp and horn,
And choral cries from multitudes of men,
But pass our palates and our ears, to reach
The senses of some sole Divinity,
Whom we thus flattered ?   When I looked below
Upon my soaring fane in Babylon,
Who was 't looked down on me ?   Who shook my soul,
But not with fear, or hate, or jealousy, —
Since each were vain, — but something fine and pure,
That made me stagger, as my feet were clay ?

PERUN.

Why, then, if such there be, I know Him not.

ODIN.

Peace, ignorant savage !   To thy Lord and mine
Dream no rebellion !   By His leave we are,
No less than Man's necessity.   But what
He is, where throned, and how upheld in power,
I fain would know.

A VOICE FROM SPACE.

Lo ! I am that I am.

(*A pause.*)

THE GODS.

We cannot understand Thee, yet we bow,
And, without knowledge, own Thee : are we Thine,
Or shall we cease when men no more believe ?

A VOICE FROM SPACE.

Mine are ye : also Man's.

THE GODS.

We feel, and must
Acknowledge Thee.   Our questioning is vain
And self-betraying, since to question is
No office of the Gods.   We yield to Thee,
Who knowest, but who wilt not answer us.

MAN.

We burned their temples, overturned their altars ;
Through force or love we learned the newer worship,
And taught our children other than our fathers.
We gave them fear, we gave them war and slaughter,
We died to keep them in their sacred houses,
We lived to crown them rulers of the nations.
But they forget, they perish or desert us,
Too weak, without us, to become immortal.
They change like us, yet claim to sit above us,
Our likenesses, of grander limb and feature,
Of stronger hate and lust, and gentler pity.
We dream of higher, yet we cannot reach them ;
We grope for something which our hands can cling to,
Our eyes behold, our minds accept and fathom ;
And, groping, seizing, holding, lo ! they fail us
As they were not — yet must we fear and worship.

SCENE II.

A Doric temple, in ruins, on a headland above the Ægean
Sea. A valley and mountains in the background. Early
dawn.

THE TREES.

Barrenly murmur through manifold branches,
   Answer the billows that tumble ashore,
Blossom or strip in the march of the seasons,
   We are but sport of the winds, and no more!

Shadow we give them where once we were holy,
   Lintel and beam for the being they stole;
Service for sacrifice, litter for garlands,
   Use for the Beauty they granted a soul.

Desolate, cold, is the shell of the Dryad;
   Still are the dances, the oracles dumb:
Playmates of old, we are slighted as strangers,
   Shorn of our honor in ages to come!

THE RIVERS.

We are loud and silent, we hasten and dally,
   We bless and waste, as in days that are dead;
We dance on the hillside and sleep in the valley,
   With the rocks as a cradle, the reeds as a bed;
But the nymphs of our fountains leave them untended,
   And the god of the stream is gone from his urn:
The term of our human beauty is ended,
   And its liquid graces shall never return.

We bless and waste, we speed in our courses,
  We urge and pilot, we cheer and call ;
We wander and widen, with fetterless forces,
  Servants and lovers and lords of all !
The pulses of Life, in our veins unbroken,
  The movement of Life, in the tides we pour,
Still bind us to men, with a secret token,
  And keep us kindred, though none adore !

THE MOUNTAINS.

Howe'er the wheels of Time go round,
We cannot wholly be discrowned.
We bind, in form, and hue, and height,
The Finite to the Infinite,
And, lifted on our shoulders bare,
The races breathe an ampler air.
The arms that clasped, the lips that kissed,
Have vanished from the morning mist ;
The dainty shapes that flashed and passed
In spray the plunging torrent cast,
Or danced through woven gleam and shade,
The vapors and the sunbeams braid,
Grow thin and pale : each holy haunt
Of Gods or spirits ministrant
Hath something lost of ancient awe ;
Yet from the stooping heavens we draw
A beauty, mystery, and might,
Time cannot change nor worship slight.
The gold of dawn and sunset sheds
Unearthly glory on our heads ;
The secret of the skies we keep ;
And whispers, round each lonely steep,
Allure and promise, yet withhold,
What bard and prophet never told.
While Man's slow ages come and go,

Our dateless chronicles of snow
Their changeless old inscription show,
And men therein forever see
The unread speech of Deity.

THE SEA.

What were the bloodless nymphs, the Triton swarms,
  The car of Cypris, Galatea's shell,
The green-haired Gods, the cold, ambiguous forms
  That in me dwelt, or only seemed to dwell?

What did I care for Glaucus by the shore,
  Or Proteus hiding in the hollow cave?
That yon blue billow old Poseidon bore,
  Or Aphrodite warmed this amber wave?

Those freaks of fancy were as dying spray,
  The foamy fringes of the strength I hurled,
Whose bosom heaves to one unsetting Day,
  The azure guard and girdle of the world.

If Man gives being, he gave naught to me,
  And of mine empire naught has overthrown:
I am, I was, and I shall ever be
  Apart in power, inviolate, unknown.

Before my myriad voices he is dumb,
  Yet probes their meaning in eternal pain:
I call him, and he cannot fail to come,
  I cast him forth, and he returns again.

So many Gods have I exalted hailed,
  So many, spurned, have rotted in my breast;
Yet mine the balanced powers wherein they failed, —
  The face of action and the heart of rest!

JOVE.

I hear thine ancient murmur, and the slow
Reverberation from thy thousand shores.
Who knows thee, cannot die : for those, thy Gods,
My brood that peopled thee, but strayed in joy
Of half-existence o'er thy restless fields.
What though Olympus props dismantled halls,
The dust of ages on their golden chairs,
And Ganymede is but a heap of bones
Beside the shrivelled eagle, — still I live,
Much as I was before my children made
Their easy ladders for the climbing souls
Of men, who dreamed while dreaming that they knew.
All chains of life they grasped led back to me ;
All aspirations pointed on to me,
And, like thyself, I bounded then the world.
If now the chains be broken, otherwhere
The eyes be turned, and features not mine own
Shine from that void beyond both men and Gods,
Shall I then cease ?   Not so : the later reign
Is built on mine, of mine the later laws
Are born, and he who rules resembles me.

ELOHIM.

Thou liest to thyself, as thou erewhile
Didst lie to men.   We saw thy hollow state,
And we allowed, foreknowing its decay.
Stretch not this tolerance, which lets thee still
Dream olden dreams, see olden visions, claim —
Since broken is thy painted thunderbolt —
The lightnings of the Law !   We led the tribes,
By changing pillars of the cloud and fire,
From On to Pisgah : we upheld their hands :
We planted them among the pleasant vales,
And they, our children, knew the Lord their God.

12

They cried, and we did hear : they went astray,
And then we smote them : as they honored us,
We gave them honor, and as they obeyed
We blessed them ; till the chosen seed became
Exalted o'er the kingdoms of the world.
Thy bestial co-mates, Baal and Peor
And Ashtaroth, have died disgraceful deaths :
Why livest thou ?

JOVE.

　　　　　Thou wert a jealous God,
And wouldst none others have beside thee.　Yet
They were, and led thy chosen seed astray.
If, knowing thee, men justice learned, and truth,
And worship, which is highest, I bestowed
Joy, beauty, grace, and with permitted toys
Coaxed my fair children to a fairer state.
I grudged thee not thy shrines and oracles,
Prophet, and judge, and psalmist, having mine.
I saw thy ways, and read what even thou
Not yet acknowledgest, but which draws nigh
To shake our thrones : for as we are, we are :
We cannot rise when clearer eyes of men
Attain our height, and strive to pierce beyond
Their own colossal shadows.　Mark where ours
Fall side by side upon the race below,
Featured alike in power and majesty,
Yet fading in a sweet and solemn light
That dawns above them !　Be not wroth with me :
I kept thy secret as thou keptest mine.

ELOHIM.

Yea, thou hast worked for us : what we foreknew
Was thy foreboding.　If, like cloud on cloud,
Something of us is dimly thrown on thee,

We are the sun whereby our shadow falls.
If thou wouldst live, teach men the way to us
Through justice, fear, and through avenging law ;
And leave thy lusts and base necessities
To those below the thunder !

JOVE.

           See, where come
The orbs of Ligth and Darkness from the East,
Across thy heavens, as 't were the cloud of stars
Beside the lone black blot of starless space,
In that far universe I know not of.
They, too, are Gods, and claim their equal seats.

ORMUZD.

Be mighty, ye, for them who look to Power ;
Be stern and just for them who bow to Law ;
Be jealous, kind, or cruel, as your tribes
Demand such discipline !   I am but one,
One spirit, effluence, operation, force,
One sweet and sovereign heart, whose beats began
With first of things, and shall be felt in all
Forever !   Void of veil or mystery
My being men behold, and with weak arms
Draw down to wed their own, and give them peace.
The lowest feels me, and the highest fails
To grasp my sole omnipotence of Good.

AHRIMAN.

Make room for me, twin of thine eldest birth !
If each bright sun in all the studded sky
Be throne, at once, and fountain of thy rays,
Yet in the unmeasured gulfs dividing them
I dwell, and ever compass thee around,
One spirit, effluence, operation, force,

One dark, relentless heart, whose beats began
With first of things, and shall be felt in all
Forever !   Men may fear me, but they love :
They seek the darkness rather than the light ;
And all thine atoms, or in them or space,
Are swallowed up in mine.   Thus am I throned
In sole omnipotence of Evil.

JOVE.

            Hark !
I hear a noise of mighty multitudes,
Confused, and crying from the fields of Earth,
And in their cries I hear your names and mine.

MAN.

We found the Gods above our ancient idols,
And worshipped them with voice and deed and duty.
Each was unquestioned, each august and awful,
And, knowing him, we rested in the knowledge.
We grew in power, we builded towns and temples;
We wrought the wider fabric of the nations,
We made the forces which we feared obey us.
Lo ! now, their spirits, as our own in battle,
Stand face to face : their dark or shining legions
Meet in our souls, and tear us and bewilder.
We yield to law, we seek eternal Justice,
We love the Good, yet we accept the Evil,
We love our lives, we cling to joy and beauty,
We render penitence, we pray for pardon,
We look past death to some serene Hereafter.
Which of these things of ours shall we surrender ?
They were bestowed : how can they be divided ?
Shall we be umpires in the high, supernal
Debate of Gods, or is there One beyond them
Whom we have heard, through them, in changing
      voices ?

Then come Thou near, enlighten and console us !
Take our own shape, be guide and God, yet brother !

APOLLO.

I come, your shepherd of the sunny hills
In Thessaly, who from the reedy pipe
Allured the hidden sweetness of your breath,
And made a music of your empty lives.
I taught ye beauty, harmony, and grace ;
I lifted and ennobled ye ; I clothed
Your limbs with glory and your brows with song.
Nature, the hard, unfriendly mother, gave
Her sweetest milk to nourish ye anew,
And all her forms, as lovers or as friends,
Moved in your life, and led your shining march
Of ages, as a triumph ! Still I walk,
Though unacknowledged, filling hungry ears
With purer sound, and brightening weary eyes
With visions of the beauty that may be.
For Beauty is the order of the Gods,
The ether breathed alone by souls uplift
In aspiration, and the crown of all,
Save whom dumb darkness and the bestial life
Tread out of being. Reaching her, ye live.

IMMANUEL.

She is not Love. I know thy proud, pure face,
And was content to see thy form as mine,
In temples where the Truth was sought through me.
In love, in meekness and in lowliness,
I did my Father's will : come unto me,
Ye heavy-laden, weary sons of earth,
And I will give you rest. I do but speak
The things He bids me, of myself am naught.
Love one another : inasmuch as ye

Shall do it to the least of these, my brothers,
Ye do it unto me.   Behold, I came
To bring ye peace, yet also bring a sword ;
For love, and diligence in doing good,
Mercy divine and holy charity,
Stir up the evil that among you dwells ;
But through the strife His Kingdom shall be based,
Who is alone from everlasting on
To everlasting : and His rule is love.

MAN.

One's face is fairer than the star of morning ;
One's voice is sweeter than the dew of Hermon
To flowers that wither : who is there beside them ?
And is there need of any one above him
Who brings his gifts of good and love and mercy ?
We climb to nobler knowledge, finer senses,
And every triumph brings diviner promise,
But Life is more : our souls for other waters
Were sore athirst, till He unlocked the fountain.
Now let us drink ; for as a hart that panteth,
Escaped from spears across the burning desert,
We think to drain the brook, yet still it floweth.

Scene III.

A vast landscape. Sunrise.

CHORUS OF SPIRITS.

In the ether of stars, in the bath of the planets,
In the darkest deeps of the severing spaces,
The force of the Spirit is working on:
And men have guessed it, have felt its glory,
Have babbled its speech, and fathomed its secrets
In earth and ocean and wind and flame.

They have conquered the phantoms themselves cre-
    ated ;
They have torn the masks from the gods aforetime,
To find the mock of the face of Man.
They sprinkle themselves with blood of atonement,
Persuade their souls to believe and be quiet,
Yet restlessly reach for the Wisdom beyond.

The years are as breath, and as sands the ages ;
'Mid a myriad suns the world is a darkness ;
The Deities die when their work is done.
But the mantle of One is wide to enfold us,
The heart of One is a Father's to love us,
The Spirit of One shall lift us and hold !

ODIN, BAAL, PERUN, AND MANITO.

We are but shadows now, we know full well,
Yet life is sweet, even that which shadows lead
In mist, and storm, and twilights of the world.
We have acknowledged Thee, the High, Unknown,

Who sitt'st above our passions : we depend
On Thee, it seems, and would behold Thy face,
If haply blood of Thine make grand our limbs,
As ours the strong, heroic shapes of men.
We give the strength which meets and overcomes;
The amorous ardor which renews the world;
The fierceness which is needful as the love,
And those indulgences to come, which lure
Where judgment threatens : shall we live or die?

A VOICE FROM SPACE.

I have allowed ye.

BRAHMA.

On my moveless throne
I hear, and, that I speak, suspend the work
Of effortless creation.   If Thou be
The primal One, whose being only IS
Forever everywhere, I work for Thee,
Thine eldest force, who fashioned Indra's peak,
And from my hand the holy Ganges stream
Poured as a long libation, — bade the gods
Be hatched in beasts and from the lotus-flower,
And with the infant races sport, until
These prayed to find me, and I was revealed.
I saw my symbols stolen, saw my laws
Transferred to other faiths, myself unknown
By those who yet obeyed me and adored :
But I am calm : no seed of meanest life
Hath missed its place in falling from my hand,
Nor any mesh in all my boundless net
Of woven law hath felt unequal strain.

A VOICE FROM SPACE.

Thou doest the work I set, yet nam'st thyself :
have no name.

ORMUZD.

Thou hast ! — thy name is Good.
I surely know Thee, since I sprang from Thee.
For Good is wisdom, Good is beauty, Good
Is even the root below the flower of Love.
I am not idle, though my nature sole
Exists therein, but like the active sun,
My sacred orb, with silent energy
Pervade the universe.

A VOICE FROM SPACE.

Good came from me.

AHRIMAN.

Whence, then, came I ? Born of the selfsame womb,
If born, or separated even with him,
From earliest stuff of Gods ! I work as well
In mine own way : I am the thing I seem,
And could not be, except in strife with him.
He may revile me, but I owe him much :
His children serve me in their ignorance,
And round his brightest altars curls the smoke
I breathe below them. If he came from Thee,
I came beside him and with him return.

A VOICE FROM SPACE.

And Evil I permitted.

JOVE.

In my youth
I called Thee Fate, and trembled at Thy name.
I felt Thou wast, but knew not what Thou wast.
Thou gav'st me fair dominions, happy realms,
Hills that inspired, and wandering seas that sang,
And noble forms of men that worshipped me.

I taught them Order, Art, Humanity,
And left them — when the time foretold had found
All these in ruin — nearer to Thy feet.
I bate no privilege of ancient pride ;
If Thou art what I dream, it came from Thee ;
And if I launched the thunder, loosed the leash
Of War and Pestilence, it was Thy will.
I do not crouch, for Thou hast made me strong.

A VOICE FROM SPACE.

Thou wast my servant.

ELOHIM.

     Art thou not ourselves ?
We spread with Thee the waters of the deep,
We hung with Thee the curtains of the heavens,
And choired the morning stars ; we gave Thy law
In thunder, and Thy mercy as the dew ;
We banished other Gods from out Thy house,
And smote the heathen : we translated Thee
In human speech to men, and sealed with them
Thy Covenant ; o'er Thy chosen seed we watched
In war, and exile, and captivity,
And the strange lusts that visited their kings.
We mean to rule forever, and we claim
Obedience of men and rival Gods.
If what we hear be but our echoed voice,
Then we have spoken.   Who besides should speak
From the unfathomed silence of the stars ?
We walk the world and hear our names implored,
Behold our power increase, our kingdom come.

A VOICE FROM SPACE.

Ye I commissioned.

APOLLO.

I but claimed a place
Among the serving Gods, yet lords of men.
Not mine to call existence from the void,
Or give reward, save what in Beauty's self
Is given forever : mine the simpler task
To build one bridge that reaches to the sky,
To teach one truth that brings eternal joy,
And from the imperfect world the promise wrest
Of one perfection. If than this Man needs
A broader hope, a loftier longing, yet
This must he have ; bereft of it, he dies.
He cannot feed on cold ascetic dreams,
And mutilate the beauty of the world
For something far and shapeless : he must give
His eyes the form of what in him aspires,
His ears the sound of that diviner speech
He pines to speak, his soul the proud content
Of having touched the skirts of perfect things.
This much in him I foster, marring not
Thy high design, but lending it a grace
Which he, insane to grasp Thee, might forget.
If Thou, as needs Thou must, be harmony,
The soft concordance of my Delphic lute
Is heard between Thy thunders, and I keep
My gentle state in dear humanity.

A VOICE FROM SPACE.

Live ! Beauty is of me.

IMMANUEL.

And thou art chief
A God of Love ! Who hath seen me hath seen
The Father. I was sent from Thee to teach
Thy Truth to souls anhungered; if I left

Untaught the things of less account, I spake
No prohibition.   Men have used my name
To mortify their bodies, maim their lives,
And plant with sorrow where I came to sow
The seeds of joy, as in that pleasant land,
In Cana's mansion and the home of Nain.
I know that I am Thine : my heart leaps up
To hear Thee, and I lean, as doth a child,
Upon Thy bosom.   I have done Thy will,
My Father, who hast not forsaken me.
Accept my work, and bless me : Thou art Love !

A VOICE FROM SPACE.

Yea, most am Love !

IMMANUEL.

            Then am I near to Thee !

A VOICE FROM SPACE.

Thou art my one begotten Son, in whom
I am well pleased.

MAN.

                  We hearken to the words
We cannot understand.   If we look up
Beyond the shining form wherein Thy Love
Made holiest revelation, we must shade
Our eyes beneath the broadening wing of Doubt,
To save us from Thy splendor.   All we learn
From delving in the marrow of the Earth,
From scattering thought among the timeless stars,
From slow-deciphered hieroglyphs of power
In chemic forces, planetary paths,
Or primal cells whence all Thy worlds are born,
But lifts Thee higher, seats Thee more august,

Till Thou art grown so vast and wonderful,
We dare not name Thee, scarce dare pray to Thee.
Yet what Thou art Thyself hast taught us : Thou
Didst plant the ladders which we seek to climb,
Didst satisfy the heart, yet leave the brain
To work its own new miracles, and read
Thy thoughts, and stretch its agonizing hands
To grasp Thee.   Chide us not : be patient : we
Are children still, we were mistaken oft,
Yet we believe that in some riper time •
Thy perfect Truth shall come.

A VOICE FROM SPACE.

Wait !   Ye shall know.

FINIS.

PRINCE DEUKALION:

A LYRICAL DRAMA.

Bestimmt, Erleuchtetes zu sehen, nicht das Licht.
GOETHE.

If thou canst not ascend
These steps, die on that marble where thou art!
KEATS.

CONTENTS.

———◆———

13

PERSONS OF THE DRAMA.

——◆——

Eos, *Goddess of the Dawn.*
Gæa, *Goddess of the Earth.*
Eros.
Prometheus.
Epimetheus.
Pandora.
Prince Deukalion.
Pyrrha.
Agathon.
Medusa.
Calchas (*High-Priest*).
Buddha.
Spirits of Dawn.
Nymphs.
Voices.
Chorus of Ghosts.
Charon.

Angels.
Spirits.
The Nine Muses.
Urania.
Spirit of the Wind.
Spirit of the Snow.
Spirit of the Stream.
Echoes.
The Youth (*Poet*).
The Artist.
Poet (*Act III.*).
Shepherd (*Man*).
Shepherdess (*Woman*).
Mediæval Chorus.
Mediæval Anti-Chorus.
Chorus of Builders.
Four Messengers.

PRINCE DEUKALION.

ACT I.

SCENE I.

A plain, sloping from high mountains towards the sea. At the bases of the mountains lofty vaulted entrances of caverns. A ruined temple, on a rocky height. A Shepherd, asleep in the shadow of a clump of laurels: the flock scattered over the plain.

SHEPHERD (*awaking*).

HAVE I outslept the thunder ?   Has the storm
　　Broken and rolled away ?   That leaden weight
Which pressed mine.eyelids to reluctant sleep
Falls off : I wake ; yet see not anything
As I beheld it.   Yonder hang the clouds,
Huge, weary masses, leaning on the hills ;
But here, where star-wort grew and hyacinth,
And bees were busy at the bells of thyme,
Stare flinty shards ; and mine unsandal'd feet
Bleed as I press them : who hath wrought the change ?
The plain, the sea, the mountains, are the same ;
And there, aloft, Demeter's pillared house, —
What ! — roofless, now ?   Are she and Jove at strife ?
And, see ! — this altar to the friendly nymphs
Of field and flock, the holy ones who lift

A poor man's prayer so high the Gods may hear, —
Shivered ? — Hath thunder, then, a double bolt ?
They said some war of Titans was renewed,
But such should not concern us, humble men
Who give our dues of doves and yeanling lambs
And mountain honey.   Let the priests in charge,
Who weigh their service with our ignorance,
Resolve the feud ! — 't is they are answerable,
Not we; and if impatient Gods make woe,
We should not suffer !

                  Hark ! — what strain is that,
Floating about the copses and the slopes
As in old days, when earth and summer sang ?
Too sad to come from their invisible tongues
That moved all things to joy ; but I will hear.

NYMPHS.

We came when you called us, we linked our dainty
    being
    With the mystery of beauty, in all things fair and
        brief;
But only he hath seen us, who was happy in the seeing,
    And he hath heard, who listened in the gladness of
        belief.
As a frost that creeps, ere the winds of winter whistle,
    And odors die in blossoms that are chilly to the
        core,
Your doubt hath sent before it the sign of our dis-
    missal ;
    We pass, ere ye speak it ; we go, and come no more !

SHEPHERD.

If blight they threaten, 't is already here ;
Yet still, methinks, the sweet and wholesome grass
Will sometime spring, and softer rains wash white

My wethers' fleeces.   We, Earth's pensioners,
Expect less bounty when her store is scant;
But while her life, though changed from what it was,
Feeds on the sunshine, we shall also live.

VOICES (*from underground*).

We won, through martyrdom, the power to aid ;
We met the anguish and were not afraid;
   Like One, we bore for you the penal pain.
Behold, your life is but a culprit's chance
To rise, renewed, from out its closing trance ;
   And, save its loss, there is not any gain !

SHEPHERD.

What tongues austere are these, that offer help
Of loving lives ? — that promise final good,
Greater than gave the Gods, so theirs be lost ?
Sad is their message, yet its sense allures,
And large the promise, though it leaves us bare.
I would I knew the secret ; but, instead,
I shudder with a strange, voluptuous awe,
As when the Pythia spake : 't is doom disguised, —
Choice offered us when term of choice is past,
And we, obedient unto them that choose,
Are made amenable !   Hark, — once again !

NYMPHS.

Our service hath ceased for you, Shepherds !
   We fade from your days and your dreams,
With the grace that was lithe as a leopard's,
   The joy that was swift as a stream's !
To the musical reeds, and the grasses ;
   To the forest, the copse, and the dell ;
To the mist, and the rainbow that passes ;
   The vine, and the goblet, — farewell !

Go, drink from the fountains that flow not !—
Our songs and our whispers are dumb :
But the thing ye are doing ye know not,
Nor dream of the thing that shall come !

VOICES.

Flame hath not melted, nor did earthquake rend
The dungeons where we waited for The End,
Which coming not, we issue forth to power.
We quench vain joy with shadows of the grave ;
We smite your lovely wantonness, to save ;
We hang Eternity on Life's weak hour !

NYMPHS.

We wait in the breezes,
We hide in the vapors,
And linger in echoes,
Awaiting recall.

VOICES.

The word is spoken, let the judgment fall !

NYMPHS.

The heart of the lover,
The strings of the psalter,
The shapes in the marble
Our passing deplore :

VOICES.

Truth comes, and vanity shall be no more !

NYMPHS.

Not wholly we vanish ;
The souls of the children,
The faith of the poets
Shall seek us, and find.

VOICES.

Dead are the things the world has left behind.

NYMPHS.

Lost beauty shall haunt you
With tender remorses ;
And out of its exile
    The passion return !

VOICES.

The flame shall purify, the fire shall burn !

NYMPHS.

Lift from the rivers
Your silver sandals,
From mists of the mountains
Your floating veils ! —
From musky vineyard,
And copse of laurel,
The ears that listened
For lovers' tales !
Let olives ripen
And die, untended ;
Leave oak and poplar,
And homeless pine !
Take shell and trumpet
From swell of surges,
And feet that glisten
From restful brine !
As the bee when twilight
Has closed the bell, —
As love from the bosom
When doubts compel,
We go : farewell !

SHEPHERD.

The strains dissolve into the hollow air,
Yet something stays, — a sense of distant woe,
As now, this hour, while the green lizards glide
Across the sun-warmed stones, and yonder bird
Prinks with deliberate bill his ruffled plumes,
Far off, in other lands, an earthquake heaved
The high-towered cities, and a darkness fell
From twisted clouds that ruin as they pass.
But, lo ! — who rises yonder ? — as from sleep
Rising, slow movements of a sluggish grace,
That speak her gentle, though a Titaness,
And strong, though troubled is her breadth of brow,
And eyes of strange, divine obscurity.
She sees me not : I am too mean for sight
Of such a goddess ; yet, methinks, the milk
Of those large breasts might feed me into that
Which once I dreamed I should be, — lord, not slave !

Scene II.

The Same.

GÆA.

I travail for my children. Babe, or youth,
Or man attempered unto utmost life,
The mother's care still follows, grows no less.
The swift impending change scarce other is
Than what my sons have borne erewhile, and thriven.
As the thin blood of boyhood, while it takes
The ripening power of increase in its turn,
Distrusts itself, half fears its own rich force,
So, now, it may be.
　　　　　　　Yet — I change with Man,

Mother not more than partner of his fate.
Ere he was born I dreamed that he might be,
And through long ages of imperfect life
Waited for him. Then, vexed with monstrous shapes
That spawned and wallowed in primeval ooze,
I lay supine and slept, or seemed to sleep ;
And dreamed, or waking felt as in a dream
Some touch of hands, some soft, delivering help, —
And he was there ! His faint new voice I heard ;
His eye that met the sun, his upright tread,
Thenceforth were mine ! And with him came the palm,
The oak, the rose, the swan, the nightingale :
The barren bough hung apples to the sun :
Dry stalks made harvest : breezes in the woods
Then first found music, and the turbid sea
First rolled a crystal breaker to the shore.
His foot was on the mountains, and the wave
Upheld him : over all things huge and coarse
There came the breathing of a regal sway,
Which bent them into beauty. Order new
Followed the march of new necessity,
And what was useless, or unclaimed before,
Took value from the seizure of his hands.

Ah me, in those old days how near and fond
Was he, how frank in fashion or in fear
His thoughtless adolescence ! To my life
The birth-cord still unsevered held his own :
He took my comforts, seeking none beyond,
And crept for shelter to my shielding arms.
But now — mistrust, and shame of aid outgrown,
And bitter enmity that springs from shame,
And faith perverse in opposite of faith,
Have made him froward. I am forced to seem
She-wolf or pantheress, a savage dam,

And lose the eager mouth that sought my dugs,
Until its native thirst returns ; but he, —
Sleep-walking in the senses once so keen,
With eyes uplifted to some distant crown,
That, while it burns, makes other glory dust, —
How long shall he thus wander ? — and how bear
The lack of all-sustaining loveliness ?
Shall fairest sights and sweetest sounds be dim,
And out of movement die the rhythm of joy,
And beauteous passion lose its power to warm ? —
All freedom, exultation, and delight
That lifted him, all energies and high desires
That bore him forth as blow the fourfold winds,
Be lashed and goaded on a single path,
One iron chariot draw ?

　　　　　　　　　　Lo ! here, the Rose ;
The woman-flower he could not choose but love,
Shall he forget it ?　Shall he turn from breath
Distilled of bliss and bountiful bright hours,
To taste the incense rank in censers burned,
Which seems to mask some odor of decay ?

　　　(A bud on the rose-tree bursts open : EROS *appears.)*

EROS.

Not yet am I barred in Hades,
　　Though a word unknown hath hurled
The Olympian lords and ladies
　　To wail in the nether world !
Let Proteus shift in ocean
　　From shape to shape that eludes :
I am one, as the heart's devotion,
　　Yet many, as lovers' moods !

GÆA.

Blithe, tricksome spirit !　Art thou left alone,

Of Gods and all their intermediate kin
The sweet survivor ?   Yet a single seed,
When soil and seasons lend their alchemy,
May clothe a barren continent in green.

EROS.

Was I born, that I should die ?
Stars that fringe the outer sky
Know me : yonder sun were dim,
Save my torch enkindled him.
Then, when first the primal pair
Found me in the twilight air,
I was older than thy day,
Yet to them as young as they.
All decrees of Fate I spurn ;
Banishment is my return ;
Hate and Force purvey for me,
Death is shining victory !

GÆA.

Thou art the same, — child of the highest Gods,
Whatever shape they wear, and child of mine !
Reclaim thy heritage ! — I give to thee
Maytime, and music, and all odorous herbs,
The whispers of the woodlands and the waves
The dewy lustre of acquainted eyes,
The thrill of meeting hands, and ah ! at last
Of lips that cannot hold themselves apart,
Save life, as beauty, perish !   Take all these,
And whatsoever else may minister
To sweet, insidious influences and arts
Which are thy being, — ply the treachery
That into blessing soon forgives itself ;
Print thy soft iris on white wings of prayer ;
Strike dangerous delight through sacrifice ;

And interpenetrate the sterner faith
With finest essence of the thing it spurns !

EROS.

With the blind desires and motions
  The innocent child that guide ;
With girlhood's shy avoidance
  And boyhood's bashful pride ;
With the arts that are simplest nature,
  And the nature that hides in art,
When the voice and the cheeks bear witness,
  And the eye confesses the heart ;
With the fond mistrust, and the frenzy,
  That falters, or sweeps above,
When the key to delight in beauty
  Is held by the hands of love ;
With the lore of the world's renewal
  In seed or in guarded bud ;
With the plunge of the sportive dolphin,
  And the heat of the panther's blood, —
The spells of my sway are woven,
  The flame of my being fed,
And I breathe in a bright existence,
  Though the eldest Gods are dead !
For Love, in the ashes of Empire
  And the dust of Faith, is born ;
And the rose of a kiss shall blossom,
  When blight has withered the corn !

                [EROS *disappears.*

GÆA.

Needless to give ! — 't is he already owns.
Before the uncounted cycles of the Past
He was, or I — even I — had caught no life
From the wide-floating elements ! Go, then,

Thou beautiful, bright secret of all suns,
All planets, and all unimaginable forms
Upon them sown !   Death and decay are things
That dissipate beneath thy radiant eye:
So thou but live, all else shall come with thee,
Now lost, or unto man's indifference
So seeming ; yet it hides in wilful sport,
And million-voicèd laughter of the waves
And winds, and million wandering smiles of sun
Forever shall betray it, and assure
Thy coming triumph !   I am calm at heart
Now that I know thou livest : was I mad,
To fear, one moment, thou couldst ever die ?

Scene III

A valley, at the base of the mountains.   On the left the en-
trance to a cavern.

PRINCE DEUKALION.
Where art thou, Pyrrha ?

PYRRHA (*coming forward*).
                              Dost thou call, at last ?
Awaiting the awakening of thy thought,
Mine own went wandering.

PRINCE DEUKALION.
                              Whither ?

PYRRHA.
                              Nay, why ask ?
What other moods have heretofore been ours
Than hope by doubt o'ershadowed, or else doubt
Made bearable by transient gleams of hope ?
But now —

PRINCE DEUKALION.

Now, courage ! — such as that we felt,
When they who made us and forefixed our fate,
The Titans, fell ! We saw the thunder-blows
Given and taken, saw the ruined world
Lie panting after fiercest throes endured,
Till milder Gods brought knowledge, peace, and power.
If, grown familiar, these have forfeited
Their ancient honor, or their term is past,
We need not question ; they consent to see
Themselves in sacred marble rebaptized,
New meanings, borrowed from an alien race,
Bestowed on their Olympian emblems, — yea,
The incense burned to beauty, grace and joy
Made dark and heavy by atoning pain
And crowned repentance !   Yet, His law is good
Who now shall rule ; for they we lose withheld
The strength of human hands from human throats,
Forced them to join, and overcome, and build, —
Create, where they destroyed ; but He compels
That strength to help, and makes it slave of Love.
Thus, from the apathy of faith outworn
Rises a haughty life, that soon shall spurn
The mould it grew from.   I foresee new strife,
Mistaken hopes, unnecessary pangs,
And yet — I wait.

PYRRHA.

And I must wait with thee.
Dost thou recall — how long ago it seems ! —
Mine ancient glory?   Nearest, then, I stood :
Our hands — ah, why not also lips ? — had met,
And o'er thy head I saw the hovering crown
Take substance from the air, and flash on me
A glow I hoped was beauty, knew was love !

PRINCE DEUKALION.

'T was when that ether, where the Ages still
Unwrinkled sit, touched by no dread of time,
Was ours to breathe, earth's only sky serene.
Why were we banished ?   Still that heritage
Exists : beyond the dark-blue, dimpled sea
Lie sands and palms, the Nile's wide wealth of corn,
And soaring pylons, granite roofs upheld
By old Osirid columns : there the sun
Sheds broader peace in all his aged beams,
And hoary splendor on uncrumbled stone.
There still the star Canopus sends the dew,
Though sound of sistrum in the dusky halls
Has ceased, and Memnon lost his morning song.
Well thou rememberest, Pyrrha ! — that which was,
Once in the Past, flies forward, like a string
Sharp struck, and straightway in the Future plants
Its brighter phantasm : more than was, shall be !

PYRRHA.

My heart is lifted, and my spirit feeds
Upon thy words.

PRINCE DEUKALION.

                    Pure, patient, brave, thou art ;
But they who set thee back, despoiled thy head
Of separate honor, and postponed my right
Through thine refused, were their progenitors
Whose kingdom cometh.   Thee they may restore
To equal freedom to renounce and bear, —
Like martyrdom : lend me thy finer sense
To see beyond !

PYRRHA.

So much the Titans gave !
14

Yet that, reclaimed, is one fulfilment more.
Pain is to me what conflict is to thee, —
A joy, when born of large necessity.
What musest thou ?   I see thine eyes' clear light
Recede within their depths, as in a lake
Its surface-azure when the cloud sails o'er.

PRINCE DEUKALION.

Erelong some spasm of the vexèd Earth shall close
This cavern's mouth, the last, sole entrance left
To Hades : I would once more see the face
And hear the counsel of my Titan sire,
Prometheus, where he sits in sunless air,
Not suffering, haply, neither glad.   And thou,
Heiress of gifts interpreted as woe,
Since the divinest fate wears evil face
To mortals, let thy steps companion mine !
Terrors shalt thou behold, and threatening forms,
And with the stress of stern, eternal words
Thy brain may falter : canst thou hear the doom
Which sifts the ages as the fingers sand,
And plays with hope, and patience, and despair,
Like beads upon a string, — inexorable,
Fixed from the first ?

PYRRHA.

So I be near to thee.

PRINCE DEUKALION.

Touch, then, my hand !   It is permitted us
To feel each other's blood, but nothing more,
Till that far day when our betrothal-kiss
Asserts the victory sure, the empire won !

[*They pass into the cavern*

Scene IV.

A spacious, arched cavern, opening upon a shadowy, colorless landscape. Enter Prince Deukalion, *leading* Pyrrha.

CHORUS OF GHOSTS.

Away !
Ashes that once were fires,
Darkness that once was day,
Dead passions, dead desires,
  Alone can enter here !
In rest there is no strife,
And memory is not life :
    We neither hope nor fear.
Like some forgotten star,
What first we were, we are.
The Past is adamant :
The Future will not grant
That, which in all its range
  We pray for — Change !

PRINCE DEUKALION.

You found the thing you sought : what fashioned else
These sunless realms ?   If change may verily come
Even to spirits, teach your dim desire
A form whereby to know itself, and seek !

CHORUS OF GHOSTS.

Retreat ! Retreat,
Unwelcome feet !
Whom doth not blast
The horror of his Past,
Who dares to see
Himself in memory,

And thus reclaim
The inevitable shame,
Him only suffer we !

PRINCE DEUKALION.

Prepare your test !

PYRRHA.

What thing is here designed ?
Thy face is pale, despite the firm-set lips,
And level glance of thine unshrinking eyes :
No passing pain awaits thee.

PRINCE DEUKALION.

Nay, but power
That grows from pain ! Hear'st thou the whistling
    rush
Of many wings that part the heavy air,
And bat-like cries, thin, impotent of sound,
That now betray the disconcerted ghosts
Huddling before us to the river-bank ?

PYRRHA.

If I behold these things I seem to see,
I know not : yonder lies a dreary marsh,
Such as at ebb for many a league deforms
A river's narrowing mouth ; gray sedges wave,
Unwhispering ever, o'er the slimy flats,
Beyond which glooms the semblance of a shore.
But who is this, so haggard, limp and old,
Approaching us ?   As with uncertain joints
He walks, still held erect by senile wrath,
That shoots dull gleams from sleep-desiring eyes,
Were sleep permitted here.

PRINCE DEUKALION.

                            'T is surely he,
The ancient ferryman of Hades !

CHARON.

                            Ay,
Nor vanquished yet ! Where wait the ghosts of men ?
Hath Death been dispossessed ? The upper world
With tears and due libations feeds no more
My sullen river : muddy shallows grow
From either side, and trespass on my right,
Till soon dishonest ghosts may wade across.
Yet, wherefore do I question ? You, I guess,
Intend no answer, and eternal Fate
Hath left for you one power of entrance still.
You seek not Lethe : so much say your eyes.
Here lies the other pool, as charged with light
As that with darkness, — awful Memory,
More dread to bear than black Forgetfulness :
Look, or go hence !

PRINCE DEUKALION.

            I look.

PYRRHA.

                        And I with thee.

PRINCE DEUKALION.

Forbear ! The knowledge must be mine alone. —
Within the moveless crystal depths, far down,
The rings of ages widen and dissolve
The while I gaze : distinct, abominable,
I see ourselves, before the Titans were ;
I see the bestial base, unpurified,
Its hideous features smeared with filth and blood,

Its rites unspoken, acts unspeakable,
Wild savage instinct beating back the brain,
Low savage greed a despot in the heart,
And all that ever since mixed foul alloy
With the bright metal of our dreams, — despair
Should the defiant God within us fail —

> [*He pauses.*

PYRRHA.

Say on, nor spare my service ! Shall I see,
Thus, only, in the mirror of thy speech,
The unfeatured truth ?

PRINCE DEUKALION.
(*To* CHARON.)
> Is there aught more than this ?

CHARON.

Look !

PRINCE DEUKALION.

> Nay ! — the forms grow dim ; and under all
There shines a face that is, methinks, mine own !
> (*Lifting his head.*)
What flimsy pride was pierced so, heretofore ?
There is no shame save what begets itself
On old remorse, that keeps its cause alive.
I see, nor shudder : vice outlived is dead,
And feeds its purest opposite in us.
No scent of mould is on the rose's leaves ;
No stain of slime degrades the lotus-cup !
Slave of the Gods, thy lease's term still holds :
Perform thy duty !

CHARON.
> Take the oars yourselves,

And, to your sorrow, cross ! My purse is lean,
So rarely comes an obolus : the boat
Leaks, the worn handles of the ancient blades
Rattle between the thole-pins. Could I push
The beggar ghosts off, crowd my bark with rich,
Enjoy authority, take delight in force, ·
My limbs were suppler; but some power grows slack
In the world's order. One gets old and lame,
And then the Gods themselves forget their words.
Do as you list : nor hinder I, nor help.

[PRINCE DEUKALION *and* PYRRHA *enter the boat.*

CHORUS OF GHOSTS.

They go !
Cleaving alone the stagnant flow
Of our deserted river :
Who thus defies the menace and the test ?
Is he some hero whom the Gods invest
With warrant to deliver ?
Though his disdain
Sharpens our slow, devouring pain,
There wakes an echo in his word
Of what in faded æons once we heard,
That change may come again !
We wait :
Uncertainty at last may bend
Divine decrees, and end
Our fixed monotony of fate !

Scene V.

The Elysian Fields.

PYRRHA.

Here can I breathe : the sight of cloudy groves
And meadows of familiar asphodel ;
The broader lift of this gray vault o'erhead
Half-luminous, as pregnant with a sun ;
The atmosphere of grand extinguished aims,
Suspended hopes or foiled ambitions, — give
Cheer to my soul ; for thus in death survives
Something that will not die.

PRINCE DEUKALION.

                    Why, death 's a thing
For who deserve it ! — We defy, and live.

PYRRHA.

What shapes are these, that, as we walk, float on
Beside us ?

PRINCE DEUKALION.

             Sovereign souls, immortal lives,
That, as a spring through myriad secret veins
Collects the dew and rain-fall, in themselves
Unite all scattered longings of the race,
All formless hope and high necessity,
Distilled through earth to be divinely clear
And flow forever ! As in them we live,
So they in us : he, with the bended brow
And parted waves of his luxuriant hair,
Shall yield his shadowy forehead to the thorn
And take a holier name : he, further off,

Within whose dim, dark eyes lie dreams of truth
He never reached, aspires in later souls ;
And yonder king who love and lordship gave
To find Humanity, and grew a God,
Now first is regal.   These are not the ghosts
Whom irreversible fiat fetters here :
They range the universe.

PYRRHA.

Can they give help ?

PRINCE DEUKALION.

Yea !   Faith in glorious possibilities
At last secures them.

PYRRHA.

See ! — our path ascends,
And near us, pedestal'd above the meads,
Towers a rocky platform, wide and vast,
Where dim Titanic forms, grouped statue-wise,
Express so much of old expectancy
As saves them from despair.

PRINCE DEUKALION.

I see those shapes,
And out of long oblivion memory breaks
To tell me who they are.   Pass we the first,
Whose haggard brows and ignorant dull eyes
No promise hold : but yonder, on the rise,
Who leans with folded arms against the stone ?
Whose forehead, trenched with subjugated pain,
Still keeps the whiteness of a rising star ?
Whose lips, that lock the wisdom of the world,
Have sweetness left for love ?   Whose huge **bare**
    limbs

Affright not, as their force were sheathed in guile,
But rest, in absence of the helping deed ?

PYRRHA.

Is he thy sire ?

PRINCE DEUKALION.

Prometheus, Titan still !
Seem not reliant, — loose thy clinging hand,
And call the proudest blood that woman owns
To prop thine equal claim !

PROMETHEUS (*rising*).

Come ye with prayers,
Depart !

PRINCE DEUKALION.

Nay, neither suppliant nor subdued !
If no celestial ichor in thy veins
Throbs warm as blood, — no instinct in thy heart
Recalls the primal purpose, and renews, —
No will rekindles, not to war with fate,
But be, thyself, the delegate of fate, —
Then are we not thy children !

PROMETHEUS.

Ye are mine.
I know ye now : will may defiance seem,
Confronted with the force that would destroy.
Thence was I punished ; but I set in Man
Immortal seeds of pure activities,
By mine atonement freed, to burst and bloom
In distant, proud fulfilment.   When that day
Has dawned on earth, I need no messenger :
My pilfered strength shall of itself return,
And all I purposed be, ere I command.

PRINCE DEUKALION.

I came to question, but thy ready words
Have almost answered.

PROMETHEUS.

Ask, and I will speak !

PRINCE DEUKALION.

Fore-knowledge, eager to fulfil itself,
And too impatient of reverse that foiled,
Provoked thy torture : how shall speech of mine
Shadow the grandeur of thine early aim,
Living in us ?   Thou knowest, without my words.
But change like this, that now hath fallen on earth,
Came never : never such consoling love
Made overthrow, such promise with one hand
Gave royally, the other taking back.
These things confuse my mind ; but all, to thee, —
Both this and what hereafter comes, — is known.
Say, only, shall thy meditated plans,
As in my soul they stir, and hold me up
O'er all discouragement of time and change,
Prevail at last ?

PROMETHEUS.

If what I planned could fail,
Were I thy sire ?   He who defied the Gods
Dares Time and Change, and all reverse of Fate.
I willed what I foresaw : because I willed,
What I foresaw shall be !

PRINCE DEUKALION.

I seek no more.

PROMETHEUS.

But will excludes not love.   Since thou, adrift,

And that immortal woman by thy side,
Floated above submerged barbarity
To anchor, weary, on the cloven mount,
Thou wast my representative.   My work
Is wrought in thee ; thy mother's deed, in her,
Shall yet be justified.   Beyond what hope
Comes to thy blood through sense of kin with mine,
Take one new comfort — Epimetheus lives !
Though here, beneath the shadow of the crags,
He seems to slumber, head on nerveless knees,
His life increases ; oldest at his birth,
The ages heaped behind him shake the snow
From hoary locks, and slowly give him youth.
'T is he shall be thy helper : Brother, rise !

EPIMETHEUS.

(*Coming forward.*)

I did not sleep ; I mused.   Ha ! comest thou,
Deukalion ?   Once I thought thee strange, distraught,
But now — so many things have happened since —
I think I know thee.

PROMETHEUS.

       Soon *thy* work shall come !
Reversely miscreated, forward mind
In thee made backward-looking, shame shall cease
When midway on their paths our mighty schemes
Meet, and complete each other !   Yet, my son,
Deukalion, — yet one other guide I give,
Eos !

PRINCE DEUKALION.

   Eos ?

PYRRHA.

   Eos ?

PROMETHEUS.

What echoes these ?
Who else than she, the genitrix of light,
The mother of the morning ?

EPIMETHEUS.

Half I know.

PRINCE DEUKALION.

Older than thou, the stealer of the fire !
More hope in thy mysterious message lies
Than certain-featured forms of prophecy.
But where, when, how, shall I approach her sky,
And win her favoring face ?

PROMETHEUS.

Come ye with me !

SCENE VI.

The highest verge of the rocky table-land of Hades, looking eastward.

PROMETHEUS.

O Goddess of the far, flushed fields of Heaven,
Swiftly enthroned between the moon and sun,
And swiftly passing as thy roses die,
To make us love thee more ; the dewy-eyed
And blossom-sandal'd opener of eyes ;
Quickener of human hearts, yea, hearts of Gods,
Not one so stubborn but thy smile subdues
To tenderness ; in whom all light and love
Are one, at whose pure lamp all rising Hours
Of hope and deed and victory snatch fire
For torches soon extinguished else, — appear !

EPIMETHEUS.

Deceived so many times, why should she dip
Her shining robes in this unfriendly gloom, —
Why smirch the star that on her forehead burns
And breathe these vapors, when the brighter earth
Forgets her?

PYRRHA.

        Speak not thus!   What virtue lies
More in achievement than its hot desire?
To shake the drowsed indifference of men
Even Gods are powerless : thy wisdom wears
Sad colors of experience ; dark thou showest
Against the light whereto we set our brows. —
But *thou*, who waitest near, as one too proud
Or to evade or spurn shame undeserved, —
Unhappy wert thou woman, angry if
A goddess, tranquil being neither, — speak

PANDORA.

No other words had opened patient lips.
I have not made complaint, though every sin
Still cheats its base possessor to transfer
Its blame to me, — though she, who now my place
Usurps, takes Egypt's serpent for the Gods,
And eats the apple, not on Ida's hill!
The passion of the race offends its pride,
So this turns back on that, and finds its source —
Where, but in us?   Wilt thou accept it?

PYRRHA.

                 No!

PANDORA.

There is no sign in yonder moveless mist

That she hath heard : thine answer bids me call. —
O Goddess, that from sleep and guilty dreams
Sprung from the dregs of day, from weary vice
And all suspended selfishness of men,
Bidst one pure moment breathe upon the world,
Renewing youth and beauty ere the sun
Shall lighten wrinkles and thin hair, — whose heart
Dreams back Tithonus and dear early love,
And morning visions of unwedded girls,
And sweet desires of uncorrupted men,
Shy as thou art, because divinely proud,
Proud as thou art, because divinely pure,
Hear thou my woman's voice !

PROMETHEUS.

Thine hath she heard.
Faint, rosy gleams, unused to Hades, steal
Forth from the sullen vapor : here no star
May rise before her, nor the clover-dews
Refresh her feet ; but every nightly crag
And jutting foreland of invisible hills
Is angered with the glory !

PANDORA.

Goddess, rise !
Forgive the darkness, not of us : so much
As we may see, so much may hear, reveal !
(*A sound, as of trumpets.*)

EOS (*unseen*).

So far away
From my high vestibule of Day,
What voices call ?

PROMETHEUS.

Titan and human, each and all.

EOS.

I, long withdrawn,
Leave to my Hours the service of the Dawn:
The Earth, henceforth, shall see
Only their lower ministry.
But when the race
Lifts unto me a fixed, believing face,
I will return!

PRINCE DEUKALION.

Say, shall not I that distant glory earn?

EOS.

Thou! — thou and she,
Inheritors of holy destiny!
Faith, when none believe;
Truth, when all deceive;
Freedom, when force restrains;
Courage to sunder chains;
Pride, when good is shame;
Love, when love is blame, —
These shall call me in stars and flame!
Thus if your souls have wrought,
Ere ye approach me, I shine unsought!

PROMETHEUS.

Yea, under thee the wavering tide
Of the Ages that, streamlike, wind as they glide
Shall mirror or lose the gleam,
And brighten as truth or darken as dream!

EOS.

If he but guard his youth,
His dream shall be wondrous truth!

PRINCE DEUKALION.

Call, command ! — I obey :
When there is Dawn, there shall be Day !

PYRRHA.

I feel, I love, I see ! —
Faithful to him is faith in thee.

EOS.

Oft shall I lift the dark
With fringe of brightness and starry spark ;
Oft shall I seem to rise
With the glory of Gods in the waiting skies ;
But the Hour shall miss its place,
And the shadow recede on the dial's face !
Say, are ye strong
To endure the wrong
That cheats the promise and mocks the trust ?

PRINCE DEUKALION.

I have borne, and shall bear, — because I must.

PYRRHA.

The end shall crown us : The Gods are just.

EOS.

When darkness falls,
And what may come is hard to see ;
When solid adamant walls
Seem built against the Future that should be ;
When Faith looks backward, Hope dies, Life appals,
Think most of Morning, and of me !

[*The rosy glow in the sky fades away.*

15

PROMETHEUS.

(*To* PRINCE DEUKALION.)

Go back to Earth, and wait !

PANDORA.

(*To* PYRRHA.)

Go : and fulfil our fate !

ACT II.

SCENE I.

A wayside shrine, opposite a fountain. Fragments of antique sculpture — among others the head of a Muse — appear in the wall of a vineyard, bordering the road. PRINCE DEUKA- LION, *seated on a rude stone bench, beside the fountain.*

PRINCE DEUKALION.

MY limbs are weary, now the hoping heart
    No more can lift their burden and its own.
The long, long strife is over; and the world,
Half driven and half persuaded to accept,
Seems languidly content. As from the gloom
Of sepulchres its gentler faith arose,
Austere of mien, the suffering features worn,
With lips that loved denial, closed on pain,
And eyes accustomed to the lift of prayer.
The suns of centuries have not wholly warmed
Those chilly pulses; scarce those funeral robes
Permit some colored broidery of joy;
And half the broken implements that fell
From conquered hands of Knowledge and of Art
Are still unwielded. From its first proud height
Humanity must bend; and so, neglecting these, —
Defenceless through its ignorance renewed, —
One pair of hands has grasped the common right,
And one intelligence the thought of all!

Are he and she, who now approach this shrine,
Other than when the conquering demigods,

Fair forms triumphant on high pedestals,
Sat where yon saint, head downwards on the cross,
Blends torture with distortion ?   What !   Shall pain
Uplift and save, spilt blood and dreadful death
The fair, discrowned serenities of Gods
Make impotent ?   But I will hear once more
The subject faith, the helplessness, the fear.

(SHEPHERD *and* SHEPHERDESS *come forward and kneel before*
the shrine.   After devotions made, they rise.)

SHEPHERD.

To her, Our Lady, Lily, Star of the Sea,
Five hundred have I told upon these beads ;
To him, now, fifty : since he keeps the keys,
Somewhat he may expect.   Save that our saints
Grow covetous of prayer as priests of pay,
And sins provoke in order to absolve,
Our faith were easy.

SHEPHERDESS.

            She, if any, hears !
Her eyes are tender, and her virgin breast
Fed not more lovingly the Child of God,
Than mine feeds mine.

SHEPHERD.

           /   Ay, safe by chrism and cross
Is he : no demons near his cradle hide !
Fast goes with feast, the penance with the gift,
Like good and evil seasons : pay your dues
And make them debtors !   'T is a plain account
Heaven keeps with earth, unless the stewards lie.

SHEPHERDESS.

And, after her, how fair the martyr-youth

Who sees his coming crown, and will not heed
The arrow quivering in his golden side !
Lover to maids, to me a brother, son
To women age-despoiled, — could once his eyes
Droop downward, he would pity, love and save.

SHEPHERD.

Why should they make the Demons beautiful,
And give our shrines to holy ugliness ?
Cecilia, sitting at her organ-keys,
And Barbara, queen-like with her large, calm eyes,
Should be my goddesses, dared I select:
One is too pure to guess men's easy sins,
The other wise to pardon.   As we go,
Sing thou with me her mellow canticle !

[*Exeunt, singing.*

For the secret faith adored,
Thou wast sent, by spear and sword,
Out of Egypt to the Lord,
            Holy Barbara !
From the sun upon the sand
And the stars on either hand,
From the glory of the land
            Taken, Barbara !
By the victory over pain
In the tower where thou wast slain, —
By thy sacrifice and gain,
            Hear us, Barbara !

PRINCE DEUKALION.

In these new names extinguished miracles
Sweetly renew themselves : disparaged types,
Torn from the pagan world and set in ours,
Become again divine.   But, stay ! who comes
With brow unbound and visionary eyes,

And nervous hands that clutch as if they sought
The antique plectrum and the chorded shell?
No wayside orison arrests his feet,
Yet doth he pause; a dream within his blood
Casts old divinity on yonder Muse,
And far Ægean echoes in his ears
Reach the forgotten sense.

THE YOUTH (*to himself*).

　　　　　　　　　Be it sacrilege,
I must adore thee!　Yea, with hands that touch
The wounds of him upon thy ruin throned,
Approach thee; none of all the hosts that save
So gaze serenely over strife and time,
Beholding Beauty, being beautiful!
I know not if I know thee; yet I know
What in my soul endeavors to thyself —
Seeks consecration!　Vacant are thine eyes,
Cold thine insulted brow and mute thy lips,
Yet, Goddess, to thy menial place I bend,
And give thee honor!

　　　(*He stoops and kisses the lips of the Muse.*)

PRINCE DEUKALION.
　　　　　　　She will give it back.

THE YOUTH.
　　　(*After a pause.*)

Who, then, art thou?　No pulse in all my soul
Hast thou abashed; but, rather, force and flame
Of scarcely self-confessed ambition rise
As I behold thee : Somewhat of *her* face
Grows into broader majesty in thine,
But human, as in them that must endure.

PRINCE DEUKALION.

As *thou* must !   Out of all that was I come,
Awaiting all that shall be ; they that know,
Behold me ever.

THE YOUTH.

Let me know, behold !
Thóu seem'st the shape of what I dare to dream.

PRINCE DEUKALION.

Do thou my work !   Through hates and battles walk ;
Eat bitter bread of strangers ; lose thy land ;
Give up thy gentle love, to find once more,
An angel guide, the lily in her hand ;
Scourge brazen power, and hunt hypocrisy
To where it hides, the olden Hades lost,
In tortured circles of your later Hell ;
Become a voice where terror sheathes itself
In music, Pity, a dove in whirlwinds tossed,
Pleads out of agony, and primal Love
And highest Wisdom set alike for thee
The gate of Dis, the mount of Paradise !

THE YOUTH.

Thou speak'st as mine own soul.

PRINCE DEUKALION.

The sight unsealed,
Without the courage, seeing, to advance,
Were but a curse ; but thou shalt be a name
Which is eternal power, and from thy pangs,
As by fierce heat, the chains be fused apart,
Which now the tears of ages rust in vain.

[Exeunt.

SCENE II.

Grand hall of a palace. MEDUSA, *seated on a throne of gold, a triple crown upon her head.* *Four Messengers standing near.*

MEDUSA.

Say to the East, her gateway of return
Stands open, though the hinges creak with rust:
Whence came the light her darkness dare not bide.
The seven lamps of Dawn have followed us,
And grown to suns, above, beneath our feet,
On right hand and on left: the Day is ours.

[*Exit First Messenger.*

Say to the South, the savor of her gifts
Delights us as of old : the faint, thin breath
Of her ascetic watches, sprinkled blood
Of self-inflicted penance, speech grown hoarse
In solitude, and visions born of brains
Dishumanized, have reached us and refreshed !

[*Exit Second Messenger.*

Say to the West, we ask no more than she
Erewhile hath given, eager and whole assent;
So flashing back the surplus of her light
As a strong sunset fires the unwilling East !

[*Exit Third Messenger.*

Say to the North, the firmest hand is love's !
Except in force there is no help : in faith
Abides no jealousy.   We hear her threats
In patience, as the frowardness of will
That brooks no other, until taught by loss.
Let her find freedom, and, as heretofore,
Finding, be cheated !   Dreams of passing days, —

Selected truth of ages, — which shall stand?
Foreseeing penitence, we pardon now!

[*Exit Fourth Messenger.*

(*Sola.*)

Not vainly did I bide my time: for Power,
A tree of cautious growth, shows stunted top
Until the meshes of its wandering roots
Have crept in secret to the choicest clay;
Then, shooting firm and spreading boughs abroad,
Resistance withers, rival force lacks room
Beneath its shade.   Now, planted for all time,
Kings are my vassals, Knowledge bids me fix
Her bounds of liberty!   By failure taught
To seem to lose for sake of later gain;
With small success, until the greater come,
Content; forgetful never of the end,
What hinders me to make my single will,
Sheathed in invulnerable divinity,
The world's one law?

(*A pause; she listens.*)

"Growth is the law, — or death."
Who spake?   Or was it some last echo blown
From ended struggles?   Growth is mine to give!
Have I kept life for all that in the Past
Men clung to, fed the old, barbaric sense
With what it loves, and paved an easy way
Between two worlds to suit the halting crowd, —
And am not potent?   'T is the single life,
Proud of small gifts, defiant in brief power,
That mocks the broad authority of time.
Through vice or perfect virtue comes alike
Obedience; this because it questions not,
And that, from need of pardon.   Having these,

Whatever third between them lies must soon
Bend, or be crushed : I rule, while I exist !

(*Enter* PRINCE DEUKALION *and* PYRRHA.)

PRINCE DEUKALION.

Hail, Cæsar's heiress !

MEDUSA.

            Who art thou?   And why
Such greeting ?

PRINCE DEUKALION.

            I declare thee as thou art.
The phantom purple underneath thy stole
We see, who nursed thy young humility
That now is pride, intrusted thee with strength
To be the strength of men, and made thee free,
That each soul's freedom find its root in thine !
How much of duty in thy power survives ?

MEDUSA.

I meet the needs and the desires of men.
What they expect, I give ; the seed whereof,
Sown ignorantly on all the fields of the Past
By dead Religions, I have reaped for them.
The passion and delight of sacrifice ;
The comfort out of self-abasement won ;
The lofty symbols, flattering lower sense
Until the thing it touches seems divine ;
The sweet continuance of miracle
That Faith implores, to feel its Lord renewed ;
The sanctioned ear, where Guilt may find release
And surety of pardon, — these I give.

PRINCE DEUKALION.

These only ?   Treadest thou thy children down,
Lest they should grow beyond thee ?   Hast thou peace
For Man's illimitable questions and desires ?

MEDUSA.

Yea !   Through obedience, peace for each and all.

PRINCE DEUKALION.

Art thou, then, more than man ?   Through him thou
    art.

MEDUSA.

Thy speech offends : the race-begotten child
Is its own father's lord.

PRINCE DEUKALION.

                    Prove lordship, then ! —
Display the rights bestowed, to balance them
Thou hast usurped !   Man's reverence is thine :
Where bides thy reverence for Man ?   The Mind
That, seated in the universe of things,
Needs all its heritage, — the haughty doubt,
Twin-born with knowledge and of equal right,
Hast thou made free ?

MEDUSA.

            I make not error free.

PRINCE DEUKALION.

Art thou, alone, establisher of truth ? —
Not also Man who made thee, the high God
Whose will permits thee ?

PYRRHA.

                Tell me what keen charm
Thou usest, that my daughters turn to thee ?

MEDUSA.

Knowest thou thyself and askest ?

PYRRHA.

Yea, I know
The strength and weakness of an instinct foiled.
Sexless thyself, the secret of the sex
Is lightly caught by thee ; yet, be thou skilled
To weave ecstatic visions from hot blood,
And call heaven down to fill Love's emptiness,
There dwells a soul in woman past thy reach,
A need that spurns thy tinkling toys, a claim
Beyond thy lullabies of sense and sound,
And sweet division of Divinity
'Twixt us and Man !

MEDUSA.

Thine ?—or felt by all ?

PRINCE DEUKALION.

A myriad speak, though single be the voice !
We know thee, Gorgon !   Though the tonsured head
Keep down thy sprouting snakes, the triple crown
Hide their renewal, yet thy stony glance
Betrays the ancient beauty, and its dread !
Why hast thou turned from that defenceless love
Which equalized all lives of men, to use
The mystery of terror ?   Why made stone
The souls that moved before thee, save in chains ?
Many thy keys of power, for thou hast learned
To govern weakness : hast thou then forgot
That force and freedom live ?

MEDUSA.

Perchance in dreams.

PRINCE DEUKALION (*advancing*).

Before thee, here, I stand !   One Power decrees
Thy life and mine : subdue me if thou canst !
My children made thee, and shall overthrow !
Take strength from all the Past, on dreams presumed
Build empire, and exalt thyself, — *I* am,
I was, I shall be !

PYRRHA.

I no less !

MEDUSA.

(*Sinking down upon her throne.*)
                              Away !

CHORUS (*without*).

As a bed where the weary sleep,
As a chest where our gems we keep
        Art thou, our Mother !

ANTI-CHORUS.

Spare us ! we stand despoiled
Of the goods for which we toiled :
Thine is the hand that foiled ;
        There is none other.

CHORUS.

We bow, and our joys endure ;
Assent, and the Future is sure ;
        Thy rule is highest.

ANTI-CHORUS.

We ask, as thy gifts decrease,
Knowledge that brings us peace,
Freedom, the soul's release, —
        But thou deniest !

CHORUS.

Power and Mystery thine,
Surely art thou divine,
    To reign forever !

ANTI-CHORUS.

Power, the child of Will,
Dares and defies thee still :
Even God shall not kill
    Man's endeavor !

SCENE III.

*Night.   An open grassy glade, between groves of ancient oak
    and ilex trees, in a deep mountain valley.   The full orb of
    the moon hanging low in the west.*

PYRRHA (*sola*).

In this pure shadow every rocky scar
Is healed : there is no lightest lisp of leaf :
The waters, only, never lose their song,
But in their swift, dissolving syllables
Some soft response to mine immortal hope
Endeavors for a voice.   Most, unto me,
The time is holy : wherefore not to him ?
Not weariness of baffled toil alone,
Nor late revenges of subjected sense,
Dare shape his dreams.   Our primal task the same,
Our purpose one, our equal bliss through each
Ordained, at need I summon him to me :

    From toil, uniting while it seems to part ;
        From visions of thyself, renewed
    To quicken men's discouraged fortitude ;

By the twin right of one inseparate heart,
    Which speaking, other voice is dumb, —
        I bid thee come !
If thee I most may comfort, or me thou,
    What need to question now ?
        We take, even as we give,
Nor, save in our unreckoned bounties, live !
Deukalion-Pyrrha, all myself in thee
        Compels thee unto me !

(*A pause.* PRINCE DEUKALION *appears.*)

One moment, ere thou speakest, let me gaze !
Though some bright rosier flush of waxing life
Forsake thy features, marbled by the moon,
Thine eyes remain, and out of shadow send
A happy splendor: am I fair to thee ?

PRINCE DEUKALION.

Fair and so near !   Ah, Love, couldst thou be mine,
Save first myself were mine !

PYRRHA.

                        Then I were less
Than thou believest; but my heart forgives
The over-fondness of complete desire.
I venture further, dream diviner end :
Each lost in each, one body as one soul ;
Endless renewals of surprise and bliss ;
A twofold touch of life, all knowledge grown
A double power through interchanging sense,
As light should warm at will, and heat illume ;
Two mingling tones to every passion's voice ;
Twin-rays from eyes, as shines from sky and stream
The single star — but that were Deity !
We will not look beyond the task designed.

Guide thou thy sons as I my daughters ; teach
Respondent honor to heroic blood
That wastes itself in self-forgetting toil;
Give rank and right, and exercise of rule ;
With lighter weapons of one temper arm
The softer strength, and in one squadron set,
To fight the world's long battle !

PRINCE DEUKALION.

                      Force is kind,
That once oppressed, and honors fade unworn.

PYRRHA.

A favor on a helm, — a tourney's crown !
Cross-hilted swords, in dying unction held,
Crimsoning scarf or glove ! In lordly bower,
Or under oriel, lute and lay espoused
In adoration that purveys to sense,
While lowly virtue is a jest of fools !
What *she* bestows, the Head whom all obey,
Degrades while it exalts, a sanctity
Conferred on bondage ! Why, methinks, the world
Is but a monstrous wizard, weaving spells,
And chanting, under breath, some siren-song,
That none escape !

PRINCE DEUKALION.

                Pyrrha, I read thy mind ;
But till the snakes upon Medusa's head
Shall turn to tresses, and be loosed to dry
Man's bruisèd feet, or Man himself shall rise
And crush them under his avenging heel,
We must endure to wait.

PYRRHA.

            How long ?

PRINCE DEUKALION.

Not long !
There are who know me, whose allegiance went
In flame aloft, to fall in thunder back.
The winds of earth are wafting to and fro
The ashes of great lives, that seem, to Her,
The Gorgon, dust ; yet are unquenchable,
Immortal ·fiery seeds of voice and act,
Her hate increases when it would destroy.
So Arnold lives, and Abelard : so he,
The youth I chose, shall with consuming song
Burn his broad way through ages !   Thou and I
Before one onset walk ; and thou shalt change
The old dependence into loftier aid.

PYRRHA.

Exact one space, where we may stand alone,
And unassailed !

PRINCE DEUKALION.

Pyrrha ! when proudest thou,
Dearest and most desired !   Full-limbed and fair,
Such perfect beauty in thy lifted head
It cannot be defiant, such clear truth
In thy large eyes, such glory as a mist
Around thee —
(Seizing her hands.)
Let it be a dream — no more !
Thy hands, a dream, and, ere the vision end,
Once let me know the lips that shall be mine !
(Thunder.   The Shadow of PROMETHEUS *rises.)*

PROMETHEUS.

Not yet !
Slow-paced is Fate :
16

All crowns come late.
Couldst thou forget?

PRINCE DEUKALION.

Since my proud task began,
Nor more nor less than Man
Am I, or may become.

PROMETHEUS.

Haste is not speed,
And Passion mars the deed;
And Love's too-early pæan soon is dumb.

PYRRHA.

But in thy scheme lie burning
Keen sparks of yearning, —
The hope that dies not,
The voice that lies not,
The dream, more bright at each returning!
Within thy reed of stolen fire
Came down the Gods' desire,
Not their chill calm of changeless being.

PROMETHEUS.

Whence they, foreseeing
Far overthrow,
Through what of them in you was planted,
Made me your Expiator!

PRINCE DEUKALION.

The One we know,
God, Father and Creator,
Himself to Man his nature granted!

PROMETHEUS.

He standeth sure.
A spark of Him in all, —
The form of faith that dies,
The tenets that surprise, —
Though falling as ye fall,
He rises as ye rise:
He will endure !

(*The moon sets : a faint light in the eastern sky.*)

PYRRHA.

Father, thou readest in my heart
What I implore, ere thou depart !

PROMETHEUS.

Though a sudden darkness fills
All the hollows of these hills,
White and large, against the gray,
Sparkles Phosphor's chilly ray ;
And the mountain-brows are wan
In the weakness of the dawn.
But the little streak that lies
At the bottom of the skies,
As the remnant-wine in cup,
Fast shall fill and mantle up,
And, where yellow coldly grows,
Burn to gold and flush to rose.
Look, and hearken, if there be
Message in the morn for thee !

                    [PROMETHEUS *disappears.*

PYRRHA.

Wait, my Deukalion ! hand in hand,
With quiet pulses, beating bliss in each,
And the immortal faith that asks no speech,

Again beside me stand!
Even now the glowing tide
Throws its first foam of fiery cloud, and wide
The heads of mountain-peaks
Feel day's fresh blood upon their pallid cheeks :
Already sings aloft the awakened lark :
Whether she come or fail, the Hour
Brings consolation and swift power,
And I am strangely happy, — Hark!   Oh, hark!

EOS (*unseen*).

Mother of them to be,
Who wast first designed in the Past
To be fulfilled at the last,
Why calleth thy soul to me!

PYRRHA.

For the beauty my daughters wear
Is made to itself a snare!

EOS.

Beauty alike shall soften and save,
Till Force shall feel,
As the galley's keel
Is lifted and sped by the lovely wave!
Under the law that holds me afar,
And Fate's immutable bar,
By the secret of something all divine,
The heart in my bosom answers thine!

PYRRHA.

Not yet uncurtain thine eyes!
I ask no more.

EOS.

The slow swift ages wait in the skies ;
The ghosts are eager on Heaven's floor.
What Darkness sowed the Light shall reap,
    And Evil that reviled,
Impregnate in her drunken sleep,
    Shall bear a purer child !

(*A pause.*)

PYRRHA.

The roses fade, the music melts away.

PRINCE DEUKALION.

It is another day !

SCENE IV.

The Roman Capitol.   MEDUSA, *throned on a platform, in front of an ancient church, in the walls of which are seen columns of a Doric temple.   An immense multitude gathered together.*

MEDUSA.

Who all possesses, dares be generous ;
And here, where fell the guardian god of Rome,
Touched by a babe's soft hand,—where Cæsar's crown,
Descending, stopped when Tibur's Sibyl spake,
Foreseeing mine, — shall go indulgence forth !
No bounty equals that which Power bestows
That might withhold : the senses must not starve,
Lest the soul clamor.   Out of what I hoard,
Prepared for me, the harvest of the Past,
Some ears may well be scattered.
                                Who demands ?

(*Two step forth : the* POET, *in a red mantle, his head crowned with laurel ; the* PAINTER, *bearing tablet and pencils.*)

THE POET.

Faithful to all thou seemest, I have sung ;
Hate is my portion, yet I sing no less.
Love for Love's sake instructed first my tongue,
That Truth so speak, and Justice so redress.
I am a voice, and cannot more be still
Than some high tree that takes the whirlwind's stress
Upon the summit of a lonely hill.
Be thou a wooing breeze, my song is fair ;
Be thou a storm, it pierces far and shrill,
And grows the spirit of the starless air :
Such voices were, and such must ever be,
Omnipotent as love, unforced as prayer,
And poured round Life as round its isles the sea !

THE PAINTER.

Faithful to all thou seemest, I have made
Thy glories visible, in beauty, grace,
Pain, death, and triumph !   I have set thy saints,
In tints exalting life above itself,
And aureoled faces caught from ecstacy,
For endless worship.   Vassal unto thee
Therein, the separate service now outruns
My vassalage ; for beauteous Art compels
Her Beauty's freedom !

MEDUSA (*aside*).

                              Freedom ? still the moon
These children cry for.
                              Yet for thee there pleads
No crownless Muse, of them that haunt the ways
Of men, and think they live : thine never lived !
But of the others whoso linger still,
Long out of service, living on men's alms,
Decoying pity through their old respect
And fallen honor, — let them now appear !

(*Enter* THE MUSES.)

So much of dignity in ruin lives ?
Save that some faces smile, and some are calm
With certainty of ancient place renewed,
Ye were defiant : but your pride is fair !
It suits me well to find dependent now
Such haught existences : as I grant leave,
Ye may endure : in them who served the old,
The newer faith rewards like loyalty.
First of the triple triads those advance,
Who nearest, lightest-natured, cheerfullest,
Were loved of men, and made the moment speed !

EUTERPE, THALIA AND TERPSICHORE.

In the woods and highlands
    We linger near ;
By the shores and islands,
    When skies are clear.
Delight of existence,
    In the feet that fly,
Calls from the distance,
    Our glad reply ;
But the joys are sweeter
    That to all belong,
When the foot gives the metre,
    The heart the song !
No more you banish
    Than a cloud the sun :
We only vanish
    To be re-won !

MEDUSA.

Good service offers ! — 't is the must of youth,
The hum, and surge, and sparkle of fresh blood,
That must have sway : be these my vintagers,

So mine the later wine !   Yea, let the vats
Even over-foam, 't is sign of potent fire
Stored in the vessels when my seal is set,
And acrid strength of age.   Without excess
Were less restraint : here may indulgence lie !
Go, altarless yet worshipped, — ye are free !

MELPOMENE, POLYHYMNIA AND ERATO.

When Music fails, and Joy is dumb
To men's exalted need, we come.
Our swords of sharper beauty cleave
The spells of senses that deceive,
And out of yearning, pain and power,
We call, and rule, one glorious hour !
Time cannot mar nor Conquest wrong
The swift, majestic march of Song,
Or Faith, in man's august desire,
Quench the least atom of her fire.
The Thought that strays, afar, alone,
We guide to speech and charm to tone :
The breathless Passions pause, to see
Their rage resolved to harmony ;
The terror of their language wooed
To music, and to law subdued ;
Till all things dread, fair, fugitive,
Touched by eternal Beauty, live !

MEDUSA.

These are suspect : whom shall they rule — or serve ?
(*A pause.*)

THE POET.

Me, if none other !   Yonder multitude
Scarce knoweth what it loves, yet loves no less, —
Enjoys, forgets, discards and craves again,

Breathing high thoughts unconsciously as air :
Without them, stifled !   Those are welcome now,
Who bring the sportive liberty of life
To the sad world's late holiday ; but these,
Seldom as odors on the arid hills,
Still keep their fond surprises !

MEDUSA.

                        Under guard,
Then, let the Three go forth !   They reach too high.
Who plucks on tip-toe at the dangling grape
Pulls down the vine : what 's Passion but revolt ?
What, save the music of illicit minds,
Is Poetry ?   Yet purposed deeds may sleep,
Lulled by the measure of their own wild dreams.
The accumulate store, saved from the wrecks of Time,
Frayed raiment, spangled thick with Pagan gems,
Is hoarded in my vaults ; but at my will
Be spent the treasure ! — easy luxury
To brains that else might coin, or claim, or steal.
These Three, of men surmised or coveted,
May walk the world henceforth ; but, under guard !

CALLIOPE AND CLIO.

Daughters, whom Zeus and she,
Wide-browed Mnemosyne,
Gave to the sons of earth,
In wisdom, might and mirth
Divinely so to lead
That word is wed with deed ;
And action, rhythmic grown,
Stands as in sculptured stone ;
And noble speech commands
Service of swords and hands ;
We wait, but do not ask
Continuance of our task !

MEDUSA.

Thou, of the keen, persuasive, perfect voice,
Thee I require ! — despite the haughty flash
Of thine unshrinking eyes, I know the spell
That rules thee : wait, I 'll feed thy tongue with fire !
Thou, too, whose stylus wanders restlessly
Across the empty tablets, at my feet
Sit down, and write me legends !   I have **store** :
Pain, penitence, and power and miracle,
Glory, disaster, blessing, — by one soul
Informed, linking the ages in one scheme
Grander than all thy fables !

                       Who art *thou*,
The last, who speakest not ?   Thine eyes are **set**
Like one who sees not, thine attentive ear
Hearkens to something far away.   Most fair
Wert thou, could Beauty, careless of delight,
Wear Wisdom's mask. — What Lamia lingers here ?
                 (*Aside.*)
No supplication, nay, but pity shines
From those firm eyes : I cannot look them down !
Is it the coldness of the serpent blood
So chills me ?   Serpent ? — one of us must writhe
When the end comes ; but ages lie between.

URANIA.

      The clear lamp, colorless,
      Of high Truth I possess.
      Hope, Will and Faith may spurn,
      While fresh their torches burn,
      What, kindling now afar,
      Seems but a dying star :
      Yet, wheeling as it must,
      This little orb of dust
      Not more the Law divine

Establishes, than mine.
Shall Faith permit me ?   Nay,
Thine standeth in my way !
The strong, unshaken mind
May shun me, but must find ;
Devotion, bowed to thee,
Is upward blown to me,
Who over Change and Time
Stand single, strong, sublime !

MEDUSA.

(Rising suddenly.)

Seize the blasphemer !   What ! — from air she came,
To air returns ?   Or doth some shadow still
Glide past yon hoary columns ? — She is gone !
Set double guards around our borders !   Bar
With fire and steel her entrance !   Say, shall we
Hold parley with such immemorial hate,
Or, being Life to men, permit this Death
Her darts to scatter ?
                    Take, new-wrought for you,
My children, chosen of the seed of Earth,
The timbrels and the flutes of joy ; the pomp
Of color, music, marble, gems and gold ;
The tender pardon of the whispered sin ;
The symbols, fitting to the weary mind
An easy load, so keeping truth alive
In dusky mysteries ; and, shadowing God's,
The universal watchfulness of Power !

[*Exit* MEDUSA : *the multitude retires.*

THE POET.

(Solus, gazing down upon the ruins of the Forum.)

Urania ! — not thy face that earliest wooed me,
And from these ancient ashes called the fire !

Thy sister, even in marble sleep, subdued me
Unto free Song's untamable desire ;
And he, in whom I feel myself united
To deed and word and vision that inspire, —
Life's homeless Prince, alone in dreams invited, —
Is of thy race, and waits afar for thee.
What now thou art, Spirit so spurned and slighted,
I know not, nor can guess what thou shalt be :
But through the light of Day thine eyes are burning,
Thy feet are on the mountains and the sea ;
The holy planets, going and returning,
Keep thy clear paths untangled in the sky :
Thy wisdom shall replace our hoodwinked yearning,
Thy living laws the mysteries that die !

SCENE V.

A pass among the High Alps.

EPIMETHEUS (*solus*).

Bright Earth !   The echo of the fateful words :
" Rise, Brother ! " scarce in twilight Hades dies,
And I behold thee !   Bath of dazzling Day,
Take these spent limbs, revive the old Titan blood,
Sharp wine of mountain-ether !   Are yon snows
Our Caucasus ? — yon melting distances
The meads of Phasis, or, on Morning's side,
The Caspian and the far Chorasmian plain ?
Here, now, the hoary, storm-tormented peaks
Stand silent : muffled thunders from below
Make brief disturbance : slopes of tender turf,
Untrampled by the steer, and flowers uncropped,
Smile a faint summer down the hollow dells,
And dark with lifeless water lies the lake.

There wheels a vulture, giving to the blue
The shade or sparkle of his slanted wings,
But seeking other quarry: not for me
Is torture, save the pang of growing sight,
And slow remembrance of the things that were.
The Past, that 'mid her ruins lay a-swooned,
In me recovers : pulse by pulse must I
Recall my life, and word by word my speech,
And age by age my knowledge !

(*Enter* URANIA.)

                       Also thou,
Whom, eminent in Babylon, I saw, —
Or wise in secrets of the Memphian stars,
Or hermitess on Samos, royal guest
In Academe, — endurest ?

URANIA.

             I endure.

EPIMETHEUS.

Where wast thou ?

URANIA.

             Waiting in the dust of earth
And the eternal splendor of the stars.

EPIMETHEUS.

Has thy day dawned ?

URANIA.

            Yea, ever is at dawn,
So men but lift their eyes !

EPIMETHEUS.

             Where goest thou ?

URANIA.

To them that seek me.

EPIMETHEUS.

Goddess, I return
To draw the forfeit forces of my youth
From dull, forgetful age : be thou my help !

URANIA.

Learn what to ask, I give : not mine to guess
The need of others.   Epimetheus, thou,
A yearning shadow, must create thyself
And thine equality of final power.
Not yet thou knowest me ; but, as I go,
Speak, soft, unsilenced Spirit of the Wind,
Speak, kindred Spirits of the Snow and Stream,
Declare my being !

[*She descends the northern side of the pass.*

EPIMETHEUS.

Spirits, I listen : speak !

SPIRIT OF THE WIND.

From the parched Numidian waste,
    From the hills of hot Fezzàn,
I sprang with a boundless haste
    That only the stars outran;
Over mountain and Midland Sea
    That strove to tire or tame, —
Over Etna and Stromboli
    That pierced me with smoke and flame ;
Till I laid, in the first desire
    That bended my pinions low,
The cheek of the sylph of fire
    On the breast of the gnome of snow !

For the powers of ruin, that meet
  In the vaults of space, must die
When the spirit that stays my feet
  Is lord of the tender sky !
I come, to wither and slay ;
  I pause, to quicken and spare ;
And the fate of the world I weigh
  In the trembling balance of air !

SPIRIT OF THE SNOW.

Homeless atoms, born in the sky,
Cling to the ledges bleak and high,
Fill the crevice and hide the scar,
And give the sunrise a rosy star ! —
Gather and grow, till a shield is won
To blunt the spear of the angry sun ;
Till from the heart of my chill repose
Power awakens and purpose grows, —
Out of my torpor the glacier goes !
Silent, certain, it crouches and crawls
Down the gorges in frozen falls,
And crystal turrets of azure walls,
Tearing the granite from crest and dome,
Hurling the torrent forth in foam !
Shepherding here my downy flock,
There I shatter the ribs of rock ;
Stayed by a hand and slain by a breath,
There I am terror, and doom, and death !

SPIRIT OF THE STREAM.

Over the mosses and grasses
  The white cloud passes,
Silent and soft as a dream;
And the earth, in her shy embraces,
  Conceals the traces

Of the secret birth of the Stream :
Till my threads are braided and **woven,**
    And speed through the cloven
Channels, and gather, and sink,
And wind, and sparkle, and dally,
    With song in the valley,
And shout from the terrible brink !
Then the whirl of the wind divides **me,**
    And the rainbow hides me,
As I midway scatter in air ;
And I bathe with endless showers
    The feet of the flowers,
And the locks of the forest's hair :
Till proudly, with waters wedded,
    My strength is bedded
By meadow, and slope, and lea ;
And the lands at last deliver
    Their tribute river
To the universal Sea !

THE THREE SPIRITS (*as Echoes*).

Thou, to power and empire born,
Stay one arrow of the Morn ;
Pluck one feather from the wing
Of the wild Wind's wandering ;
Breathe to air the flakes that blow
From the chambers of the Snow ;
Hold one speck of drifting Force
From the measures of its course ;
Then of these hast thou the chain
Binding Man's immortal brain !

(*Enter* PRINCE DEUKALION *and* PYRRHA.)

PRINCE DEUKALION.

faint, clear music of the elements

Makes all these mountains rhythmic, and this air ?
Thou hearest, Pyrrha ?

PYRRHA.

                    Not the same that fell
From fair Ionian stars, and found afar
Reverberant echoes on the mounts of Song;
But Earth awakens !   Hope I breathe, and power,
Losing my burden of remembered ill.

PRINCE DEUKALION.

New realms, yet not unknown, invite us.   See,
How, yonder, where the piny gorges fall
Northward, it spreads ! — a land of tempered air,
Where Beauty's enemy, rough Toil, abides,
And all the joyous Muses bind their brows
With straightening fillets : never Daphne shakes
Her glossy head, or Pallas' hoary tree
Makes moonlight on the hills.   But Druid oaks,
Univied, stretch their stubborn arms abroad,
The firs bend black beneath their weight of snow,
The gray walls gloom, fire mocks the absent sun,
And Life, no more a lightsome gift of Earth,
Defends itself by battle : voices there
Call thee and me.

PYRRHA.

                    So but my daughters call,
They shall behold me !   Under placid brows
Of Nymph or Goddess, and the chaste cold breasts,
And beating through the snow of perfect limbs,
Is Woman !   Beauty's soft inheritress,
Let her uplift her downcast lids, and see
Power abnegated, dignity unworn,
And equal freedom sheltering equal love.

17

PRINCE DEUKALION.

There lies Medusa's secret : with such bait
Long hath she fished ; but thou shalt dis-immure
Her slaves, and give them their abolished sex !

       [*Perceiving* EPIMETHEUS.

Here were a face — save that the kindled eye,
And April bourgeoning of sunny locks
Around the seamless forehead, might deceive —
I looked upon in Hades : is it thou ?

EPIMETHEUS.

Am I so young, then ? What Prometheus mused
I know not yet.   With sight indrawn he sat,
And seemed to listen, while our starless air
One weary hour hung dead, — then hoarsely spake :
" Rise, Brother ! " and the thin, gray, crowding ghosts
Whirled on and would have risen ; but I was here !

PRINCE DEUKALION.

What doest thou ?

EPIMETHEUS.

I listen.

PRINCE DEUKALION.

      Unto whom ?

EPIMETHEUS.

The Wind, the Snow, the Stream.   The mighty Muse
Bearing an orb, the star upon her brow,
Commanded speech of them, and passed beyond
To Thrace or Scythia.

PRINCE DEUKALION.

      She ? — and thou ? — Again,
O Pyrrha, let our severed hands unite !

Not mine the eternal secret of the Gods
To fathom, yet their purpose in my blood
Beats prophecy.

        Go, Epimetheus, sunward,
And seek thy childhood in the dust of ages !
Burrow in buried fanes : wash clean the altars,
And spell forgotten words on mouldering marble.
Perchance thy limbs shall fail, thy lids be weary,
And thou shalt sleep ; fear not, I will awaken !
Thy brother's words fulfil : " Take one new comfort,
Still Epimetheus lives ! " and now the morning
Shall not withhold the unseen eyes of Eos !

                   [Exit Epimetheus.

PYRRHA *(as they descend the pass).*

Arching aisles of the pine, receive us ;
   Dells of alder and willow, be fair !
Something of ancient beauty leave us, —
   Gift for promise, and deed for prayer !

ECHOES.

In the shadows of the pine
Beauty waiteth, still divine :
   She is thine !

PRINCE DEUKALION.

Will of manhood and blood of valor,
   Leap as of old to the day at hand :
Free of doubt and of craven pallor,
   Rise and ransom the captive land !

ECHOES.

In the forge and in the mine
Weapons for the battle shine :
   They are thine !

                   [Exeunt.

ACT III.

Scene I.

A valley among hills covered with forests of oak and beech. Below, in the distance, a richly cultivated plain, a city with Gothic towers, and a broad river, dotted with the sails of vessels.

POET (*passing*).

EARTH, thou art lovely as any star,
  With rest so near, desire so far !
Peace from the tree-tops on the hill
Sinks, and the blissful fields are still ;
While tender longing, pure of pain,
Dwells in the blue of yonder plain ;
And all things Fancy, faring free,
May clasp or covet, come from thee !
Something of mine is everywhere,
Trodden as earth or breathed as air ;
Giving, with magic sure and warm,
Voice to silence and soul to form,
Calm to passion and speed to rest,
Borrowed or lent of mine own breast
By that swift spirit that mocks the eye,
As over thee the unfeatured sky,
Heaving its blue tides, endlessly,
To planets that fail to lift the sea !
I am thy subject, yet thy king :
Give me thy speech, and let me sing !

                              [Exit.

GÆA.

Step to the music of the song I gave,
My Poet, homeward ! Lovers, find in me
Your voiceless eloquence and balm of bliss,
That else were pain !   Mine ancient life revives
With sweeter potency : I am a Soul
Responsive unto all that stirs in Man,
Transforming passion to a natural voice,
From airy murmurs of the fragrant weeds
To the hushed roar of pines, the tramp of waves,
And bellowing of the ocean-flooded throats
Of headland caverns ! Wafts of odorous air,
The thousand-tinted veils of dawn and day,
The changeless Forms, that from the changing Hours
Take magic as a garment, stellar fire
Sprinkled from hollow space, and secret tides
Lifted by far, fraternal planets, — these
Have grown to speech, companionship and power.
Tired of the early mystery, my child
Hearkens, as one at entrance of a vale
Never explored, for echoes of his call ;
And every lone, inviolate height returns
His fainter self, become a separate voice
In answer to his yearning !   Not as dam,
With hungry mouth, — as goddess, with bowed heart
He woos me ; or as athlete, million-armed,
Summons my strength from immemorial sleep.
He comes, the truant of the ages, — comes,
The rash forgetter of his source ; as lord
He comes, — lord, paramour and worshipper,
Tyrant in brain, yet supplicant in soul,
With fond compulsion and usurping love
To make me his !

     Still scorned are ye, fair Forms
I sheltered ?   Under yonder beechen shade

Hath human longing set ye ?   Hide my streams
Your beauty still, my mists your loosened hair ?

NYMPHS.

(At a distance.)

As the night-air pants ;
As the wind-harp chants ;
As the moonlight falls
Over foliage walls ;
As gleams forerun
The smile of the sun
When clouds are parting,
Our beings are.
We are held afar
By a knowledge burning
In the heart of yearning ;
For the necromancy
Of the fonder fancy
Breathes back into air
The Presences fair
It would fain restore :
We are Souls and Voices,
But Forms no more !

GÆA.

Ye highly live, more awful in the spell
Of unseen loveliness !   No need to quit
Your dwellings, strike the dull sense into fear,
And win a shallow worship : Man's clear eye
Sees through the Hamadryad's bark, the veil
Of scudding Oread, hears the low-breathed laugh
Of Bassarid among the vine's thick leaves,
And spies a daintier Syrinx in the reed.
For him that loves, the downward-stooping **moon**
Still finds a Latmos : Enna's meadows yet

Bloom, as of old, to new Persephones;
And 'twixt the sea-foam and the sparkling air
Floats Aphrodite, — nobler far than first
These bright existences, and yours, withdrawn
To unattainable heights of half-belief,
Divine, where whole reflects the hue of Man.

NYMPHS.

In the upward pulse of the fountain ;
On the sunny flanks of the mountain;
Where the bubble and slide of the rill
Is heard when the thickets are still;
Where the light, with a flickering motion,
From the last faint fringes of ocean
Is sprinkled on sand and shell ;
In the ferns of the bowery dell,
And the gloom of the pine-wood dark,
And the dew-cloud that hides the lark,
The sense of Beauty shall feel us,
The touch of delight reveal us !

[Exeunt.

GÆA.

Fear not, sweet Spirits, what unflinching law,
Tracking creative secrets, Man may find
In my despotic atoms !   Who denies
Confirms ye to the sense that bade him seek.
But thou, mine Eros, through whose ministry
Stole back the banished Beauty, — as, at first,
The harmless tear-like trickle of a stream
Through some Cyclopean dam, that softly wins
A vantage, till the whole collected lake
Sets its large lever to the trembling stones,
And freedom follows, — thou, who, well I know,
Hidest beneath this roof of summer leaves,
Or where the minty meadow-breath makes cool
Thine ardent brow, — appear, and speak again !

EROS.

I am not he whom Hermes overcame,
Nor always from my brother's grosser flame
    Held my pure torch afar :
New bows I span, new arrows fill my quiver.
Those twain, mine enemies, avoid me now,
Stung by the steady radiance of my brow,
      Nor, save in secret, mar
My lordship over them that I deliver.

The penance of the ages was in vain ;
Old sweetness sprang from each invented pain,
    And Love increased by wrong,
And won supremacy by sharp denial.
Faith dungeoned him, till, pining for the day,
He stole the wings of Faith and soared away :
    So grew my nature strong
Through conquered violence, and pure through trial.

What though new strains enrich my airy lute,
The primal ecstasies are never mute ;
    No throb of joy is missed,
Nor from the morn is any splendor taken.
But nuptials of the senses now repeat
The mystery of equal souls that meet, —
    That kiss when lips are kissed,
And each in each to sovran life awaken !

GÆA.

Not mine to guess thy riddles, — yet I see
Near manhood in thine adolescent limbs,
Proud lustre in thine eyes, as, through the joy
That still around thee sparkles, other joy
Made prophecy, but never of an end,
And mystic sweetness in thy budded lips.

Nathless, whenever my strong spouse, the sun,
Stoops nearer, sets his bosom unto mine
And stirs all fond, sad raptures of my frame,
Then most I note thee, hurrying to and fro,
Sure in thy speed; or when he lingering leaves
My bed of long delight and summershine
With last caresses, thou on every hill
Dost walk in light, and breathest through the woods
Voluptuous odors of the yearning year!
Exalt thyself past limits of my law,
I feed thee still!   What soaring mist of mine,
Sun-gilded, but the iron frost of space
Shall seize?   What odor reaches to the stars?

EROS.

Nor the soul of the wandering odor, nor the light of the
    mist, is thine,
Who art rolled through day and darkness, at the will of
    a star divine;
Who claim'st the arrows of beauty, alone from its quiver
    sped, —
Thou readest but half the riddle in the dust that else
    were dead!
Thy life is blown upon thee, as a seed from another
    land,
And the soil, and the dew and water, are the bounty of
    thy hand;
But the secrets of whence and whither are mine for my
    children's need:
I go with the flying blossom, as I came with the flying
    seed!

SCENE II.

A spacious square, at the extremity of a city. In front, a church: on one side a cemetery, with an open gateway: on the other side a market.

PYRRHA.

(*Looking towards the gateway.*)

There, out of stubborn wrong and thwarted hope
And helpless ignorance, Earth has only gained
A heavier mould ; and she must heap her dead —
As the slow ages on her bare emerge
Gathered the dust for grass, the deepening sod
For forests — ere our seeds of total life
Find rootage, and with undecaying green
Redeem this desolation !

PRINCE DEUKALION.

Yea, but eyes
That once behold, and souls that once believe,
Lend faith and vision as a lamp its flame !

PYRRHA.

Ay, Faith ! that limits where it should enlarge, —
That sees one only color, where the sun
Brands ever three, nor suffers even them
To burn unblended !

PRINCE DEUKALION.

'T is the curse of souls
That selfless aspiration looks above
To find joy, knowledge, beauty, waiting there,
Because abandoned here !

PYRRHA.

So mine await:
They doubt me, not forbid me.

PRINCE DEUKALION.

Doubt but feeds
The callow faith that has not tried its wings.
Be comforted !

PYRRHA.

Deukalion, is it time ?

PRINCE DEUKALION.

How often, Pyrrha, have we watched the morn
Divinely flush — and fade ! How often heard
Music, that, ere it bade us quite rejoice,
Died, echoless ! Yet Patience cannot be,
Like Love, eternal, save at times it grow
To swift and poignant consciousness of self ;
And something veiled from knowledge whispers now
Prometheus stirs in Hades !

PYRRHA.

Darest thou call ?

PRINCE DEUKALION.

I dare not. Epimetheus slowly clears
Back through the gloom and chaos of the Past
The path of his return. The widening sphere
His keener vision measures now for Man
Discrowns Tradition, shrinks the span of Time,
And throws the primal purpose of our fate
Once more upon us. Thus the Titan stands
Nearer than when the frosty fetters burned
His limbs on Caucasus!

PYRRHA.

And also she,
Pandora, freed from long disgrace of Time,
Since now her Hebrew shadow flings away
The fabled evil!   When the Past is purified,
We shall possess the Future.

PRINCE DEUKALION.

Yea, our source,
As from the bosom of a mountain mist,
Leaps out of Nature, innocent at last!
In our beginning Destiny divine
Set the accordant end ; and this, obscure,
Makes that with monstrous intervention dark
To human souls.   Already Earth is red
With ebbing life-blood of the wounded Faiths
That shriek, and turn their faces to the wall,
And shut their vision to the holier Heir,
Who, unproclaimed, awaits his lordship.   Lo!
How he who governs these austerer lands
Withholds his gifts, betrays his promises,
Gives freedom for repentance, not for change,
Nor other answer than his own, to doubt!
Foe to Medusa, in his secret dreams
He wears her triple crown, — allows, perforce,
Urania, banished from her first abodes,
Chill hospitality, an exile's fare, —
No right of home !   What will his welcome be,
When Epimetheus, hand in hand with her,
Tells the new story of the human Past ?

(*Enter a Man and Woman.*)

PRINCE DEUKALION.
(*To the Man.*)

Say, dost thou know me ?

MAN.

At a distance, I
Have seen thee pass : I never heard thy name.

PRINCE DEUKALION.

I speak it not.

MAN.

Thou movest my desire
To know, yet, save the knowledge be allowed,
No less my fear : there 's brightness on thy face,
As one who sees no pitfall in delight,
Nor snare in science, nor the burden bears
Of fallen nature.

PRINCE DEUKALION.

Whence is thine so dark ?
Art thou in love with pain ?

MAN.

I cannot help
Some joys of life, and guilty dreams of more :
But He who suffered for my sake forbids
That I rejoice too greatly.

PRINCE DEUKALION.

Wisdom, then,
Wilt thou accept ?

MAN.

The wisdom of the world ?
Nay : 't is vain-glory.

WOMAN.

(*To* PYRRHA.)
If indeed for me
Thou hast a message, as thine eyes declare,
Thou knowest my need.

PYRRHA.

I know thine ignorance.

WOMAN.

I would have knowledge, were the entrance free.

PYRRHA.

Want forces entrance, justifies itself,
As hunger crime!   But learn what Beauty is,
And this, thy present weakness and reproach,
Becomes immortal power!

WOMAN.

When I behold

Thy face, I seem to own it.

PYRRHA.

Set thou, then,

Whatever visage unto thee I wear
Within the shrine of thy desires, thereon
To brood in longings born of motherhood,
That so thy daughters shall inherit it,
And I in them be nearer !

MAN.

(*To the Woman.*)

Strange the words,

Their meaning doubtful : how shall thou and I,
Bearing Eternity's full weight alone, —
Ours all the debt, foreclosed if other coin
Save what our Faith supplies be given as due,
And poor in deeds that earn it, — how shall we
Accept such help ?   He wears the face of Power,
She that of Beauty ; what if both mislead ?

WOMAN.

Her spirit touches me, as doth the sun
A folded bud : if I become a flower,
The hue and fragrance locked within my life
Without my will are scattered.

MAN.

                Come away!

                  [*They pass on.*

PYRRHA.

No more the shepherd and the shepherdess,
Our children ! 'T is the wisdom of the school,
So grave in childish self-sufficiency,
That turns on Nature and disowns her bliss.
I know not what large hope awakens now :
Pandora, Titan-mother ! rise and see
How speeds thy purpose !

PRINCE DEUKALION.

                Ere thou summon her,
Or he unsummoned rises, let us seek
The stately High-Priest who hath ruled so long
These broadening realms, advancing nobler fate
Even where he willed it not, the instrument
Of that diviner mystery than his God !
The sky-cast shadow of a Hebrew Chief
Fades o'er his altars ; and the aureoled Love,
That later veiled the tyranny, reveals
A change in its intensest splendor wrought
Invisibly : if he hath eyes to bear,
His ear may hearken, when Prometheus calls.

Scene III.

The interior of a spacious church. In the chancel a lofty altar, on the front panel whereof is carved a rayed triangle: on the top of the altar rests the Ark of the Covenant, above which towers a Cross. Calchas, *High-Priest, stands upon a raised platform before the altar, clad in an ephod of gold, blue, purple and scarlet, with mitre, girdle and breast-plate of twelve stones, as described in Exodus xxxix.* Prince Deukalion *and* Pyrrha *in the nave.*

PYRRHA.

Still old the symbols ! — and the spirit looks
Backward to whence they came.

PRINCE DEUKALION.

                 So should it look,
But free, across a conquered realm ! The Past
Is Man's possession, not his mocking glimpse
Through loopholes of the jail where Reason pines.
It gives the Prophet vision, as a root
Declares the measure of the branch it feeds ;
But here are teachers, who, to lead the blind,
Hoodwink themselves.   What common eye can see
Past things as present, ancient miracle
To-day's dull fact, God's hand upon the man
It looks at ?   Over gulfs of ages these
First find their sanctity, as our dark orb
Drinks light from ether till it grows a star.

PYRRHA.

It is the heart that dares not look too near,
Nor yet too high.

PRINCE DEUKALION.

                    The heart, that doubts the brain, —
Feeling, divorced from knowledge, — this it is
That neither loves us nor can be estranged ;
That dimly plays with our conjectured will;
Obeys, mistrusts itself and grows ashamed, —
Then turns apostate !

PYRRHA.

                    Nay, Deukalion, nay ! —
That, born anew, retains the old desire ;
That, kindled once, keeps memory of the flame ;
That out of thwarted yearning, baffled peace,
And endless pangs of vain self-surgery,
Still floods all life with fond presentiment
Of thee and me !

                    (*Sound of the organ.*)

CHANT.

From this body of death deliver,
     This burden of woes !
We call, as they called where the river
     Of Babylon flows.
Like the wail of a captive nation
Is the sound of our lamentation.
From the pleasures that still delight us ;
From the daily sins that smite us ;
From the difficult, vain repentance
And the dread of the coming sentence ;
From the knowledge that gropes and stumbles ;
From the pride of mind that humbles ;
From beauteous gifts that harden,
And bliss that implores not pardon ;
From the high dreams that enslave us,
     We beseech Thee, save us !

                    18

PRINCE DEUKALION.

Joy in Thy world divine,
And the body like to Thine ;
Pride in the mind that dares
To scale Thy starry stairs,
Rising, at each degree,
The least space nearer Thee ;
Strength to forget the ill,
So Thy good to fulfil ;
Freedom to seek and find
All that our dreams designed,
Driven by Thine own goads
Forth on a thousand roads ;
Patience to wrest from Time
Something of Truth sublime,
Or of Beauty that shall live, —
     We beseech Thee, give !

CALCHAS.

(*Perceiving* PRINCE DEUKALION *and* PYRRHA.)

I do mistrust these strangers.   Since that she,
Medusa, thrust them out from all her realms,
What time she banished her of orb and star
I sheltered (threatening now with adder sting
For life revived), they wander to and fro —
Or others in their likeness, — and disturb
My settled sway.   Freedom I gave, because
Free-will must choose me, — bade men seek the truth,
Because the truth conducts them back to me.
Urania, with her forward-peering eyes,
Saw not the vestments, which, to mark her mine,
I laid upon her shoulders : suddenly now,
Full-statured, with uplifted head she walks,
And drops her loosed phylacteries in the dust.
These, too ! — whate'er they purpose must be mine,

If good, since other good exists not : yet
They stir some quick perversity of heart
In man and woman, teach abolished needs,
And open gates I shut — but may not bar.
They come this way.   I 'll question them.

PRINCE DEUKALION (*advancing*).

High-Priest,
Thou shouldst proclaim us, and thou know'st us not !

CALCHAS.

Much have I heard.

PRINCE DEUKALION.
What most ?

CALCHAS.

That ye do breed
Confusion.

PRINCE DEUKALION.
Nay ! — but out of thine we build
The ruined harmony.

CALCHAS.
Then, enemies
Ye now declare yourselves, where I but deemed
Some seed of pride had sprouted o'er its fall.
What is 't ye do ?

PRINCE DEUKALION.
What thou hast never done,
Who hast one purpose where thy sons need all,
Who keep'st them puppets lest they grow to Gods !

CALCHAS.

I seek to save them.

PRINCE DEUKALION.

They will save themselves,
Not by one anchor which may drag them down,
But carried outward by all winds that blow
Into the shoreless deep !   Give knowledge room,
Yea, room to doubt, and sharp denial's gust
That makes all things unstable !   Tremble not
When stern Urania writes the words of Law :
Make once more Life the noble thing it was
When Gods were human, or the nobler thing
It shall be when The God becomes divine !

CALCHAS.

Blasphemer !

PRINCE DEUKALION.

Curse, if so it comfort thee,
Thy weapon, too, is terror ; but when men
Cease to be cowards, idle Hell shall close.

PYRRHA.

Yield what thou canst : there still is time.   Give up
Dead symbols of the perished ages : doff
The trappings of a haughty alien race
Whose speech was never thine : keep but the spark
Of pure white Truth which nor repels, forbids
Nor stings, but ever broadening warms the world !
Think what thy lips have promised, how thy hand
Rent suddenly our chains !   Nearest thou art
Of them that sway the torpid souls of men :
So, then, be *all* where thou art but a part, —
Be all, teach all, grant all, and make thyself
Eternal !

CALCHAS.

Am I not so, now?

PRINCE DEUKALION.

                 Not yet,
Save in the taste of that thou offerest, —
Repentance.

PYRRHA.

And thou mightst be, in thy love.

CALCHAS.

Repentance? Love? What words are these you speak?
One wins the other: I announce them both,
And all beatitude that follows them.
Beyond the curse inherited by flesh,
Beyond this cloudy valley, where as rain
Fall human tears, and sighs of vain desires
Make an incessant gust, I know the way
To refuge, and the one permitted bliss
Of living souls.

PRINCE DEUKALION.

             Let me behold that bliss!
I have the right of entrance; fear thou not!
The phantom key thy hand yet seems to clutch
Lend me a moment; or, canst thou not yield,
Then stand aside! — O Father is it time?

PROMETHEUS (*rises*).

What matters, whether soon or late?
Thine is the burden, thine the fate.
Long hast thou waited, not too long,
For patience is the test of wrong;
And thee the slow years may allow

Some right of deeper vision now.
The trial art thou strong to bide,
Explore thy way! — there is no guide.

[Disappears.

PRINCE DEUKALION.

(Seizing the horns of the Ark upon the altar.)

I know what holy mysteries were thine
In the old days : but what art thou become ?
Yield up thy spells to one who saw thee pass
Through the dusk halls where Amun-Ra was lord,
Or Nile-borne on thy barque of flowers ! What lore
Of wandering souls — of life beyond the end —
Is thine to give us ?

(A pause.)

Nothing more than this ? —
Gray emptiness of space, with here and there
A flying shadow, whether man or fiend
The eye detects not : something vast of form,
Yet Hebrew-featured, stirred to mighty wrath
By hostile Gods, defending, as it seems,
A throne secure, — uncertain of His will,
And undecided if His sons shall live.
They, too, poor ghosts ! must hover on the verge
Betwixt two worlds : they reach no firmer soil
Of airy substance, yet which may upbear
Thin feet of spirits, but in endless whirl
Drift through the shapeless void. I 'll look no more.

(He lays his hand upon the Cross.)

Symbol of Fire, the oldest, holiest !
Forget thy speech on Asia's hoary hills,
Dip thy pure arms in blood of sacrifice,
And tell me what thou heraldest !

CALCHAS.

Avaunt !

PYRRHA.

There is less profanation in his act
Than in thy prayers.   Be silent, — wait the end !
(PRINCE DEUKALION'S *eyes close: he slowly sinks down and
lies, leaning against the altar.*)

SCENE IV.

THE VISION OF PRINCE DEUKALION.

As out of mist an unknown island grows,
It swam in space, surrounded with repose.
" Behold," an airy whisper said, " the sphere
Through hope existing, as yon pit through fear ;
For what men pray for — while they pray — shall last,
Since Faith creates her Future as her Past."
No light of sun, or moon, or any star
Touched the white battlements that gleamed afar,
Or painted with strong ray the pastures wide
Between slow stream and easy mountain-side,
But over all such cold and general glow
As moonlight spreads upon a land of snow,
Yet fairer, shone ; and myriads wandered there,
Giving no stir to that unbreathing air,
White as the meadow-blossoms, and as still,
And white as clouds on each unshadowed hill.
A city vast, that bore an earthly name,
With thousand pinnacles of frost and flame
Stood in the midst ; and twelvefold flashed unrolled
The pavements of her avenues of gold,
Where harps and voices one high strain did pour
Of " Holy, holy, holy ! " evermore.

And out the centre, from the burnished glare,
A golden stairway sloped athwart the air,
And faded upward, where a Phantom shone
That changed in form to them that gazed thereon.
These, side by side, and wing caressing wing,
Rested like wild doves on their wandering,
Innumerable : and o'er them seraphim
Winnowed rich plumes to make the glory dim,
And children's faces, kissed with sweeter light,
Circled in swarms around a Throne of white.
Shapes of no sex, too beautiful for man,
Too cold for woman, spread the rosy van
And slanted, shining, far amid the space.
Some pleasure came on each uplifted face
To see those messengers, — some rapid awe,
When that high Form, with hidden brow, they **saw**, —
But else their eyes were weary, and the fold
Of each white mantle slept upon the gold.
Dead seemed their hands, save when the harps they smote
    smote
And made accord of one perpetual note.
The entrance of a living spirit there
Gave a quick motion to the torpid air,
Startled the light with shadow, and breathed out
Keen earthly odors ; yet of dread or doubt
Among the myriad myriads was no sign.
A listless wonder woke in souls supine,
But made no speech, for consciousness was numb,
Save to the awful voice of what must come,
As on dead continents the live sea's roar :
    " Forevermore !   Forevermore ! "

PRINCE DEUKALION

Angels, a moment stay
Your heavenly errands, and betray

What nature, beautiful and dim,
As in some twilight dream of power
  Is born for one bright hour,
  Ye have received from Him !
  Shorn of all kin are ye,
  Companionless, unwed
With primal mortals, loveless, passion-free,
  Not living, neither dead !
    Declare me this :
    Is it your only bliss
To sail, soft-shining, with your wings outspread ?
To cheat the ecstacy ye cannot share,
  With apparitions fair ?
  To give each holy dream
  Its warranty supreme,
The palm to promise, and the lily bear ?

ANGELS.

  We cannot know :
We are the feather, His the breath to blow.
  Though human yearning mould
  Our passive being, we are cold.
  Pity, to eyes that mourn ;
  Passion, to hearts that burn ;
  Reward, to lives that dare ;
  Salvation, unto prayer, —
  What face men look for, such we wear !
  Unborn, we have no destiny,
  Nor other being than to be ;
  Nor service, but to soar
'Twixt One Adored and many that adore.
  What should we further tell ?
  Thou hast no message : so farewell !

PRINCE DEUKALION.

But ye, Transfigured, whose denial
  Endured the life-long trial, —
Pure souls, whose only human terror
  Made Thought an ambushed error, —
Who now possess, secure from losing,
  The bliss of your own choosing,
Speak, are there needs ye here have sighed for,
  More than on earth ye died for ?

SPIRITS.

Is it permitted ?

PRINCE DEUKALION.

I am here.

SPIRITS.

We tremble, yet we must not fear.
The bright temptation of thy brow
We once resisted, conquers now ;
But thought unused and voice unheard
Deny us the consenting word.

PRINCE DEUKALION.

Look on me, and it shall be given !

SPIRITS.

  O joy ! O pain !
As leaves from autumn boughs are driv
  At last, at last,
Thy will hath torn us from our Past,
  And half we live again !
Yea, here is glory, here is bliss,
Arms that sustain us, lips that kiss,
And rest, and peace, and pain's rev

In that pure light which seems the Lord ;
But — bliss without endeavor,
  And lips that cannot part ;
And rest that sleeps forever
  In each immortal heart ;
And light whose splendor hideth
  The Face we burn to see —
What is it that divideth
  Eternity and thee ?

PRINCE DEUKALION.

I am eternal, even as ye.
But your concealed, undying woe
Is this : ye have not sought to know.

SPIRITS.

We did obey.

PRINCE DEUKALION.

But whom, ye may not say.
Have ye beheld Him ?

SPIRITS.

Nay.

PRINCE DEUKALION.

Once more upon Him call :
Uplift awakened eyes !
Though falling as ye fall,
He rises as ye rise.

SPIRITS.

His Will in dreams we saw,
And left unlearned His guiding law ;
  We forced our lives to crave,

Through bondage, what His freedom gave ;
  Till, having fondly wrought,
We own the Paradise we sought, —
  Self-bound, and over-blessed
With endless weariness of rest !

One multitudinous sigh was breathed along
The golden avenues, and shook the song :
But far aloft they heard a trumpet blown,
And keen white splendor gathered round the Throne.
Then slowly up the ether-darkened blue
The meads and hills and battlements withdrew,
Till all the sphere became a silvery moon,
With ever-lessening disk, and star-like soon,
And faded out : but in the hollow space
All suns and planets kept their ancient place.

SCENE V.

A wide plain, uninhabited, dotted with ancient mounds. EPI-
METHEUS, *seated on a fallen pillar, at the doorway of a half-
exhumed palace, with a broken tablet in his hand.*

EPIMETHEUS.

It is the speech I heard but yesterday,
When all this buried pomp stood bright in air,
Terrace on terrace, till the topmost seemed
Fit for the feet of some descending God,
While bannered masts and galleries of sound
Hailed him, invisible ; and whispered words
To consecrated ears, these tablets bore ;
And the wide shadow of this power was thrown
O'er half the world.   What said Prometheus then,

When, groping first on fields of unblown mist,
I sought to hold the ever-vanishing forms
With stable vision ? — "'T is the Future's gift,
To know the Past ! "

      Yet I had mused, not slept,
Through weary ages : 't was alone their dust
That made me seem so hoary.   Action, now,
And waxing knowledge, destiny fulfilled,
Restore the ardors of Titanic youth.
Though lost the primal struggle, lost the joy
That even defeat to high defiance yields,
I am at last a Power, and challenge Powers, —
A truth, and thus a terror !   In my veins
Burns eager blood ; I know my brow is fair,
My voice hath music, and the ears of men
Perforce must hearken, as I tell the tale
Of ever older and of mightier Pasts,
Lost tongues and sacred secrets, stolen faiths,
Perverted symbols, and the favor shed —
One tribe usurped — upon the Chosen All !

    (*Enter* URANIA.)

URANIA.

What doest thou here ?

EPIMETHEUS.

    I triumph !

URANIA.

      Wherefore now,
More than erewhile ?

EPIMETHEUS.

    I have remembered that
Forgotten, when I saw nor understood ;
And now remembered since I know.

URANIA.

(*Taking up a handful of dust.*)

                                            And I
Have found in this the secret of all worlds.
Thy Past? I know no Past! Thou dream'st of time, —
It is not, was not! Nothing is, save Law.
Thy feet are on my paths : not heeding them
I guided thee, yet in so much of power
As may be given thee, more of freedom lies
For them that follow me and cannot turn.

EPIMETHEUS.

Proud wast thou ever.

URANIA.

                          Proud, because assailed,
As who, with full hands bearing gifts, is spurned.

EPIMETHEUS.

Yet pause! I am no longer slack of thought :
I know thy being.   Though I give return
Of needed help, the will which sent me forth
Hath still some ancient empire over thee.

URANIA.

Yea, thou art wakened! Why should I conceal
From thee, thus proud, associate soon with him,
Thy brother, whose large vision moves with mine,
The ultimate barrier where I needs must pause ?
But thou, and every Titan yoked with thee,
And every track that other knowledge treads,
And all the visions unto Faith allowed,
Reach not so far : what matter if I halt,
Not impotent, where no disturbance comes
To vex me, resting but a little while ?

Push back that point where thou rememberest not
Through countless æons, still thou find'st my trail !
Grasp thou the seeds of life in sun and star,
And sink then, fainting, where I stand and smile !
'T is not subjection, but a limit, rules :
My work is baffled since I could not give
The primal impulse.

EPIMETHEUS.
　　　　　Neither thou, nor he,
Prometheus !

URANIA.
　　　　Cease ! — thy words renew the chill
That seizes me at each new victory.
The cry of old affections shakes my hand;
The gush of human heart's-blood comes to dim
My crystal eyesight ; and a something lost,
Because unsought, perchance unsearchable, —
Unknown, because unknowable to sense, —
Assails my right.

EPIMETHEUS.
　　　　There is no enmity
Where neither can be lord : do thou thy task,
I mine, and each eternal Force its own !

SCENE VI.

The shore of the open ocean: morning.

PRINCE DEUKALION.
Thou lookest eastward, past the gem-like round,
The sky of opal and the sea of pearl :

I surely misinterpret not thy hope,
Or is 't thy longing ?

PYRRHA.

Say, my haughty faith,
That will not pray for what it must expect.
Once have I called on Eos, but I call
No more : the silver echo of her words
Repeats itself within me, as their vows
To happy lovers.   Thus it was she spake :
   " Faith, when none believe,
      Truth, when all deceive,
      Freedom, when force restrains,
      Courage to sunder chains,
      Pride, when good is shame,
      Love, when love is blame, —
These shall call me in stars and flame ! "
Thence call I not; but, yonder, as I gaze,
The twin stars, visible no more to sense,
Glimmer, the phantoms of her eyes ; the red,
Now fading, is her cheek's immortal flush,
And the loose golden opulence of her hair
These clouds untangle.

PRINCE DEUKALION.

Here her face revealed
Would doubly promise, as the mirroring wave
Doubled her loveliness.   The conquering Gods
Made too much haste to seize a mountain-throne :
This were their seat; but old Poseidon took
The realm that should be Jove's, where, set between
The unknown silence and the noise of earth,
Are too pure elements, pavement and dome.
Here glimpse upon the soul imagined shores ;
Here Fancy out of changeful air may build

Her far-off palaces ; yet what of truth,
Accepted fate or world-defying will
Exists, confirms as well its being, here.
Time is the billow, Destiny the shore.

PYRRHA.

Deukalion !   Seest thou naught ?

PRINCE DEUKALION.

       I see the gray
Of waves that first shall darken to the sun ;
The distance, where no separating line
Cuts the soft web of sky-inwoven sea ;
And all the dipping rondure of the world
Beneath it, where the mighty Day looks down,
Or sadly lingers for the word and deed
Undone, unspoken !

PYRRHA.

     Ah ! as out of air
It suddenly grew, I see a glorious barque
With bellied canvas of the morning cloud,
The cordage of translucent vapor spun,
The hull a curve of sea-foam, foamlessly
Borne onward, silent, with unruffled prow
Approaching us !   Two forms direct her speed,
And either's arm is on the other's neck,
And locks of gray and gold are mixed above
Their equal brows.   Thou hast not called them ?

PRINCE DEUKALION.

         Nay,
And yet, beholding not, I know the twain.
Oh, come ye hither from the unmeasured Deep,
And not from Hades ?   Come ye with the morn,

19

Unsummoned, though the morning's goddess fail?
Come ye, at last, whose birth reversed your fates,
United, one in knowledge, one in power?
Father, and thou, alike a father, hail!

(PROMETHEUS *and* EPIMETHEUS *appear.*)

PROMETHEUS.

What language hath, to-day, the sea,
To chill, inspire or menace thee?
What eager hope or spleen forlorn
Blew on thee through the gates of morn? —
Or were thy power and purpose dumb
To speak our coming, ere we come?

PYRRHA.

Not in dejection did we brood,
Hearkening the many voices of the sea.
    But for the scattered spirits free
Which lure, yet mock, the captive multitude;
        And for these last, who yet
Can neither learn new things, nor old forget;
        And to fulfil thy plan
That woman shall be woman, man be man,
        We pondered, here apart,
One wisdom for the brain and heart!

PRINCE DEUKALION.

Not in dejection, no! — while every Force,
Once idle, formless, unto Man becomes
A god to labor and a child to guide;
While Space, obstructing human will no more,
Makes Time a tenfold ally; while the draught
Of knowledge, once a costly cup, invites
Free as the wayside brook to whoso thirsts,
And aspiration, trying lonely wings,

Escapes the ancient arrow !   These are gains
We cannot lose ; but what new justice comes
With them, to right Earth's everlasting wrong ?
The weariness of work that never sees
Its consequence ; chances of joy denied
To noble natures, prodigal for mean ;
Helpless inheritance of want and crime ;
The simplest duties never owned untaught,
The highest marred by holy ignorance ;
Crowned Self, that with his impudent hollow words,
Is noisiest, and Vanity that deems
His home the universe, his day all time !

PROMETHEUS.

These are, and they shall be ;
Nor less, though thine impatience fret.
Man is a child upon thy knee,
And earth his cradle yet.
Unto thy voice his quickening ears
Open a little space,
Till, taught by dreams of countless years,
His eyes shall know thy face.

PYRRHA.

I stand as one that after darkness feels
The twilight : all the air is promise-flushed,
Yet strangely chill, and though the sense delight
In sweet deliverance, something in the blood
Cries for the sun.   Ye know, who set my work,
It is no selfish passion.   Shorn are they,
And by the fondest fate, of action's crown,
My daughters, — so, denied their part
In old divinity and balanced right
Of man's prone worship, losing thence
Some honor Time is ignorant to restore,

They need their equal half of all there is,
Uniting, not dividing, Life.   Who twains
What once was one, makes both more grandly **one**;
Or thou and I, Deukalion, could not be !

PROMETHEUS.

Now should Pandora speak !
Withdrawn the demigoddess **sits,**
And silent, yet there flits
A flush across her cheek,
A soft light o'er her eye,
And half her proud lips smile :
Unto thy hope, the while,
Be this enough reply !

PRINCE DEUKALION.

(*To* EPIMETHEUS.)

What bear'st thou from thine East ?

EPIMETHEUS.

The living **Past**

That from its grave my former being caught,
And left me youth.

PROMETHEUS.

Which, backward sent
To Man's dim childhood, where thy memory dies,
Foresees with me.

EPIMETHEUS.

And active even as thou !
I bring dread knowledge : change and overthrow,
Despair of creeds, and shaking of the shrines,
And fruitless building till the Builder come,
Are in my hands.   The Gods of races I

Unseat, as Time or Tyranny of old
Unseated them, by one subversive lore
Of equal truth revealed to them that seek,
None self-elected as depositors,
But His eternal Covenant with Life
For all, forever !

PRINCE DEUKALION.

Who shall teach that lore ?

PROMETHEUS.

Its whisper now sets every wind of earth
Vibrating : hearken, here ! — the subtle sea
Hath learned it from the happier stars, and bears
The message to his loneliest isles ; the buds
Expand it in their blossoms ; helpless souls
Discover it and rejoice, forebode and flee.
Truth gathers being as the fire in air,
Until, surcharged, it drops a blazing bolt
And speaks in thunder.

PRINCE DEUKALION.

Who shall hurl those thrones,
Untenanted, beside all wrecks of Power,
And dwell above them, that mankind may rise ?

PROMETHEUS.

He is unknown.

ECHOES.

Unknown ! — yet known.

PROMETHEUS.

He is alone.

ECHOES.

Alone ! — yet with His Own.

ACT IV.

SCENE I.

A vast flowery meadow : the sea, cities and mountains in the distance.

AGATHON (*a child*).

(*Solus.*)

SOULS know their errands, — yet must live,
    Ere speaking, all the truth they give.
Sad must their brooding childhood be
Who teach the old captivity,
And ah ! how sad, perplexed and strange
Is theirs who see, but cannot change ;
How dark who build not, yet destroy, —
But mine, at last, but mine is joy !

No herald star announced my birth ;
Men know not that I tread the earth ;
I fashion not the doves of clay
That, when I bid them, soar away ;
Nor twine the rose, in sportive need
To make prophetic temples bleed ;
Nor look, from eyes of early woe,
The agony I shall not know !
O Purest, Holiest ! — not thy path
'Twixt tortured love and ancient wrath
Is mine to follow : none again
Wins thy beatitude of pain :

But all the glory of the Day,
All beauty near or far away,
All bliss of life that, born within,
Makes quick forgetfulness of sin,
Attend me, and through me express
The meaning of their loveliness.

Yonder, the weary, longing race
Conjecture my maturer face,
Nor dream the child's — when they behold.
Beneath its locks of sunburnt gold —
That only says : " My life is sweet ;
The crisp, cool grasses love my feet ;
The lulling air my body takes
To slumber, and the wave awakes ;
And pleasure comes from soil and flower,
And out of lightning falls a power,
And from the breath of ancient trees
The vigor that enriches ease,
And from the mountain-haunted skies
The will that ruins, save it rise ! "
Be the white wings of Duty furled
To-day, and let me own the world ! —
The azure flag-flower basks in heat,
Yet cools, below, her plashy feet ;
The footsteps of the breezes pass
In shadow-ripples down the grass,
And glimmers, where the pool is thin,
The slide of many a silver fin.
Beam on my bosom, warmth divine,
Until its pulsing currents shine
Like yonder river's ! — pour the flame
Of supple life through all my frame,
Till consciousness of beauty there
Gives me the glory I should wear !

My limbs shall float, my motions be
Each a new change of ecstasy,
Nor shall I breathe except to know
What savors the swift airs bestow,
While pure, as when its beats began,
The heart to music builds the man !

I know I AM, — that simplest bliss
The millions of my brothers miss.
I know the fortune to be born,
Even to the meanest wretch they scorn ;
What mingled seeds of life are sown
Broadcast, as by a hand unknown,
(A Demon's or a child-god's way
To scatter fates in wilful play !) —
What need of suffering precedes
All deeper wisdom, nobler deeds ;
And how man's soul may only rise
By something stern that purifies.
But here I gather, ere my hour
Shall call, the fresh, untainted power
Of Nature, half our mother yet,
And angry when her sons forget.
Far as the living ether bends
My being through her own extends ;
Free as a bird's to sink and soar
O'er meadow, mountain, sea and shore ;
One with the happy lives that breed
Their like in spawn, and egg, and seed ;
One with the careless motes that stray
To gather gold for dying day,
And with the dainty sorcery
Of odors blown far out to sea,
That say to mariners on the wing :
The unseen earth is blossoming !

But farther, finer, airier yet
A soul may spin its mystic net,
And, with unconscious heart-beat sped
Vibrating on each gossamer thread,
Declare itself and all it gives,
Though, speaking not, it simply lives !

Scene II.

The interior of a spacious church, as in Act III., Scene III.
Noon: the windows are open, and the nave is filled with sun-
shine. URANIA, *slowly pacing down the main aisle.*

URANIA.

An added step, and these groined arches fall !
The mine beneath the fortress of my foe
Is dug, the fuse is laid, and only fails
One spark of fire, but such as must be stolen
Elsewhere than from mine atoms.   How, save I,
Myself, create, shall I creation solve ?
Exalted thus, and throned on rigid Law,
That bids a million universes whirl
In the inconceivable Immensity, —
Earth but a mote, and all humanity
Its faint result, — shall I admit desire
As cause, not sequence, fondest dreams as fact,
And vast inflation of the vapory Self
Beyond all spheres of sense ?   With my large scheme
This last breathes interference : unto me
Myself suffices : no fond paramour
Shall woo me for my beauty, save as truth
Makes beautiful, or knowledge stands for love.
Men's minds grow wider : my serener light
Probes the dark closets of the mystic Past,

And many a bat-like phantom, blinded, shrieks
For the last time, and dies : yet — one more step,
The final one, awaits me.

AGATHON.

(*Appearing from behind the altar.*)
                              Yea, and that
Thou canst not take.

URANIA.

                    What hinders me ? — speak on !

AGATHON.

Then thou wert God !

URANIA.

              The Cause ? the first impelling Force ?
The Ages yet may make me so.

AGATHON.

                              And Man,
Who, knowing thee, is everything thou art,
Shall find himself created by his will,
And all his faith in one advancing life
Through fairer spheres is thine in being his !
Almighty Love, lord of intelligence,
Anointed Prophet of Eternity,
Lives, even as thou.

URANIA.

              And dies, when thwarted law
Prohibits.

AGATHON.

        Nay ! — not dies, howe'er obscured

Or mutilate, — not dies, in that dense dark
Where thou art impotent, but is the ray
That guides men to thy feet and far beyond !

URANIA.

I know thou canst not be mine enemy ;
Yet why, to flatter life, wilt thou repeat
The unproven solace ?

AGATHON.

               Proven by its need ! —
By fates so large no fortune can fulfil ;
By wrong no earthly justice can atone ;
By promises of love that keep love pure ;
And all rich instincts, powerless of aim,
Save chance, and time, and aspiration wed
To freer forces, follow !   By the trust
Of the chilled Good that at life's very end
Puts forth a root, and feels its blossom sure !
Yea, by thy law ! — since every being holds
Its final purpose in the primal cell,
And here the radiant destiny o'erflows
Its visible bounds, enlarges what it took
From sources past discovery, and predicts
No end, or, if an end, the end of all !

URANIA.

I know this dialect, so many strive
To make it mine, or bend my tongue thereto.
Let there be truce while perfect knowledge waits !
Here cometh one whom I must serve, — and thou,
If thou wouldst live.
      (*Enter* PRINCE DEUKALION.)

AGATHON.
My father !

PRINCE DEUKALION.

                                    Have I, then,
In some exalted trance begotten thee ? —
Ah, not from her who only should have nursed
Thy babyhood, — *our* race is yet to come.
Thou hast my features, and from heart and lip,
As thus I hold them swiftly unto mine,
Flows sweetness ; and the light in thy young eyes
Is as a hope within me.

AGATHON.

                            And my work
Shall bring me nearer, since, if thou wert not,
I could not be !   My hands are tender yet,
My feet too lightly borne, my soul alive
With too much joy : I feel, but cannot teach,
And wander, guided by a shaft of light
That shall illumine knowledge as I need.
Whither, I question not : I only know
It touches thee, or thy far phantasm set
Where fades from earth the beam, so linking us
In one design.   The first art thou to know,
The first to love me, — and wouldst first command !

PRINCE DEUKALION.

I have awaited thee a thousand years.

AGATHON.

I waited for my time.

PRINCE DEUKALION.

                            Our blood thou hast :
So might Prometheus speak.   But wilt thou, here
Where gray Tradition hews each separate stone,
And vainly gropes decrepit Faith to clutch

The outflown Deity, transform the shrine
Where He, so starved by penance, comes no more,
But elsewhere stays until His feast be spread ?
Some natural odor of the happy earth
Breaks in with thee : the arches clasp above
With leafy lightness of the summer boughs :
The oriel drops rose-leaves, and the font,
Bubbling and brightening with an inward life,
Spins up in silver, tinkling as it falls.
What hast thou done ?

AGATHON.

                    At first I took away
The High-Priest's mitre, long since threadbare grown,
Eaten by moths, dust-soiled and shapeless.   He,
As one forgetful, sought, then seemed to wear,
And with a customed hand to set aright, —
Then missed, forgot again.   His ephod, next,
Of fine-twined linen, scarlet, blue and gold,
The girdle and the breast-plate of the tribes,
I hid from further use, — a sorer loss,
Awhile in his bewildered looks betrayed
And halting speech ; but now he scarce recalls
That such things were nor could be otherwise.

PRINCE DEUKALION.

What next ?

AGATHON.

What still remains ; and — now — I do !
(AGATHON *removes the tablet with the rayed triangle, takes the
   Ark of the Covenant from the top of the altar, and conceals
   them.*)

PRINCE DEUKALION.

The Cross endures.

AGATHON.

Till some diviner type
Of man that loves and gives himself for men,
Shall plant his emblem !

PRINCE DEUKALION.

O'er it, set a star, —
Beneath, a sphere !

AGATHON.

Man must invent his own ;
And this, that his far memory antedates, —
Descended with him from the world's cold roof,
Where, past the Indian peaks, on high Pamere
His race was cradled, — from a single death
Took sanctity forever !   Whether mine
Be star or sphere, it is not mine to choose ;
For I must pass ere I am known of men,
Who seeing, hearing, loving me, perchance,
Behold the brother, not the future god !

[*Exeunt.*

Scene III.

The court of a grand, dusky temple, with beams as of cedar-
wood, supported by gilded pillars. At the farther end, a
veil, through which sculptured cherubim are indistinctly seen.
On each side are thrones, overlaid with gold, set in the in-
terspaces of the colonnades.

PROMETHEUS (*solus*).

The sportive genii of illusive form,
Of hidden color and divided ray,
Have built me this, the ampler counterfeit
Of thine, O Solomon ! that lifted up

Moriah into flashing pinnacles,
And spoiled umbrageous Lebanon to roof
Its courts with cedar!   Less than air is mine,
The ghost of thy barbaric fane, yet meet
To hold the ghosts that deem themselves alive,
As in a truce of spirit, when the Dead
Float gray and moth-like through their wonted rooms,
Are shaped in dusky nooks to living eyes,
And send the hollow semblance of a voice
To living ears, — the law that parts them both
Being all inviolate.   Such unconscious truce
I now proclaim, as ever in large minds
Holds back the narrower passion, and decides.
The conflicts of the earth must sometimes pause,
Breathless : some hour of weariness must come
When each fierce Power inspects its battered mail,
The old blade reforges, or picks out a new,
While measuring with a dim and desperate eye
The limbs of Man's new champion.   Agathon!
Thy soul is yet outside the fiery lists :
The trumpet hath not called thee: as a child
Thou waitest, but the wisdom of a child
Must first be spoken.   From their seats of rule
I summon them whom thou shalt meet, — and thee!

> King of the glorious reign,
> To whom thy glory slain
> Returned for all men's gain, —
> Queen of the triple crown,
> Whose haughty eyes look down
> From heights of old renown, —
> Priest, that wast sent to be
> Deliverer, but mak'st free
> Only who follow thee, —
> Muse, that hast grown so high

Through the unmeasured sky,
Man knows thee but to die, —
Come, or the phantom send,
Commissioned to defend !

(*The forms — or phantasms — of* BUDDHA, MEDUSA, CAL-
CHAS *and* URANIA *appear, and seat themselves upon opposite
thrones.* AGATHON *enters and advances to the centre of the
temple-court.*)

BUDDHA (*dreamily*).

Across my bliss of Self absorbed in All,
And only conscious as a speck of dust
Is of its Earth, there creeps such faintest thrill
As to the lotus-bulb or rose's root   •
Strikes downward from the sweetness of the flower, —
The sign that somewhere in the outlived world
A God-selected soul is ripe to ask
A question that compels reply.   I wake,
As one that, hammock-cradled under palms
Beside a tropic river, drinks the breath
Of clove and cinnamon orchards, seaward blown,
And through the half-transparence of his lids
Sees from the golden-gray of afternoon
The sunset's amber flush, but never fade.
Art thou, fair Boy, the questioner ?   Thine eyes
Demand Life's secret: learn thou to renounce,
And grow, renouncing, sure of Deity !

AGATHON.

But I *accept*, — even all this conscious life
Gives in its fullest measure, — gladness, health,
Clean appetite, and wholeness of my claim
To knowledge, beauty, aspiration, power !
Joy follows action, here ; and action bliss,
Hereafter !   While, God-lulled, thy children sleep,

Mine, God-aroused, shall wake to wander on
Through spheres thy slumbrous essence never dreamed.
Thy highest is my lowest !

MEDUSA.

                        So speaks Youth,
That fans a calenture in spirits light :
With such I deal not, but its answering chill.
What refuge hast thou for the weary soul
That says : " My feet are bleeding ; carry me,
And I will serve thee " ?   Fretful is the race,
And breaks its playthings like a petted child.
But, looking backward o'er the heritage
That makes me holy, thee nor like of thee
Do I perceive : whose warrant sent thee here ?
If Man's half-lost and consecrated Past
Thou canst restore, be welcome ! — otherwise
New heresy and hate are born of thee.
Lo ! my commands are heard ; I do not change ;
Nay, though the headlong world transform itself
And speak strange tongues, in me all truth begins,
In me is finished !

AGATHON.

(*Advancing to the foot of* MEDUSA's *throne.*)
                    Wake, O Sorceress,
Caught fast in thine own toils !   Wash thy filmed eyes
And look around thee !   Why, what things are these ?
Terror is gone from men, and Ignorance
Girds his weak loins, and all usurping hands
Of mediation grope for lost appeals,
Since that dread simulacrum thou didst frame
From breath of prayer, and altar-smoke, and gold,
Falls, and is God no more !   A thousand years
Have passed since thou, in plenitude of power,
                    20

Didst set thy house in order, smile well-pleased,
And softly say : " Now may I sleep awhile ! "
Yea, though the night-lamp bearing, thou hast walked
The chambers to and fro, 't was still in sleep,
And drowsed from changes of the sunlit life
Outside, till all thy Past slid down, and drifts
Where now it harms not : waken, if thou canst !

MEDUSA (*starting*).

What place is this ?   Who else is throned, where I
Alone am crowned ?

AGATHON.

Let them declare !

CALCHAS.

(*Lifting his hand mechanically to his brow, then suddenly rec-
ollecting.*)

No crown

He needs to wear whom happy followers love ;
And unto these have I enlarged my gifts
Even as their souls discovered and desired.
I hold them not from seeking, but above
High wills and actions set the highest Good,
His gift, not mine.   I war but with their pride
That, looking inward, finds too clear a light,
Too large a license, — looking upward, sees
A Deity too dim for mortal sense.

AGATHON.

Nay, Priest ! — thou warrest with pure intelligence
That rays allwhither from its central flame,
And reaches God on Power's or Beauty's side,
As on Devotion's !   Since thou wast content
With One whose human spite and jealousy,

Though veiled by later love, still shows the badge
Of clanship, men have passed thy visible fanes
To kneel in that invisible, whose wide walls
Surround all tribes, all upward-lifted lives,
All downward driven by ignorance and wrong.
Who reigns there sits above thy reach of soul:
Denial cannot 'scape Him, sacrilege stray
Beyond His pity, nor by any path
The seeking spirit miss !

URANIA.

                  Save, indeed,
He be not else than universal Force,
And all His worship out of fibres born,
That, changing texture, change Him unto Man.
What eye hath known Him ?   What fine instrument
Hath found, as 't were a planet yet unseen,
His place among the balance of the stars ?
But selfish fancy and insatiate love,
Chilled by almighty Law, demand to feel
A human heart-beat somewhere in the void,
And rescue their imagined essences,
Distinct and conscious, from eternal dust !

AGATHON.

That selfish fancy and insatiate love
Are thine, not knowing !   Thou, without thy will,
Art the most glorious of the hosts that serve,
Proclaimer of the measureless scheme divine
That makes men tremble !   In that universe
Thy lore hath found for His activity
Earth's petty creeds fall off as wintered leaves,
When April swells the bud of new.   Men grow,
But not beyond their hearts, — possess, enjoy,
Yet, being dependent, ever must believe ;

So with thy knowledge rises Him believed,
Shakes off as rags what once were holy names,
Treads under foot as crackling potsherds all
The symbols of old races, with one breath
Puffs into air defilement of their hates,
And stands alone, too awful to be named !
This is thy service.

PROMETHEUS.

Hast thou aught to ask ?

AGATHON.

Verily, one seed is Truth's; but they who clip
The sprouting plant to hedge their close domains,
How should they know its grace of natural boughs
And blossoms bursting to the startled sun ?
I ask them naught, fore-hearing their replies.

PROMETHEUS.

Forces that work, or dream ;
Shadows that are, or seem ;
Whether your spell sublime
Fades at the touch of Time,
Or from the ages ye
Take loftier destiny, —
I, of the primal date
As of the final fate,
Having compelled, release :
Depart, but not in peace !

(*The four figures disappear from the thrones.* PRINCE DEUKA-
LION *and* PYRRHA *enter the court of the temple.*)

PYRRHA.

O Son, thou last and sweetest hope for us,
Since men shall clasp thy truth in loving thee ;

Where tarriest thou ?   The vault of golden air
Above thy meadows, knowing thee no more,
Is emptied of delight : the scattered homes,
Wherein thy face was precious, yearn and wait :
The cities and the highways of the earth
That know thee not, yet having seen thee, miss,
Are calling on thy name.   Lo ! we have sought, —
I and thy father, — sorrowing, for thee.

AGATHON.

How is it that ye sought me ?   Wist ye not
That I must be about my Father's work ?

Scene IV.

*A vast, natural platform, thrust forward from the extremity of a
mountain-chain. Upon it rise the unfinished walls of an edi-
fice, only half the pillars of the façade being lifted into place ;
yet every block suggests the harmony of the complete design.
Beyond it the height falls away into broad terraces, the first
dotted with woods of oak and chestnut trees, those below with
fig, olive, and fields of vine, and finally sinking through
orange groves to the palms and tamarinds of a great plain,
divided by an inlet of the sea. PROMETHEUS, PANDORA,
EPIMETHEUS, PRINCE DEUKALION and PYRRHA, on the
marble steps leading to the portal.*

EPIMETHEUS.

We know ourselves.

PANDORA.

And love !

PROMETHEUS.

And work as one !

Divided by the Gods that portioned out
Parts of a single destiny to each, —
Divided by the darkness of the race
That sees in fragments, and by highest Will,
Forerunning Time so far with prophecy
That even hope grows faint, and faith benumbed,
We stand united now !

PRINCE DEUKALION.

                        Thou in design,
We in fulfilment ; what is Time, henceforth ?
I know thee as the Titan who defied
Man's violent Gods, defending Man's own right,
And who, foreseeing triumph in the end,
Hast never made surrender.   What I am   .
Is thine : I am thy form of victory,
First kindled with the stolen fire of heaven,
To make all wisdom, worship, power, faith, joy,
And beauty, one !

PANDORA.

                        And thou, my daughter pure,
My Pyrrha, fear not thou that this shall be,
Till Woman owns her equal half of life,
And, following some supernal instinct, finds
Her half of Godhead !

PYRRHA.

                        'T is not hers to doubt.

PROMETHEUS.

Once did we walk the earth unseen ; but now
Men pause, and with a holy, sweet surmise
Behold us dimly : Pyrrha, Deukalion
Grow dear to many an eye that looks afar,

And vanish in the nearness.   Brother, thou,
Whose mind reversed interprets all the Past
And so o'erlooks the Future, even as one
That scales a mount between two mighty vales, —
Who readest thus Faith's awful secrets, — thou
Art loved and feared ; but still our perfect day
Sleeps in the womb of an unrisen morn.

SHEPHERD.

(On the terrace below, singing.)

Where the arch of the rock is bended,
   Warm, and hid from the dew,
Slumber the sheep I tended,
   All the sweet night through.
Never a wolf affrights them
   Here, in the pasture's peace,
But the tender grass delights them,
   And the shadows cool their fleece.

I blow, as a downy feather,
   The sleep on my eyelids laid,
And rise in the twilight weather,
   Between the glow and the shade.
Too blest the hour has made me
   For a speech the tongue may know,
But my happy flute shall aid me,
   And speak to my love below !

PROMETHEUS.

These simple lives may own contentment now,
Unscared ; for happiness it is that gives
Sweet savor unto worship.   Men, as trees,
Take from the elements their separate food
And grow in concord with the season's will, —
Exempt not yet, unsheltered even as these

From fated evils, gnawing drouth at root,
Bough-shattering winds, the lightning's sudden spear,
And blackest ruin, when the forest's heart
Breaks in the vortex of the hurricane!
But each discerns his place, or, failing it,
Is gently guided, — honors, in himself,
Symmetric health and noble appetites
He once insulted, — hears the choric chant,
Unenvious of the singer's golden throat,
And smiles when Genius speaks, as who should say:
" He knows me, and his mighty words are mine."

SHEPHERDESS.

(*Singing in the valley.*)

Uncover the embers !
With pine-cone and myrtle
My breath shall enkindle
    The sacred Fire !
Arise through the stillness
My shepherd's blue signal,
And bear to his mountain
    The valley's desire !
The olive-tree bendeth ;
The grapes gather purple ;
The garden in sunshine
    Is ripe to the core :
Then smile as thou sleepest,
His fruit and my blossom ;
There 's peace in the chamber,
    And song at the door !

PROMETHEUS.

The suns of milder centuries must gild
The snow of this young marble, ere one block
Shall cap the pediment, and flash to heaven

Its finished glory!   Oft the laborers
Shall pause, grown weary of the vast design ;
Oft shall old apathy return, old strife
Shake like a chained volcano 'neath the sea ;
But ere men change it, every stone shall turn
To adamant, or rise by hands of air !
As from the evangels of all races God
Begins to be, the tongues of every race,
Quiring a strain that silences the stars,
Alone can worship Him !   Not yet Earth hears
More than the quarriers' and the builders' hymns.

CHANT.

(*From the opposite side.*)

Fashion your chisels well
With the steel from a hero's hand,
  Who conquered, as he fell,
The freedom of a land !
  Forge, out of chains that break,
Hammers and clamps alone ;
  And cut from a martyr's stake
A wand to mete the stone !
  But sing, as ye work, a strain
Of joy and of triumph pure,
  Of deeds that were not in vain,
And blessings that most endure, —
  As a hope and a happier grace
Round the lives of duty poured ;
  And the stone shall find its place
In the Temple of the Lord !

PRINCE DEUKALION.

Quick, fiery thrills, which only are not pangs
Because so warm and welcome, pierce my frame,
As were its airy substance suddenly

Clothed on with flesh ; the ichor in my veins
Begins to redden with the pulse of blood,
And, from the recognition of the eyes
That now behold me, something I receive
Of Man's incarnate beauty.   Thou, as well,
Confessest this bright change : across thy cheeks
A faintest wild-rose color comes and goes,
And, on thy proud lips, Pyrrha, sits a flame !
Oh, we are nearer ! — not suffice me now
The touch of marble hands, reliance cold,
And Destiny's pale promises of love ;
But, clasping thee as mortal passion clasps
Bosom to bosom, let my being thus
Assure itself, and thine !

PYRRHA.

                    Thine eyes compel ;
Thy words are as a wind that bends me down,
And thou art beautiful as I to thee.
What holds me back ?   Is it that I perceive,
O Titan Mother, thy reproving face,
Immortal patience consecrates, and haste,
That pours too soon the beaker of the Gods,
Must ever trouble ?   Aid me with thy words !

PANDORA.

Take counsel of thy heart !   The Gods themselves
Have seasons to rejoice ; when happier eyes
Illume their ether, and unwonted lips
Meet, and their large refreshment falls on men.
Think what thou art, then follow thy desire !

(PYRRHA *muses a moment, then turns towards* PRINCE DEU-
KALION. *He clasps her to his breast, and they kiss each
other.*)

SCENE V.

The Same.

SPIRITS OF DAWN.

Hark ! has the Sun-god's Hour
Smitten her cymbals, dreaming him nigh ?
We are called by a sound, and sped by a power,
 To break the sleep of the sky !
 Æolian echoes blow
From the fourfold realms of the air,
And a torch, not ours, with a mightier glow
 Burns where the East is bare !
 We hasten, we scatter the cloud :
We quench the beam of the great white star ;
 But the pæan is over-loud,
And the splendor comes from afar !
 It flushes our halls of rest,
 As the sun were a rose in hue,
And it paints the Earth, as she bares her breast
 To the emptied urns of the dew.

 (*Sound of Æolian harps ; the face of* EOS *appears.*)

EOS.

Is this mine Earth ?
The many-headlanded, the temple-crowned,
Which the great purple sea so whispered round,
 When earlier Gods had birth ?
 Mine Earth, I loved so well,
Rejoiced in, as it welcomed me,
And fed with unexhausted hydromel,
 While the young race was free !
 I know its curving strands,
Its dimpling hollows, bosom-budding hills ;
I scent large fragrance of the life that fills

The joined or parted lands.
Old hopes, and sweetest, burn again ;
Old words are stammering on my tongue :
Was it your lips that kissed, Immortal Twain,
Or is Tithonus young ?

PYRRHA.

As a gift unsought ;
As a joy unbought ;
As a fair hope fed
From a hope that is dead ;
As a diadem set
When the brows forget, —
Thou, the dearest,
Uncalled, appearest !

PRINCE DEUKALION.

Eyes of hope, and promise-laden
    Lips, that smile before they speak,
Are they thine, divinest Maiden,
    Blushing morning from thy cheek ?
Unto prayer thy face denying,
Unto deed at last replying,
Linger near, and turn not from us
Present bliss and holier promise !

In the glory thou unfoldest,
    Tranced with music of thy tongue,
Young is all that once was oldest,
    Love and Faith and Will are young !
Stay with us ! — thy smile assuages
Pangs bequeathed by weary ages,
And thine eyes are sweet forewarning
Of the world's eternal morning !

GÆA.

The blushes of thy cheeks descend on me,
Thy glance is glorious upon my mountains :
I breathe in ampler wind and prouder sea,
And beat, strong-pulsed, thro' mine unnumbered fount-
 ains.
Though filled with seeds of unimagined powers,
I cannot spare my beauty : now, from thee
Fresh silver stars the dewy-beaded flowers,
And rosy mists the fading forelands cover,
Until, far northward, thou dost pour
The rainbow's dust on every ice-built shore,
To make even sun-forgetting Death thy lover !

Am I not fair ? — yea, though thy face should bow
Thus near and fond, and find no child that knew thee :
But, having nursed Humanity as thou,
I feel what pure, prophetic rapture drew thee.
Stay thou with men ; take not away thy hope,
The endless answer to an endless vow :
Touch only, here, the risen Temple's cope,
And every glen and darksome lowland alley
Shall hail it as a herald ray,
And wait in happier patience for the day
When morning's mountain-gold shall flood the valley !

EOS.

Another must fulfil :
 I am the promise, not the will.
Men dimly guess, through me,
 The distant glories that may be,
Renewed, as each grows pale
 In coming, through my roseate veil.
But, seeming o'erpowered
 When sunrise is strong,

Faith, Courage, Devotion,
　　My being prolong!
I fade, for the coward;
　　I flame, for the bold;
And noble emotion
　　My face shall behold.
I grow from their yearning
　　As they from my vision,—
No longer the Eos
　　Of spaces Elysian,
But ever returning
　　With promise sublime,—
First victor o'er Chaos,
　　And last over Time!

PYRRHA.

To the gracious heart of Woman and the love that
　　fondly bends,
Thou hast given the juster manhood that shelters it
　　and defends:
For the Man's immortal ardor and the breadth of his
　　soul's demand,
Thou hast set the woman beside him, and weaponed
　　her equal hand;

As the palm by the palm in beauty, the female and the
　　male,
When the south-winds mix their blossoms, and the
　　date-sheaf cannot fail;
For one is the glory of either, since the primal Fate
　　began
To guide to a single Future Earth's double-natured
　　Man!

CHORUS. ·

(*From the valleys.*)

Mother, thy work hath blessed us !
Honored, we wear thy cestus ;
Honored, we lay it aside,
Crowned with the bliss of the bride ;
Honored, we loose from eclipse,
Unto the sweetness of lips
Sweeter for innocent need,
Moons of the bosoms that feed !
Tender, for difference' sake,
Serve us man's haughtier powers ;
Strength from his being we take,
But to restore it from ours.!

PRINCE DEUKALION.

In the kiss of our lips that reddened
 With a perfect passion's dawn,
Met the bliss pure women yearn for,
And the noble truth men burn for,
When the youthful fancy is deadened,
 But the human heart beats on !

By the light of the dawn within them
 Their weakness my children see,
And Self and its greeds are broken
By the longing that dares be spoken,
And the warmth of the deeds that win them
 The courage to be free !

Still shy is the best endeavor
 That hath set its goal so high ;
But Good, when the heart betrays it,
And Love, by the lives that praise it,

Shall cradle the earth forever
  In the arms of a happier sky!

CHORUS.

(*From the valleys.*)

We hear thee and know thee, Father!
  As a flock the Shepherd leads,
We follow to thy pastures
  Of great and generous deeds.
Though suns to come may brand us
  And sudden frosts may blight;
And Crime, the prowling were-wolf,
  Steal on us in the night;
Though Self, that builds unwearied,
  May stain the purer will,
Or Apathy, slowly dying
  Of his own mortal chill;
Yet thou hast healing fountains
  Replenished from above,
In heart, brain, soul, renewing
  The triple strength of love!
Planted through all the ages
  Thy trees shall yield us food,
And goldening for our harvest
  Shall grow the natural Good!

PROMETHEUS.

Retrieve perverted destiny!
'T is this shall set your children free.
The forces of your race employ
To make sure heritage of joy;
Yet feed, with every earthly sense,
Its heavenly coincidence, —
That, as the garment of an hour;
This, as an everlasting power.

For Life, whose source not here began,
Must fill the utmost sphere of Man,
And, so expanding, lifted be
Along the line of God's decree,
To find in endless growth all good, —
In endless toil, beatitude.
Seek not to know Him ; yet aspire
As atoms toward the central fire !
Not lord of race is He, afar, —
Of Man, or Earth, or any star,
But of the inconceivable All ;
Whence nothing that there is can fall
Beyond Him, — but may nearer rise,
Slow-circling through eternal skies.
His larger life ye cannot miss,
In gladly, nobly using this.
Now, as a child in April hours
Clasps tight its handful of first flowers,
Homeward, to meet His purpose, go ! —
These things are all ye need to know.

THE END.

21

NOTES.

THE PROPHET.

THE plan for the *Prophet* was conceived as far back as 1866 or 1867. The drama was not written, however, until 1873. A curious circumstance connected with it is, that about the same time Mr. T. B. Aldrich had formed a similar plan for a drama, which, after having given up all intention of working it out himself, he communicated to Bayard Taylor whilst walking with him one day in the streets of Boston. The latter at that time had almost entirely completed his own plan in his mind, and was startled to find that he and his friend had both busied themselves with the same theme.

In 1872 he left this country for a stay of two years in Europe. It was meant for rest, after the completion of his Faust-translation had made recreation from work and study necessary for him. But his ever active brain would not let him rest, when he might have done so. It was one of his seasons of song, over which, as to time, he had no control, and the poetic faculty claimed its dues. Hardly had he arrived on the other side of the Ocean, and refreshed himself somewhat at the baths of Bormio, in the Italian Tyrol, where he was sent to recruit, when he wrote the poem of "Lars," in the autumn of that year. The following year, after exhausting literary labors, the plan for the *Prophet* presented itself again to his mind, and would not leave him until it found utterance.

It was at the end of August, during a short stay at Gotha, Germany, that the first scenes were written. In the month of September the first Act was completed, and the second Act begun. Then came the " Autumn Days," at Weimar, in the course of which, during the months of October and November, the drama was continued. The editor at that time was in almost daily correspondence with the poet, and was enabled by references in his letters to follow closely the growth of the poem under his pen. On October 18th he wrote : " I have nothing more to send you, for I shall bring the new scenes with me. I write something, whether much or little, every day, and find it the only way to prevent the Goethe-interests from interrupting me. I want to go on with the main action while I am possessed with it." So much, indeed, was he possessed with his work, that it went on involuntarily in the midst of social engagements, researches, and visits paid to neighboring towns. On the railway to Gotha, on November 9th, the second stanza of Livia's song (Scene IV. of Act IV.) was composed and noted down in pencil. In the middle of October, after having completed Act IV., he resolved not to begin Act V. until a week later, when he expected to have a few quiet days at Gotha. But before getting there, on November 18th, he wrote: "I began Act V. last evening — could n't help it. To-day, D. V., I shall finish Scene II. There 's no use of waiting, while I am in the humor to write."

The last two scenes of the drama were written during a visit to the editor at Leipzig, on November 24th and 25th. The diary of the latter says on the former of these days : " B. came at noon, and sat down at once to write the last scene but one of the *Prophet.*" On the 25th it says : " He wrote the last scene in the forenoon. It is quite time the work should cease, for his nervous system has been considerably strained by it."

Whilst Bayard Taylor was so intensely occupied by this drama in Germany, there came a letter from New York, written by his friend, Mr. E. C. Stedman, in which literature, and especially poetry, were largely discussed, and wherein this sentence occurred : " I strongly advise you to try a dramatic poem on a strictly American subject." It was just what he was then doing.

The subject of the *Prophet* is in fact so thoroughly American that its realism has been made a reproach by the critics.

We have the farm-life and talk ; the camp-meeting — so essentially American ; the religious element which, in the absence of other themes of interest beyond farm matters, enters to so large a degree into the daily routine of American country-folks ; the emigrant train ; the development of a religious sect, such as could take shape nowhere but in the unbounded and untenanted West.

This latter circumstance led of itself to the adoption, in some measure, of the Mormon history for the historical background of the drama. But the characters and the plot are the poet's own, and have nothing to do with the Mormons, as he himself stated. It was, in fact, a trial for him to find that his design was misinterpreted, and that the critics would see Joe Smith in David Starr, there being indeed nothing in common between them. The prototype for his hero which the author had in his mind was rather the Rev. Edward Irving, the founder of a sect in the first half of the present century, which still exists in Scotland and in Germany. This sect believes in the miraculous renewal of the spiritual gifts bestowed by the Apostles on the early Christians. The dramatic poem, however, was worked out in the author's mind (to use his own words) "without reference to that or any other sect. I designed only to represent phases of spiritual development and their external results, which are hardly possible in any other country than ours. For the same reason, the tragic element in the poem is placed chiefly in its moral and spiritual aspects, rather than in the action."

Persons intimately acquainted with the Bible will read this poem with a better understanding of the author's intention, than others who are not familiar with the sacred book. Bayard Taylor knew the Bible thoroughly, and in it, like Shelley, "he took a great and peculiar interest." Scriptural allusions abound in the *Prophet ;* the drama turns, indeed, on a literal interpretation of the Biblical text, which grows out of the belief that it is dictated by the Holy Spirit, and consequently must be accepted as it stands. This belief (to use once more the author's own words) "is the power which impels him [David] ; and this is the Fate which makes the tragedy of his life inevitable."

In the camp-meeting scene, David comes in contact with doctrinal Christianity, of whose preachers he says later, on page 14 : —

> " And are not all alike
> Giving their husks of doctrine for His bread?"

and confronts it by his simple faith, which returns to the original source, the Bible, for guidance and inspiration. But there, in making the fatal mistake of seeing the letter only, and not the spirit, he allows himself to be misled from the outset, and thus is forced step by step to follow up his error to its last developments, which cannot but destroy him.

The vision of David, after he has gone to the Wilderness (Scene V., Act I.), is partly based on a personal experience of the author, of which he tells in "At Home and Abroad," vol. 1, p. 146. Whilst travelling on horseback in California, in 1849, he lost his way near the foot-hills of the Sierra Nevada. Night came on, and he was obliged to halt in a wooded dell. He had taken no food for some time, and he lay down supperless on the bare ground, taking the saddle for his pillow. The neighborhood being "famous for bears," he slept but little. "I lay awake half an hour at a time," he relates, "watching the culmination of the stars on the meridian line of a slender twig over my head. It was perhaps an hour past midnight, when, as I thus lay with open eyes, gazing into the eternal beauty of Night, I became conscious of a deep, murmuring sound, like that of a rising wind. . . . . A strange feeling of awe and expectation took possession of me. Not a dead leaf stirred on the boughs ; while the mighty sound — a solemn choral, sung by ten thousand voices — swept down from the hills, and rolled away like retreating thunder over the plain. It was no longer the roar of the wind. As in the wandering prelude of an organ melody, note trod upon note with slow, majestic footsteps, until they gathered to a theme, and then came the words, simultaneously chanted by an immeasurable host: ' *Vivant terrestriæ !* ' The air was filled with the tremendous sound, which seemed to sweep near the surface of the earth in powerful waves, without echo or reverberation."

David in his monologue, speaking of his vision (page 23), says : —

> " The trees were filled with whispers; and afar
> Called voices not of man; and then my soul
> Went forth from me, and spread and grew aloft
> Through parting lights — His arrows here and there,
> Shot down on earth."

And farther on he continues thus : —

> " The dark, invisible pillars of the sky
> Breathed like deep organ-pipes of awful sound :
> A myriad myriad tongues the choral sang."

At the conclusion of his narrative the author says in explanation of his own " wonderful visitation " : " I was undeniably awake at the time, ... but I was fatigued, famished, alone in the wilderness, awed by the solemnity and silence of the night, — perhaps even more than I suspected, — and my excited imagination, acting involuntarily and unconsciously to myself, produced the illusion. I have often observed that complete repose of the body, after great fatigue, is accompanied — when continued to a certain time — with a corresponding repose of volition, a passive condition of the mind, highly favorable to the independent action of the imagination. Then, if ever, are we in a fit state to hear

> ' The airy tongues that syllable man's names
> On sands, and shores, and desert wildernesses.' "

The crashing of the rock at the end of Act I., when David (page 37) says : " Be thou removed ! " is an incident which is said to have taken place during the preaching of the so-called " Prophet " Matthias, who, in the early part of this century, made a stir among the people of the State of New York.

The " exercise " of the " gift of tongues " bestowed on Livia, in Act II. (page 53), is analogous to an episode in the career of the Rev. Edward Irving, who, when preaching in London, in 1830, was suddenly interrupted by a lady, speaking in a strange tongue. Thereupon the coming down of tongues became so frequent an occurrence among the sect

that he used to pause in his sermons at certain times, in order
to allow a fair chance to this manifestation of the Spirit.

In Act III. there occurs a passage which the author considered the most tragical one of the whole poem. It is at the
conclusion of the Act (page 96), when Rhoda, alone, in the
depth of night, searches the New Testament in vain for the
text which she had thought must be there — the words that
would arm her against the new commandment which David
is to proclaim to the sect. But she does not find the truth
pointed out that would save her, the one lawful wife of the
man she loves, from being superseded by another ; — that
would make her husband shrink from committing the deep
wrong he is about to inflict, not upon her alone, but on womankind. This one fatal omission in all the holy teachings left
her without a defence, a prey to despair. All is lost to her
now.

In Act IV. the curse of sin, that one guilty step compels
another, has descended upon David. He is led to contem-
plate the taking of the life of a member of the council considered to be dangerous. Whilst he still debates with himself,
he falls into a revery, and soliloquizes (page 117), beginning
thus : —

> " I see the poor beast's eyes,
> And that tremendous question hid in them,
> I tried to answer."

This and the following lines commemorate a real event, which
was tragical enough, although merely concerning two favorite
dogs ; one large and most affectionate, the other young, small
and intelligent. By day they were constant companions of
the family, when at home on the farm, but at night they had
to sleep out of doors, to keep watch. One morning, early,
there came on the place a mad dog. He was seen by the
colored man in the act of springing upon little " Beppo " and
worrying him. There was no sign of bite or scratch on him,
or on poor " Picket," the large dog ; both, however, were put
in confinement, and as " Beppo," after a day or two, showed
some doubtful symptoms, the safety of the household and
the neighborhood seemed imperatively to demand the killing

of both dogs. They were killed accordingly, but the last look the poor beasts, who seemed to feel by instinct that they were doomed, gave to their master and mistress, was never forgotten. The latter mourned for these poor animals, to whom they had to act as Fate ; and the question came up between them in those days, whether dumb creatures, like these, do not in some measure recognize in man that Providence to which we ourselves bow down, even though we are not capable of fathoming it. The author in this passage set up an expiatory monument to poor " Picket " and " Beppo."

The simplicity of language and diction in the *Prophet* was a part of the author's plan. He found it not easy to restrain himself and to tone down his characters from beginning to end ; but he certainly proved his art in making the poem one harmonious whole of subdued coloring. As to an acting play, it was far from his intention to consider this drama as such. His own words in this respect are : " It would simply be an absurdity to attempt its representation upon the stage."

THE MASQUE OF THE GODS.

If chronologically ranked, this drama should have preceded the *Prophet*, since it was written more than a year before the latter was begun. The editor, however, has deemed it best not to separate this dramatic poem from that which follows it, because of its connection in theme and order of thought with *Prince Deukalion*. Although not intended to be such, the *Masque of the Gods* is a concordant prelude to the larger and more important work. So close, indeed, is the intellectual kinship of the two poems, that the former seems to strike the opening chords, whilst the latter sets in full-toned, and with orchestral power sweeps through its growing centuries.

The *Masque of the Gods*, when it appeared, differed from anything the author hitherto had sung. It touched upon a much higher and loftier theme than had been chosen by him before, though the poem of " Harpocrates," written in 1865, already seemed to point in the direction that his mind and his poetic faculty were to take. This drama marks the ripeness of the new intellectual development which had been preparing itself in the author's mind. It came after his translation of " Faust," that had taught him a masterly handling of form, and after a long and rare season of congenial labor and study. For several years past the volumes he " loved," — to which he alludes in the " August Pastoral," — " the heartful, whispering pages," " the yearning voice from the garden in Jena," and the " answering voice from the park-side cottage in Weimar,"

> —" the sentimental echo from chambers of office in Dresden, —
> Yea, and the feebler and farther voices that sound in the pauses,"

had been his intimate companions, and the close intercourse with this august company had opened new avenues of thought, and had imparted to his mind that largeness and universality which characterize in so high a degree the latter years of his life.

With this first of his dramas he ceased to sing to his old audiences : — he now sang to himself and to the few who were able to understand him. It was written whilst residing in New York for the winter, in 1872. He had been obliged to leave his temporary home in that city for a fortnight, in order to fulfil some lecturing engagements in the West. When he returned he brought with him, as the fruit of his lonely journeying from place to place, the plan for this dramatic poem, on which he began work at once. He wrote the first scenes of it on February 16th, and finished it three days afterwards, in the evening. This was shortly before sailing for Europe, where " Lars " was written in the autumn of the same year, and the *Prophet* the year after.

The *Masque of the Gods* is the purely poetical expression of one large thought, which had taken possession of the author's

imagination, and which could not rest until uttered. It paints
the growth of the religious aspects and aspirations of the
human mind : — its steady spiritual advancement from the
worship of the rude forces of nature to a clearer perception
of the Deity. The Gods of old and the idols that find themselves set aside, correspond to respective degrees of civilization over the world ; they are creations of the human mind,
and became rulers over men and nations by right of those
moral powers and spiritual ideas which they personified to
the perception of mankind. They were allowed, as a part of
the great and universal all, to prepare the mind of man for the
dawning and perception of that higher truth which culminates
in the humble declaration on the last page of the poem : —

> " We dare not name Thee, scarce dare pray to Thee."

There are lines of exquisite beauty all through the poem, —
lines which strike the ear with melody all their own ; but the
idea conveyed is greater than the rhythmical charm. The
entire last passage (pages 188 and 189), where Man speaks, is
full of ample suggestiveness. The lines,—

> " If we look up
> Beyond the shining form wherein Thy Love
> Made holiest revelation, we must shade
> Our eyes beneath the broadening wing of Doubt,
> To save us from Thy splendor,"

express so grand a thought, and one so original, that we cannot help wondering why it was not pointed out in any of the
reviews of this poem, and of the " November Pastoral " ; for
it was first expressed in the latter, thus : —

> " Be calm, for to doubt is to seek whom
> None can escape, and the soul is dulled with an idle acceptance.
> Crying, questioning, stumbling in gloom, thy pathway ascendeth ;
> They with the folded hands at the last relapse into strangers.
> Over thy head, behold ! the wing with its measureless shadow
> Spread against the light, is the wing of the Angel of Unfaith,
> Chosen of God to shield the eyes of men from His glory."

The reference made to science, farther on in the same passage, is one of the links that connect this drama with the following larger one, where we see Urania taking an active part,

not to mislead and confuse mankind, but to assist in conduct-
ing the human race towards the daybreak of a purified and
enlightened age. The *finale* of Man's speech, however, seems
to be the chance key-note, struck for the intonation of the
later drama : —

> —"we
>
> Are children still, we were mistaken oft,
> Yet we believe that in some riper time
> Thy perfect truth shall come."

PRINCE DEUKALION.

THIS drama was begun three years before the death of the
author, at a time which, to all seeming, would have been most
unpropitious to poetical production, especially of a purely
ideal character. Owing to recent circumstances, he was forced
to apply himself to hard, practical work. He had been for
months past on an extensive and very fatiguing lecturing-tour,
and during that time — the winter of 1875 — the conception
of *Prince Deukalion* was matured in his mind, and the opening monologue written on a day in March, whilst at home in
New York. From this time forth, the manuscript-book, in
which each scene was copied from the first carefully revised
draught, was his constant companion wherever he went, until
the whole poem was completed at noon, on October 7th, 1877.

. After the completion of Act I., in May, 1875, the work
rested for a while, until, at the beginning of winter, and towards the spring of the following year, Act II. was written
and Act III. begun. Of the latter, only two scenes were put
on paper then. Lecturing engagements and professional
work, and, later in the spring of 1876, the honorable duty im-
posed upon the author of furnishing the Centennial "National Ode," prevented him from continuing his drama. Yet
there was still another reason for the long pause that inter-

vened before the poem was taken up again and brought to conclusion. A difficulty had presented itself to the poet at the
beginning of Act III., as to the elaboration of his conceived
idea, and, as was his wont, he waited until the lacking inspiration should present itself, and help him to solve the problem
in his mind. It came to him at last, while on a visit on the
coast of New England, towards the end of August, 1877.
Work on the drama was resumed immediately after returning
to New York, and the whole was completed between September 1st and October 7th.

The author at first intended to call his drama " Eos," but he
soon afterwards changed this title for the present one. His
hero, as he conceived him, being no common person, but an
exalted and regal character, he called him Prince Deukalion, instead of Deukalion. He borrowed the names of Deukalion and Pyrrha from the old Greek myth, to which he
adhered in a slight manner, but he was anxious at the same
time that they should not be identified with that ancient couple.

Whilst the drama was in progress, the author repeatedly
expressed his intention of waiting several years after he had
completed it, before he gave it to the public. About the time
the work was done, however, an earlier publication seemed to
be desirable for various reasons. All the different parts of
the drama had undergone several strict revisions, and had
been filed considerably. Some passages, indeed, had been
rewritten more than once before they would satisfy him. This
was not an unusual occurrence. He never published any
poem from a first draft, as his copiously corrected and rewritten manuscripts of poems show. He felt now that he had
done his best with this drama, and that he could not alter it
materially. But there was a still more urgent reason. It
seemed as though, all the world over, the intellectual atmosphere were pervaded with thought akin to that expressed in
this work ; and when two different poems appeared, touching
on the same subject, he became alarmed lest his idea should
be forestalled by the earlier publication of a work, similar to
his own in design and purpose, by some other author.

The first of these poems was a short one, which gave its

title to the whole "Volume of Verse." It is called "Aurora;" the author's name is not given. It appeared in 1875, in London, but not till 1877 did it come into Bayard Taylor's hands. The second was a German poem of some length, by a new poet, Siegfried Lipiner. It is called "Prometheus Unbound," and was published at Leipzig in 1876. Bayard Taylor's attention was called to this work in the autumn of 1877, after he had finished his own poem, by a review of it in the "London Academy," which gave an extract that came very strikingly near his own idea as incorporated in *Prince Deukalion*. The volume was ordered from Germany, and a startling resemblance between the two conceptions was discovered in more than one place. This circumstance was of the greatest weight with him, in deciding him to publish his drama in the autumn of the following year; and before he left for Berlin, in the spring of 1878, he contrived to read the entire proof for publication.

The author was aware that in this poem he addressed himself to a small class of readers, and he was resigned to it from the first. Still, its lyric and rhythmical beauties are so varied and manifold, that they might lure all lovers of poetry to ponder over the thought which is clad in such garments. In time the idea underlying the poem will reveal itself to all thoughtful readers, — there is no necessity for explaining it. What the editor purposes to do in the following brief remarks, is to elucidate a few poetical disguises, or allusions, for those not familiar with them : — to throw some stray light on a passage here and there, that might otherwise be considered dark. By so doing we would not be thought to be wiser than most readers ; we merely hope that, through our intimacy with the work during its progress, some informing light may have been imparted to us.

ACT I.

PAGE 205.

—yonder sun were dim,
Save my torch enkindled him.

According to Hesiod, Eros was one of the original creative Powers.

PAGE 208.

Dost thou recall — how long ago it seems ! —
Mine ancient glory ?

Pyrrha refers here to the elevated social position accorded
to woman in the civilization of ancient Egypt. We learn
from authentic sources, discovered in papyri and inscriptions,
that not only was woman considered the equal of man, but
that superior right and privilege was accorded to her in some
respects. A papyrus, preserved in the Louvre at Paris, tells
us that she had the right to hold property and dispose of it as
she pleased. In the inscriptions on the oldest monuments
she is frequently called the " Mistress of the House," and on
most of the paintings in tombs and on the papyri of the dead,
man and wife sit side by side, — oftentimes with their arms
put around each other, — as being united in true and lasting
wedlock.

PAGE 210.

Heiress of gifts interpreted as woe.

The gifts here referred to are those wherewith the gods and
goddesses endowed Pandora, when she was sent down from
Olympus to entice Prometheus to wed her.

PAGE 214.

— despair
Should the defiant God within us fail —

The defiant God can be no other than Prometheus, who
stole the fire from heaven to kindle the soul of Man, which
brought down on him the wrath of the Gods. After his
atonement for this daring act — when Hercules had liberated
him from his tortures — he was admitted into the assembly of
the Gods, on Mount Olympus.

PAGE 216.

— he, with the bended brow
And parted waves of his luxuriant hair,
Shall yield his shadowy forehead to the thorn
And take a holier name.

22

In the National Museum at Naples there is a beautiful bronze head, said to be that of Plato, which answers to this description. It was found at Herculaneum, and the resemblance between it and the typical head of Christ is very striking.

PAGES 219 AND 220.

Since thou, adrift,
And that immortal woman by thy side
Floated above submerged barbarity.

In these lines and the following an allusion is made to that part of the ancient myth which clings to the names of Deukalion and Pyrrha. They, because alone righteous, were saved when the flood came to destroy all other human beings.

In the fifth line of the same passage, Prometheus clearly and distinctly points out the significance of the hero of the drama, whilst in the following line he alludes to Pandora, his spouse, who stands in the same relation to Woman as he to Man. Pandora's " deed," means, of course, her opening the forbidden casket from which escaped all the evils with which the human race has been afflicted ever since.

A little farther on, the line, —

Take one new comfort, Epimetheus lives !

brings us suddenly face to face with one of the subtler ideas of the poem. For those who have been following the wonderful progress of human knowledge, the lighting up of dark ages, in our own days, it ought not to be difficult to see what is meant in Epimetheus. A long vista into the Past has been opened before our amazed eyes by discoveries and researches, until we see our race almost young again. But Epimetheus is not merely an intellectual force : he is also an ethical power. If Prometheus — will, aspiration, genius — leads us onward and upward, Epimetheus, through perception of and insight into all that is past without us and within us, gives us self-knowledge, which is the awakening of the soul — its re-juvenescence.

PAGE 222.

— though she, who now my place
Usurps, takes Egypt's serpents for the Gods.

This allusion to Eve is made in the spirit of the Titan's spouse, who feels deeply the wrong done her in imputing the blame of all the sin and evil of the world to her. In this spirit she sets herself up as the prototype of the Mosaic Eve, who was tempted, not like herself, by the Gods, but by the serpent, which, in the most ancient lore of Egypt, represents sin and wickedness under the name of Apep. She then adds scornfully —

And eats the apple, not on Ida's hill !

referring to that other apple of old renown which caused the war and the destruction of Troy.

PAGE 223.

—whose heart
Dreams back Tithonus and dear early love.

Eos, who heralds the morning with the splendors of Dawn, is one of the most soulful conceptions of the Greek mythology. Dr. Emil Braun, in his " *Griechische Götterlehre,*" says of her : " She gives rise to elementary phenomena which prove distinctly that in her we have no frosty allegory, but that we see before us incorporated the ideal aurora, who at every recurring break of morning is greeted with holy awe by every living creature." It would have been impossible for the Greek mind to imagine a being like her without an ethical background. To it she was instinct with life and warmth and passion. Wherever she appears she is love-compelling and victorious. Her earliest love was Orion, the beautiful youth — the pupil of the Palæstra. But he was a mortal, and fell a prey to age ; he was lost to her. Her love then turns to Tithonus, who is represented with a lyre, as a favorite of the Muses. For him she besought the gift of immortality, which Zeus granted. Unluckily, however, she forgot to ask at the same time that eternal youth be bestowed on him. When he grew old and weak with age, he grew a burden to her, **and** she at last, for very pity, turned him into a cricket.

ACT II.

In the "Contents" which are found at the head of the drama, "A. D. 1300" is mentioned as the time in which the second Act takes place. This is meant to comprise the whole era, which was one of the greatest importance to the development and progress of the human race. It was the time when the Church of Rome had reached the climax of its power; when new ideas were taking root, and were stirring the minds of men; when art and literature put forth fresh shoots and blossoms, and the spiritual legacies of the antique world — spurned so long in the triumphant march of the newer civilization — became patent once more and acted like a new leaven.

PAGE 230.   THE YOUTH.

In him we easily recognize Dante, the greatest genius of the age. In Scene IV. we meet him once more as "The Poet."

PAGE 231.

The gate of Dis.

Dis is another name for Pluton, the Greek God of the nether world.

PAGE 232.   MEDUSA.

Medusa, the Gorgon of old, was of a wondrously dazzling beauty, but whosoever looked in her face was transformed into stone. The name is fittingly chosen for her, who would grasp all things, and compel them to her sole service.

PAGE 240.

A favor on a helm, — a tourney's crown!

In this line and the following ones Pyrrha refers to the chivalrous display of the Knights and Minnesingers, which **was** empty of true regard for woman, whilst seeming to confer honors upon her. Farther on, in the same passage, she continues to feel as a degradation the spiritual servitude of women in cloisters, in spite of the sanctity which, in return for it, is bestowed on them.

PAGE 241.

The winds of earth are wafting to and fro
The ashes of great lives.

Dissension was rife within the Church and without. More than one powerful mind had already arisen in opposition to its despotism and sore abuses, and had been crushed by flame and torture. Arnold of Brescia for such endeavor was burnt in Rome, in 1155. The French monk Abelard, famous for his learning, was persecuted relentlessly his whole life long for the liberal theological views he entertained and taught.

PAGE 245.

— where Cæsar's crown,
Descending, stopped when Tibur's Sibyl spake.

When Augustus thought of making himself Roman emperor, he consulted the Tiburtine Sibyl in regard to his probable success. The Sibyl then showed him the future in a vision. She bade him look up, and there he beheld the Cæsar's crown he coveted, hovering, not over him but over a lowly child, lying in a manger.

PAGE 246. THE PAINTER.

He is no other than Giotto, the friend of Dante, whose youthful likeness he has left us on the wall of the Bargello, at Florence. Giotto was the regenerator of art, who freed it from the bondage of the stiff forms of the Byzantine school, and restored movement to the human figure.

PAGE 246.

Yet for thee there pleads no crownless Muse.

Medusa comforts herself not only with the fact that the Muses no longer wear the crown of divinity, but that there is not even a separate Muse, whom the painter can invoke.

PAGE 247.

First of the triple triads.

The author follows the example of Classic Art in introducing the Muses in groups of three. A triad is of frequent occurrence in mythological formations. There being nine Muses, they are represented either as a triple triad, or in pairs, in which latter case one of the Muses appears as the leader of the whole chorus, — or she forms the centre, connecting thus the two half-choruses. There was no set schedule for such combinations : the poet or the artist was left free to form them as it suited the purposes of his art. The author of our drama has availed himself of this. He introduces as the first triad the Muses expressive of the gladsome enjoyment of the passing moment — of Music, of frolicksome Comedy, and of the Dance. The next triad is led by the tragic Muse, denoting thereby its serious tenor. Linked with Melpomene are the Muses of Song and lyric Poetry. This triad is followed by the Muses of epic Poetry and of History, independent and apart from whom stands Urania, the Muse of applicable Science, as the most potent of all — the only one who terrifies Medusa.

PAGE 250.

—What Lamia lingers here ?

The author himself gives the explanation of "Lamia" in one of his "Notes" to the Second Part of "Faust."

"The original Lamia, the daughter of Belus and Libia, was beloved by Jupiter, and then transformed, through Juno's jealousy, into a hideous, child-devouring monster. Lilith, the nocturnal female vampire of the Hebrews, mentioned in Isaiah, is rendered *Lamia* in the Vulgate. In the plural they appear to have corresponded, very nearly, to the witches of the Middle Ages, who, indeed, were then frequently called *Lamiæ*. Keats's poem of 'Lamia,' in which the bride, recognized by the keen-eyed sage, returns to her original serpent-form, represents another of the superstitions attached to the race."

ACT III.

PAGE 260. POET.

In him we see the representative of modern Lyric Poetry in its relation to Nature. He is no longer indifferent to her, as were the poets of ages gone by. He has recognized her beauties ; he loves her, and is in sympathy with her aspects and moods. He appeals to Mother Earth, and is heard. Gæa now proclaims herself "a Soul," and exults.

PAGE 262.

Ye highly live, more awful in the spell
Of unseen loveliness !

In the passage commencing thus we are reminded of Schiller's poem of " The Gods of Greece," in which he laments the loss of that time when —

— " of Poesie the veil enchanted
Sweetly o'er the form of Truth was thrown."

The author of our drama, in the lines before us, draws quite another conclusion from that which Schiller sets forth in his beautiful poem ; and we feel very much inclined to accept this speech of Gæa as an answer to the following verses of Schiller, taken from the above-mentioned poem. In singing of all the fair forms of Nature that are no more, he says that then —

" Misty Oreads dwelt on yonder mountains ;
In this tree the Dryad made her home ;
Where the Naïads held the urns of fountains,
Sprang the streams in silver foam.

. . . .

" From these rushes Syrinx once was crying,
From this forest Philomela's pain.
For her daughter Proserpine, the mighty
Ceres wept beside the river's fall ;
Here, upon these hills, did Aphrodite
Vainly on Adonis call.

. . . . .

" Meads and woods are lifeless, hushed the voices,
And I seek divinities in vain ;

Of that world where nature bright rejoices,
But the shadow we retain.
Heaven's vault I scan, the stars in motion, —
Thee Selene, I can find no more,
And my cries to forest and to ocean
Echo from a desolate shore!"

PAGE 278.

Yield up thy spells to one who saw thee pass
Through the dusk halls where Amun-Ra was lord,
Or Nile-borne on thy barque of flowers!

The ark formed a conspicuous feature in the religious cere-
monies of ancient Egypt. It sometimes had the shape of a
boat, and sometimes that of a shrine, and was used to receive
the image of the deity when carried about in grand proces-
sion. Such was the case during the sacred mysteries of
Amun-Ra, the Sun-God of Thebes and Heliopolis (the On of
the Bible), and during those of Osiris, which were the most
solemn of all. The latter rites were celebrated each year in
rejoicing for the inundation of the Nile and the new life that
sprung up from it. The ark of the God, who had been dead
and was now resuscitated, was then seen floating on the Nile,
in a festive bark, trimmed and entwined with garlands of flowers.

PAGE 278.

Symbol of Fire, the oldest, holiest!

In the remotest Past, when on the high table-land of Asia
men knew of no other deity than the life-giving Fire of the
sun, the cross was worshipped as its emblem.

PAGES 290 AND 291.

And aspiration, trying lonely wings,
Escapes the ancient arrow!

We have an allusion here to the myth of Icarus. His
father, Dædalus, having made wings for him which he fast-
ened to his shoulders by means of wax, warned him not to
soar too high. But the youth, unmindful of this counsel, rose
up higher and higher into the ether, until he came near the

chariot of the sun, whence Apollo, driving along the vault of heaven, espied him. Incensed at this presumptuous daring of a mortal, he shot one of his arrows at him, and, pierced to death, the poor youth sank until the waves of the Ægean Sea covered him.

After Act III. there is no occasion for any further explanatory notes; for the fourth and concluding Act being of a purely imaginative and ideal character, the reader will need no other guide than his own mind.

THE END.